PIONEER NEVADA

Copyright 1951 by

HAROLDS CLUB

Reno, Nevada

LITHOGRAPHED IN THE UNITED STATES OF AMERICA IN NINETEEN FIFTY-ONE

THIRD PRINTING

FOREWORD

This book consists of reprints of a series of newspaper advertisements based on pioneer history of Nevada, and published by Harolds Club of Reno. These advertisements were published once a week during 1946, 1947, 1948, 1949, 1950, and 1951 in every legal daily and weekly newspaper in Nevada, and the selection included here is almost complete, but omits a few which tended to repeat or duplicate other material, or which did not bear directly on the history of the state.

This volume is not represented as a history of Nevada, although the material it contains is as accurate as known records permit. The reader should bear in mind that each page represents a complete advertisement, designed and written to appear as a single anecdote having some significance in Nevada pioneer history. Much of Nevada's past is still to be established in detail, and many incidents are still debated by authorities.

When this series of advertisements first appeared in newspapers of the state, many requests for reprints were soon received. Harolds Club then announced the same subject matter would appear in full color illustrations on the walls of the gambling club, and would be available in booklet form. Signs were also erected around the state where these incidents took place. Later the pioneer western theme was followed in the interior decoration of Harolds Club, and the Covered Wagon Room was added. Roaring Camp, a virtual museum of western Americana followed, to be climaxed with the construction on the third floor of Fort Smith.

The advertisements were prepared, designed, and written under the direction of the Thomas C. Wilson Advertising Agency of Reno. Members of the agency staff conducted research work for six years. Artwork in pen and ink was based on old records, and careful research was made into costumes, furnishings, and architecture common to pioneer days in Nevada. Adaptations of the same subjects for the paintings on mirrors in Harolds Club were the work of Theodore McFall and his staff, of San Francisco.

The Paiute Creation

EVERY TRIBE and race has its stories of origin, and American Indians are no exception. In fact, they have an abundance of legends and myths about "the first Indians" in almost every section of the country, and many years ago this story was told to whites by patriarchs of the local tribes.

Many thousands of years ago, the desert between the Rocky Mountains and the Sierra Nevada was an immense garden of unimaginable loveliness. A happy and wonderful race of giants lived in this vast "Eden," so large they stepped a rod, and taller than the average pine tree. The men were handsome and brave; the women were "surpassingly lovely and extremely faithful." They lived in happiness without quarrel or discord, needing no laws to govern their ideal existence, and were known as the Lelangonappess people.

In the center of the great garden was a magic mountain of fire, whither those who were maimed or bruised went to breathe the vapors and smoke, and be instantly healed. The dead were cast into the fires of this mountain and the Great Spirit reclothed their souls with flesh, and transported them to the happy hunting grounds. Around the garden-country of the Lelangonappess were high mountains covered with snow. And beyond these mountains dwelt a tribe of fierce, gaunt, hungry men known as the Zhashmock. The Zhashmock were forbidden to enter the garden-country, but now and then would succeed in raiding with vast hordes, which were always desperately repelled by the Lelangonappess.

After these battles, the wounded and dead were borne with ceremonies to the mountain of fire, where the injured were healed, and the dead consumed. During one of these ceremonies a woman was terrified at the sight of a bear. Months later she gave birth to a child, so deformed it excited ridicule everywhere it went. The vapors of the magic mountain of fire failed to heal this case, and it grew up taunted and jeered by everyone, until its very existence became a torture.

The youth finally could stand the burden of his life no longer, and slowly and painfully made his way to the summit of the mountain, preparing to plunge into the fires.

At this instant a mighty roar of thunder split the heavens, the valley glared in a great light, the Great Spirit emerged from a cloud, and stood on the mountain top. With a terrible frown at the Lelangonappess, he spoke deep into the mountain, picked up the deformed youth, and dipped him thrice into the flames. Lo! He became a figure almost as perfect and glorious as the Great Spirit himself!

Another blast of thunder crashed overhead, and the Great Spirit vanished. Then the garden became dark. Black clouds piled overhead, the earth shook, huge cracks split the surface, and from beneath came the bellowing of a great giant. Two days this continued, and on the third a sheet of flame suddenly split the magic fire-mountain and melted rock gushed forth into the valley.

The Lelangonappess fled, but the molten rock grew to a fiery lake that drove them to the ends of the valley, shrinking them in size, burning their skins to a dark brown. And at this moment, they were attacked by the fierce Zhashmocks and massacred to the point of extermination except for one man named Paiute and his wife, who had hidden in a cave. The two survivors were forced by the Zhashmocks to walk forever on the cooling surface of the melted rock, living on the few birds that perished there. Thus lived the Adam and Eve of the Paiutes; and to this day you will never see a deformed or crippled Paiute treated by his people with anything except the greatest kindliness and respect.

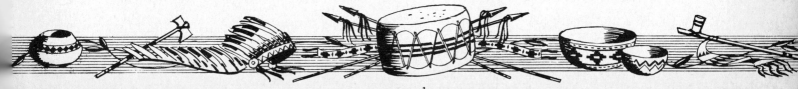

The Creation of the Washoes

IN THE BEGINNING, the Wolf ruled over all beasts, birds, and reptiles, with the Coyote next in power. And the Wolf, to demonstrate his great magic, conceived the idea of creating mankind. Accordingly, he called together the Coyote, the Jack Rabbit, who was the warrior and scout; the Sagehen, custodian of fire; the Lizard, and the Yellow Hammer or the gambler of the land.

The Wolf filled a jar with rushes or cattails and coyote grease, and allowed it to rest for hours at a point on the Carson River near the present day Indian School. Scratching, talking, and strange sounds within the jar were heard, and when the Wolf emptied from it, there appeared a multitude of men and women Indians. There stood the Diggers, the Washoes, and the Paiutes; and the Wolf ordered them to live respectively "west of the Sierras; Carson Valley; and to the east."

But then it was noticed the Indians were perfectly formed except they had no hands! A tremendous argument rose among all the animals as to which should furnish the form for the hands. It resolved between the

Coyote and the Lizard, the Coyote claiming the hands should be like his paws which were ideal for every conceivable purpose and use. The Lizard shouted that the four fingers and thumb of his forefoot were best for basket weaving, sewing, arrow and bow making. And the Wolf finally decided to let the debaters hold trial by combat.

The Coyote sprang at the Lizard, snarling and snapping, but the Lizard flashed into a tiny rock crevice. The Coyote then heaped a vast pile of sagebrush around the crevice and set an immense fire, 'round which he pranced in gleeful triumph. But the Lizard had inhaled some gaseous substance which distended his body, and when the fire was hottest, blew a jet of gas from his mouth which opened a passage through the flames. Through this he waved his hand, exclaiming, "Here I am, alive and unhurt."

And so delighted were the animals at the Coyote's discomfiture, they declared the Lizard victor, and to this day, you will find the Diggers, and the Washoes, and the Paiutes all have hands like the little Lizard.

Shoshone Saviour

S PURRED BY the promise of gold in California, civilization pushed relentlessly westward in '49. The dusty Humboldt trail became main street of the nation across Nevada's wilderness.

Other arterials like the Goose Creek-Fort Hall trail, Hasting's cutoff, Lassen's route and Simpson's cutoff added their slow moving traffic to the migration. At times the wagon trains met with open Indian hostility, on occasion they faced only sullen, silent resentfulness. As the network of trails grew and traffic increased, the tribes withdrew gradually to the back country, and with them they took the secrets, the customs and legends of their races. Few are the tales that White men learned concerning the centuries old beliefs of their red brothers. One that has been passed along, however, is the story of the Shoshone Saviour.

"Many suns ago," according to the aged medicine man, who passed the legend along, "a mountain in the Goose Creek range, tribal territory of the Shoshones, began to rock and rumble. The tribesmen who had assembled to gather pine nuts, were terrified. They huddled at the base of the mountain, men pale with fear, women and children crying. For several days the rumbling continued. Suddenly one dark night a shaft of light shot into the sky from the mountain peak. In a matter of seconds the sky was brilliant with a rosy glow.

"Fascinated, the Shoshones watched as a giant figure began emerging from the mountain. Clad in beaded buckskin, nose and ears decorated with rings and wearing an eagle pinion headdress, the full figure finally came into view.

"Gazing thoughtfully at the astonished Indians, the figure turned, fixed an arrow to his bow and loosed the missile at the barren hills across the valley. A streak of light like the tail of a meteor followed the path of the arrow and when it struck the ground, pinon trees, heavily laden with pine nuts miraculously appeared. A second arrow struck a bubbling stream at the foot of the mountain. In the flash of light Shoshones could see that the stream was suddenly teeming with fish.

"Without a word the giant then pointed toward the rock on which he was standing, and disappeared into the mountain.

"The next morning, Salamahowich, chief of the Shoshones, ascended the mountain and stood upon the rock where the giant had appeared. The stone gave way and the Shoshone chief found himself in an immense cavern with a floor like silver and a 'roof like icicles.' From one of the far reaches of the cave the giant appeared and explained to Salamahowich that he was the saviour of the Shoshone tribe, and that as long as tribesmen obeyed his code he would be their guardian and protector. He warned that no human should enter the cave, that constant guard should be maintained, and that the Shoshones were to dance in his honor whenever they heard him strike on the silver boulder at the cave's entrance." From the legend appears to have grown the customary Shoshone dance, Neg-ga-kin, later called a fandango. But, of greater importance, is the fact that the tale was related long before discovery of Lehman and Whipple Caves in eastern Nevada. Although these cave areas are over one hundred miles south of the legend locale, they are in a direct southerly line!

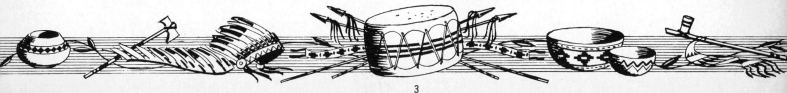

Tsawhawbitts the Evil Spirit

AMERICANS THE NATION over are familiar with the "Legend of Sleepy Hollow," and "Rip Van Winkle." Westerners are intrigued by the tales of Paul Bunyan and Babe, his big Blue Ox, but little is known of ancient folklore, predating these almost contemporary legends by centuries. Filled with superstition, tales originating in the stone and flint age, have been passed from generation to generation among the Indians long before white men ever set foot in the Great Basin.

Such a story is the tale of Tsawhawbitts, evil spirit in human form, who drove an ancient civilization of Redmen from lush hunting grounds of the Bruneau river where Nevada's present day border bumps into the rugged mountain country of southern Idaho.

Eons ago a peaceful tribe of Redmen inhabited the shores of the Bruneau river and roamed the fertile country between Jarbidge and Charleston in northern Elko county. The grass there grew tall, the trees were green; wild game abounded and fish were plentiful in the streams. Small bands of the tribe made their homes in many of the rolling valleys, enjoying a life of plenty, but the serenity of existence could not be maintained.

Gradually a tale of superstition and fear passed among the encampments concerning an evil spirit, Tsawhawbitts, a giant who stalked the Indian hunters with the same sure cunning they in turn employed in hunting wild game.

Tsawhawbitts was huge! In one step he could cross the turbulent Bruneau . . . in a few fleet strides he could climb a mountain . . . no one was safe! On his broad back Tsawhawbitts carried a basket which he filled with Indian hunters for his own feast. From his great height Tsawhawbitts could spy lone wanderers and swoop down upon them before they could flee. Snatching them up from the river bank or a tall pine thicket, Tsawhawbitts would stuff them in his basket and then disappear into a crater where he made his home.

First in small numbers and then in a great panic-stricken migration, the Indian bands fled in all directions. Gradually they were assimilated by lesser tribes, and, with each passing generation memories of the verdant north country diminished, but the fear of Tsawhawbitts, the evil spirit, remained constant as it was told and retold. It is known that for generations, this lush hunting area in northern Nevada, was avoided by Indians of all tribes as though it were a plague. The tribal memory of evil spirit was handed down for centuries.

Today's name, of Jarbidge, is an emasculated contraction of the legendary name, and as if to lend a note of truth to the ancient tale, relics of a flint age civilization have been found along the Bruneau. Could it be simply circumstance that one of the ragged mountain peaks, once within the domain of Tsawhawbitts, today bears the name of Mt. Ichabod?

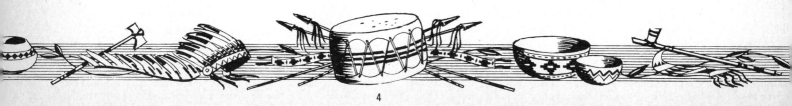

4

Why the Pinon is Dwarfed

THE ETERNAL struggle between good and evil is also told in the legends of the Washoe, who still relate how the good Wolf God tried to preserve Carson Valley as an "Eden" and how the wicked Coyote God debauched the tribe.

The Wolf God directed a prehistoric river north past Job's Peak, and taught the Washoes to bathe in it, cleansing away all sin and disease, and gaining immortality. Paiutes, Shoshones, and Diggers came from points later called Bodie, Mason Valley, Walker River, and Pyramid, and they came as friends, dancing, feasting, singing. Fish, deer, and rabbits were plentiful and there was no pain or sickness.

But Gou-Wet, the Coyote God, who is the devil of the Washoes, taught them evil ways. Even warning them their hands would become like his; they would become old and die; they would forget how to make bows, arrows, and fire, and in time he would eat them . . . with that warning, he won them to licentious ways of evil. And soon all game disappeared and there was no food, no warm rabbit robes. The babies cried from cold, and sickness came. The Paiutes made war and took all the ponies. The Washoes had been many, but now they died and the tribe dwindled in size. Even the pine nut forests were destroyed by fire.

Bitterly the Washoes reflected if it had not been for the Coyote God they would have been immortal and numerous. But their friend the Wolf God had not forsaken them. Out of pity he made vast numbers of hunting arrowheads and cast them over the land. But the cunning Coyote God poisoned them so that any unwary Washoe who picked them up died a lingering death. (To this day, a Washoe believes it very unlucky to pick up an arrowhead with the point toward him.)

Again the Wolf God tried to help his friends, this time scattering pine nuts which sprang magically into forests. But the Washoes were so weak with hunger they could not reach the pine nuts on the trees. Again the Wolf God came to the rescue and he started to strike the pinon pines on the tops, making dwarfs of the trees so the Washoes could gather the cones. Desperately the Coyote God wheedled, and argued, and talked, trying to get the Wolf God to stop shrinking the nut pines. Every trick, every argument, every enticement he could devise, the Coyote God tried, but the Wolf God remained firm. He shrank thousands of nut pine trees and the hungry Washoes harvested the crop and were saved.

And ever since, the Washoes have depended on the pine nut for food, and the pine nut trees have obeyed the Wolf God, and remained short; so the Washoes, young and old, strong and weak, rich and poor, could harvest the nuts with ease.

Lake Tahoe Monster

AN OLD STORY has it that the Washoes once knew of a terrible monster which lived at the bottom of Tahoe. From its nest rushed the waters that filled the Lake. With an evil human face, giant wings, and webbed feet, this cowardly bird loved human flesh, and all Washoes knew their spears and arrows could not pierce his armored scales and feathers.

The Washoes were holding their final hunt of the year before snows drove them down from the Lake to Carson Valley. And the Chief was to betroth his beautiful daughter to the bravest warrior of the tribe, at the big feast after the hunt; the choice to be made after each warrior boasted of his feats of valor and strength.

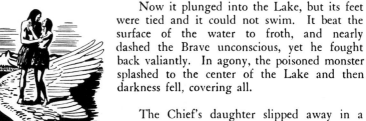

Now the Chief's daughter loved a handsome young brave, too young to have won a reputation in the last war with the Paiutes, and he had been praying for a chance to demonstrate his bravery when he saw the waters of the Lake part and a gigantic bird, the Ong, take wing! Quickly he moved to catch the giant bird's eye, and in a flash it swooped and bore him high among the clouds. Below, the Washoes screamed in horror. Hurriedly the young Brave lashed himself with buckskin thongs to the vast webbed toes of the Ong. Higher and higher soared the Ong, 'til they could see Carson Valley, and suddenly the bird opened its claws to plunge the Brave to his death. But he did not drop. In rage the bird tried to seize him with its teeth, but the Brave took cover behind the webbed toes, and the Monster cartwheeled through the sky. Every time the Ong opened its vile mouth, the Brave hurled poisoned darts down its throat and the Ong screamed with fury!

Now it plunged into the Lake, but its feet were tied and it could not swim. It beat the surface of the water to froth, and nearly dashed the Brave unconscious, yet he fought back valiantly. In agony, the poisoned monster splashed to the center of the Lake and then darkness fell, covering all.

The Chief's daughter slipped away in a canoe, and quietly paddled out to the center of the Lake, resolved to die with her young lover. But a strange sight met the gaze of the astonished Washoes at daybreak. The great rigid body of the Ong floated on the Lake and near it was an overturned canoe. Approaching the shore drifted a raft fashiond from a single vast wing of the Ong. Standing on it, and clasped in each other's arms, were the young Brave, called "Tahoe," and the Chief's beautiful daughter. The story, (unverified), claims this gave the Lake its name.

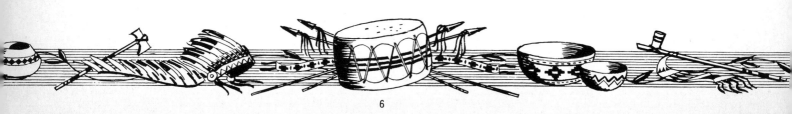

6

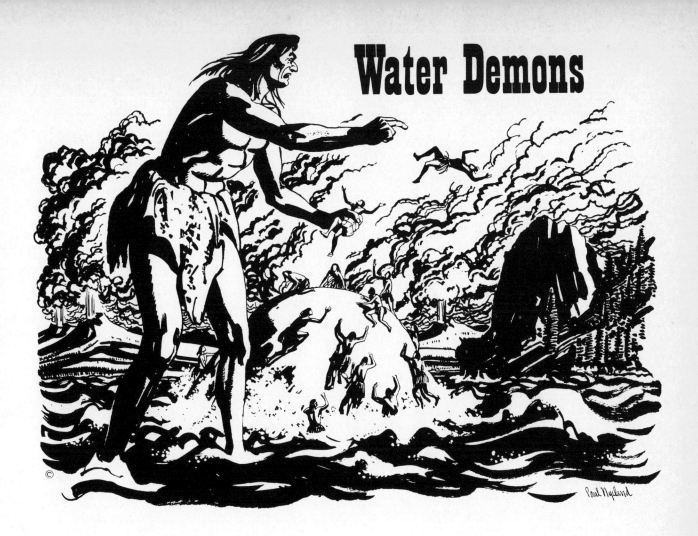

Water Demons

THE WASHOES say if you listen at Cave Rock, Lake Tahoe, in the spring when the water rises, you can hear the moaning of the water demons imprisoned below in the sacred Spirit Lodge. They were placed there according to an ancient Indian legend which is amazingly faithful to the modern scientific geological theory on the formation of Tahoe and Western Nevada areas.

"Ages ago (goes the legend) the Tahoe region was a flat fertile plain through which a great river flowed to the western sea. The happy people lived on salmon, sweet fruits, vines, and trees. But they were brutally conquered by a cruel people from the north who forced them to build a temple to worship the sun, and enslaved them.

"Then came a great tidal wave from the western sea, sweeping away all but a few oppressors and slaves cowering on the top of the temple. When the flood subsided, the earth was convulsed, heaved, rocked, and cracked open. Great vents spewed ashes, fire, and molten rock rained for days! The terrified masters fled inside the temple and locked out the slaves, who seized the canoes and escaped down the great river to the west.

"Suddenly the whole plain began to rise. Mountains formed all around, and spouted fire and smoke, melting the stars. Snow fell for the first time. The mighty river was cut off from the western sea and began to flow to the east! It formed a great new inland sea to the east of the mountains.

"The sun temple now stood in a deep cleft, surrounded by high mountains. Snows filled the chasm with rising water 'til the conquerors clung to the temple roof for refuge. The God of the World, terrible in his anger at their tenacity, walked out upon the water, seized them, and hurled them across the lake and into the Spirit Lodge (Cave Rock). There these imprisoned people became water demons, terrified to this day at the rising waters of Spring.

"The escaping slaves on the great river were swept eastward, settling along the shores of the great inland sea which geologists today have labeled Lake Lahontan." Their descendants are the Paiutes who still dwell on the shores of the remnants of this vast sea . . . Pyramid Lake, Honey Lake, Walker Lake, and Humboldt Sink. The cleft filled with snow water and dammed by volcanic Mount Pluto, is our own Lake Tahoe, formed, says science, much like the legend told by the Washoes to the first white man to visit the beautiful "Lake of the Skies." And to this day, the Washoe tribes hold Lake Tahoe and the Cave Rock areas as sacred to their religion.

Legend of the Whistling Swans

Paul Nyrland

ANCIENT PAIUTE legend tells of a battle fought between the tribes more than 100 years before the white man came. So fierce was this struggle that the waters of the Carson Sink ran red with the blood of its victims, before the victorious, bitter, and exhausted Paiute warriors gathered on the shores of the sink to count their dead.

To their astonishment there came a sudden vast rumbling in the sky, with the deep roar of thousands of wings, beating the desert air. Then the sun was abruptly blotted out by thousands of graceful white birds. Countless . . . White Whistling Swans, with black bills and feet, wheeled and soared far into the distance. The air vibrated to their quacking, and the waters of the sink splashed, as they sank to rest upon miles of its surface.

Food had been brought to the Paiutes, and they thankfully killed many of the big birds. Soon cooking fires twinkled along the banks of the sink, and fast runners sped across the desert to summon former enemies to join the feast. A great banquet, with tribal peace dances followed, and the white feather of the swan was adopted as the symbol of peace and prosperity among the tribes.

Much later, white settlers came to the Carson Sink, but they laughed at Indian tales of "white swans." In 1862 the town of Stillwater was established as an overland station, and in six years it became the county seat. In 1871 a woman, Ella Redman, built a toll bridge, and the first school was opened. In 1896 a post office was established on the Mike Fallon ranch. Then Congress passed a reclamation act, and in 1902 the county seat moved to Fallon.

The reclamation act, first of its kind, provided for a dam and canals to irrigate the rich desert lands near the sink. Construction started in 1903.

Then, on a January afternoon in 1905, the brooding quiet of the placid Carson sink was shattered by a great rumbling roar, filling the sky and echoing back from the barren hills. Thousands of beautiful big Whistling Swans swam in the sky, and circled out over the sink. Eye-witnesses swore they blotted out the sun, extending nearly three-quarters of a mile in width. Soon they were splashing down on the waters of the sink, feeding and quacking by the thousand.

It was then the Fallon Standard recalled the ancient Indian prophecy of prosperity and well-being after a visit by the great birds. The Standard observed that prosperity in this case would seem to follow completion of the irrigation project, making the Indian prophecy come true.

And so it did, for the Lahontan Dam, first reclamation project in America, was completed three years later and turned thousands of acres of barren desert into a rich garden of prosperous farms.

Duck hunters say that a few Whistling Swans still come to the sink, but they are very rare and supposedly nearly extinct.

But who knows? Perhaps any day now, another visit by the magical swans will tell of another great prosperity in western Nevada!

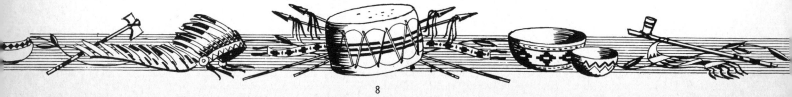

Nevada's Cannibal Problem

HUNDREDS OF YEARS before the exploration parties of Jedediah Smith or John C. Fremont set foot along the western rim of the Great Basin, savage cannibals, wild, freckled-faced redheads, roamed the arc of the Humboldt Sink.

Tales of their actions and final extinction have passed from generation to generation of the Paiute tribe and numerous artifacts unearthed in deep caves near Lovelock appear to bear out at least part of the tale. Archeologists say there are definite evidences of the existence of a civilization which may have thrived as far back in history as two thousand years ago.

Paiute legend indicates that the fierce wild fellows were cannibalistic, that their inordinate greed for the taste of human flesh led them to stalk Indian hunters much in the same way the Indians' stalked game.

As a result numerous small Paiute hunting parties failed to return and investigation by the tribe pointed to the belief that they had been preyed upon by the redheads. The situation became so acute the Paiutes agreed upon action to settle once and for all the bothersome cannibal problem.

Marshalling their forces for war the Paiutes gradually drove the entire tribe of fierce redheads into a high horseshoe-like cave on the north face of the limestone bluffs overlooking Humboldt Sink. The cave area had long served as home for the cannibals and they gradually assembled their entire tribe in the big horseshoe cavern to make a stand against the Paiutes.

Approaching the cave entrance Indian warriors warned the redheads unless they agreed to put an immediate end to their practice of cannibalism the cave would become their funeral pyre. No answer came from the cave as the cannibals awaited the next move of their adversaries. A repeated request for truce brought no answer so the Paiute chief gave orders to ring the cave entrance with fagots.

Huge piles of wood were stacked along the rim of the cave and again the redheads were warned of their danger, but they still refused to yield, whereupon the order was given to fire the wood and the entire tribe of man-eaters died in the cave which had once served as their home. Some members of the tribe, particularly the women were reputedly of small size.

The cannibal legend is only one of many concerning early inhabitants of the Lovelock Valley area. Traces of ancient peoples were first found in 1911 when some of the caves were worked as guano mines. Since that time thousands of artifacts attesting to the existence of an ancient civilization have been unearthed and now rest in the museums of Nevada and California.

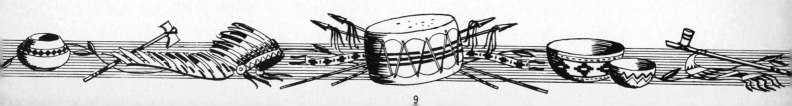

Mary's River

THE TORTUOUS TRAIL of the Humboldt through Nevada was well remembered by the Forty-niners. Along its banks hundreds died during the westward journey. The dust that rose from the hooves of plodding oxen and the lumbering wheels of covered wagons clung to memories of pioneers like a nightmare, for this three hundred mile journey down the winding, muddy river represented one of the worst hardships in all western travel.

Strange it was that for a quarter of a century before the Golden Army began its migration this very river was a magic name which conjured dreams of riches and adventure in the minds of men who longed to "go west."

Peter Skene Ogden, Hudson Bay Company factor and one of the foremost explorers of the great basin area, had led his trappers along the Snake, down the Owyhee and to the headwaters of the Humboldt as early as 1828. Ogden called this desert stream "Unknown River" and he systematically trapped it westward to the present site of Winnemucca. Luck was with him and he returned with many pelts. The name of "Unknown River" became a by-word with the hardy trapping fraternity, possibly because its name held all the mystery of the great uncharted west where extremely few white men had yet set foot.

Although Ogden preferred to call it "Unknown," numerous other names were applied to this twisting desert stream. Many of his trappers referred to it as Paul's River, honoring one of their friends who had sickened and died along its banks during one of the trapping expeditions.

Others called it Ogden's River after their leader, but the name that met with general fancy was Mary's River, an appellation traced to fact and fable surrounding the legendary Indian wife of Peter Skene Ogden.

Like Sacajewa, who guided Lewis and Clark, Mary reputedly led Ogden's trappers safely along the Snake and to the Humboldt headwaters. Tales of her daring are all but erased from the scanty notes of these early explorers, but one legend tells how she rescued her child without bothering to ask the aid of Ogden's men.

One day when the trappers had rendezvoused along the river the horses stampeded toward another distant trapper's camp and hanging to the saddle of one horse was Mary's baby in a carrying basket. All of the other animals were heavily loaded with furs taken from the trap lines. Rivalry for furs was keen, and any act aimed at securing the stampeded horses was fraught with danger. Mary, however, gave no thought to this possibility, and mounting her horse, she rode straight to the rival camp, seized her child and grabbed the halter of one of the fur-laden packhorses. So quick had been her action that the rival trappers had no chance to recover from surprise before Mary was well on her way back to Ogden's rendezvous.

When John C. Fremont traversed the great Basin and came upon the winding river, he promptly named it Humboldt in honor of the German explorer Baron Alexander von Humboldt, who never so much as saw the desert stream.

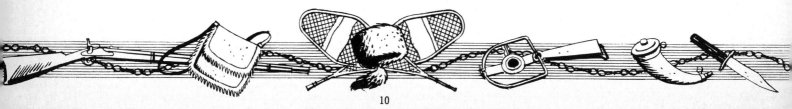

First Battle

LIKE SO MANY conflicts in the history of the world, the first battle fought in Nevada was the needless product of suspicion and fear between two alien groups. It came in September, 1833, when Joseph Walker and his party camped at the mouth of the Humboldt River.

Walker was seeking beaver streams for Captain Bonneville, although some authorities believe he was a secret agent investigating possible future expansion of the United States to the coast. While coming down the Humboldt some Paiutes stole beaver traps, and two Indians were slain by the white men, against Walker's orders and wishes. Indian feelings were high, when the party of 40 whites camped near Lovelock in the tall grass and reeds.

Suddenly the group was surrounded by several hundred Paiutes, poorly dressed in reeds, and slowly advancing from smoke fires in the tules from all directions. They were led by five chiefs who signalled they wished to parley. It is probable the Indians wanted some restitution for their slain men, and meant no harm. It is certain that Walker wanted no trouble; but the Indians were armed, and kept advancing.

Walker asked the Paiutes to halt. He feared to have his camp filled with armed Indians. He showed the wondering Paiutes how the white men's guns could kill by shooting ducks. The mob of Indians withdrew that night, but returned the next morning 800 strong. Again they seemed determined to overwhelm his camp. So the baggage was barricaded and horses readied.

At last Walker decided to use violence. The barricade was manned and all guns loaded. As the Indians again moved closer, Walker ordered a volley fired, and his mounted group swept out, shooting and stampeding the Indians into a panic and flight. Many Paiutes were wounded and 39 killed outright.

The Indians fled, and Walker's party was no longer followed. Some accounts say they continued on up the Carson River to Eagle Valley and over the old Kingsbury Grade, but it is generally believed they took another route, as on this trip Walker discovered Yosemite. The party wintered in California, returning by Walker Pass, Walker River, and again to the mouth of the Humboldt River, where they found the Indians so hostile that another battle took place on the site of the original fight. Again the Indians lost, this time with 14 men killed, and Walker's party continued on up the Humboldt and back to Bonneville without further trouble. Accounts of the first battle at that time depicted Walker as a bloodthirsty killer, but later study of the diaries kept by his men revealed he had made every effort to prevent bloodshed, consistent with what he believed to be the safety of his men.

The Paiutes were angry and became unfriendly, almost with the sole exception of Chief Truckee, who persisted in befriending the invading white parties of the following years. But the Indian weapons were hopelessly outclassed by the whites. Walker later became embittered at the publicity given Fremont, who later "explored" this area.

Rabbit Drive

JOHN C. FREMONT was prepared for surprises when he traversed Nevada in 1844. His western explorations had accustomed him to many strange sights, but he was highly intrigued by his first view of a Rabbit Drive as conducted by the Paiutes along the Truckee River* in Nevada. He deemed it of sufficient interest to include it in his travel notes.

"We had scarcely lighted our fires," Colonel Fremont remarks, "when our camp was crowded with nearly naked Indians; some of them were furnished with long nets in addition to bows, and appeared to have been in the sage hills to hunt rabbits. These nets were perhaps thirty to forty feet long, kept upright in the ground by slight stakes at intervals, and were made from a kind of wild hemp."

Colonel Fremont's notes were made on the evening of January 31, 1844, which is normally a pretty chilly season along the Truckee, but the Indians seemed immune to the cold, probably because the rabbit drive was a rather active form of exercise and it provided winter food for the tribe as well as skins from which to manufacture blankets and clothing.

Normally about two hundred bucks and braves of the tribe, along with numerous children gathered for the drives in the winter months. They used a slight hemp net about five feet in width to enclose a huge circle of sagebrush hillside where jackrabbits and cottontail were known to be plentiful. When the circle was completed the tribal braves would secure the net in a vertical position with pointed sap-ling stakes which would be driven into the ground. Just enough of the net was left to dangle along the ground to ensnare the frightened rabbits. At each stake was stationed a Paiute brave who was armed with a club. The remainder of the hunting party scattered themselves within the circular enclosure and beat the brush with clubs and switches to frighten the rabbits from their burrows and hiding places.

As the rabbits leaped toward possible escape, they either became entangled in the net or were clubbed in their flight. Within the space of a very few minutes after the actual brush beating commenced, the hunting party succeeded in killing several hundred rabbits, enough food for a few weeks, and enough fur for several warm blankets.

Though the sight of a rabbit drive was new to Fremont, it had long been the Paiute's way of augmenting their winter's food supply, since the desert land and hill country offered little other means of livelihood during the season snow lay thick upon the ground. Even after the whites began to settle the country, the Indians staged their Rabbit Drives several times each winter. In later years, they took the easier course and used rifles and shotguns for the actual killing, rather than resorting to the more primitive use of clubs.

* Fremont's notes said "The Salmon Trout" (or Truckee) River but actually he was on the east fork of the Carson. With broken sextant, his navigation was often in error on this trip.

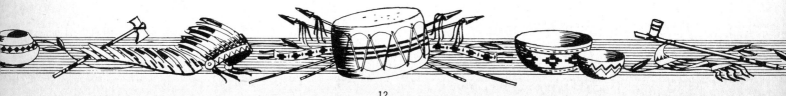

Captain Truckee

Big CHIEF over all Paiutes in western Nevada at the time of the arrival of the first white men, was the father of Chief Winnemucca. And for him the Truckee River and town of Truckee are named, today. If the pioneer whites had shown the Indians the kindness and fairness given them by Chief Truckee, there would have been no Indian wars in pioneer Nevada.

This Paiute chieftain believed all men to be sons of a common ancestor, and that "the white brothers were to return someday in peace." Accordingly, when he heard of fair-skinned, blue-eyed men coming across eastern Nevada, he sent word to his warriors to make them welcome. The Chief himself went to see the whites, but they were suspicious and hurried on, ignoring his greeting. The next year a much larger party of whites under a Captain Johnson camped three days at Humboldt Lake. This time the Chief called and dropped his rabbit skin robe to show he was unarmed, shook hands in the fashion of the whites, and presented gifts. Again and again he repeated the Paiute word for "it is all right" or "okay" . . . "truckee, truckee." The whites thought it was his name, and called him "Chief Truckee" and so the word has come down in history. They gave him a tin plate, which he took for a hat, bored holes for a chin strap, and proudly showed it to his tribesmen.

Next year came Fremont, and he, too, was greeted with the robe-dropping ceremony. Like the others, Truckee offered to guide him over the Sierras to California, and with Truckee for a guide, this 1845 trip took the direct route over Donner, and from that time on, many a party of whites reached the coast with a guide encouraged by Chief Truckee.

When Chief Truckee decided to go to California for a lengthy trip, he appointed his son, Po-i-to, Big Chief, who became known to the whites as Chief Winnemucca. Old Truckee made Po-i-to promise to keep peace with the white brothers, and a study of Winnemucca's life reveals he made every effort to keep this promise to his father, often even relinquishing command when war was unavoidable.

Old Chief Truckee took 12 Paiutes with him on one trip to the coast. He served under Fremont in the Mexican War, and as an officer of scouts became more proud of his rank as "Captain" than his title of "Big Chief," with power over all sub-chiefs of the Paiutes. He was remembered by many early settlers, wearing his blue officer's coat with brass buttons. Captain Truckee learned fast, and came home to tell of the wonders of far off places and to laugh at what a fool he had been to mistake a tin dish for a hat!

Authorities still disagree over who first called him "Truckee" but all stories over his friendship for the whites coincide. He died, just as the wrongs inflicted on his people by the pioneer whites were inflaming the Paiutes to the waging of a bloody war that cost scores of white and Indian lives. Winnemucca at times favored war on the whites but at the point of conflict, always rode off into the Humboldt River country, where his father had spent most of his life, where the grass was deep, and where the hunting was most plentiful.

History has no record how many big and little parties of whites were safely guided over the Sierras to Sutter's in California by Paiute warriors on Chief Truckee's orders.

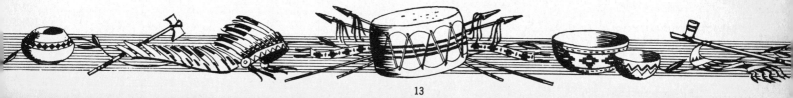

The White Dragon

STORIES HANDED down from old Indians to younger tribesmen, reveal that a pinto pony brought fabulous good luck. An Indian would risk anything to gain a pinto pony.

A true Indian tale of over a hundred years ago tells how a Paiute hunting party was surprised to see a vast cloud of dust, far different from the usual desert whirlwind. Cautiously watching from the protection of high sagebrush and rocks, they were astonished to see that the cloud moved, and horrified to discover it was "following them."

Panic stricken, they bolted through the brush, but the cloud still followed. Luckily it stopped at dusk, and as the Paiute hunters watched, they saw a long, moving white object crawl into a coil, and stop.

Hours later, when the stars were out, a scout returned. His report was not reassuring. It seemed there were pale ghosts who walked around the camp fires. Dawn revealed the long white object uncoiling and crawling down the valley, a huge white serpent. Keeping pace with it, the Paiutes flitted from rock to brush, and from hilltop to gully, chattering and whispering.

Scouts still watched every move of the ghosts, from as close as they dared. In the afternoon one scout came back with the report that the ghosts drove buffalo (oxen) but the big news was that among the ghosts was a magic pinto pony! By nightfall the lure of the pinto pony was so irresistible that several members of the tribe dared to walk right up to the white men's camp. That night the Paiute hunting party camped where they could watch the white men, their wagons, and the magic pinto pony.

The next morning the Paiutes wanted the pinto so badly they could hardly stand it. This time they walked right up to the white man, and the chief of the tribe offered to trade for the magic horse. The white man refused to talk or trade with them. He turned his back and shrugged.

Then, before the startled gaze of the ox drivers, the wagon train scouts, and the Paiutes alike, the Indian chief made a sudden rush. Swiftly he vaulted to the back of the pinto. Both hands dug into the mane and grasped big handsful of hair. Two moccasin clad heels dug deep into tender flanks and a wild war cry split the quiet of the morning camp.

The astonished and indignant pinto gave a snort, jumped straight up into the air, and came down running. Rolling the whites of his eyes and panicked, he bolted out over the desert, leaping the rocks and sagebrush.

It was a tense moment for a battle could break out with a single false move on either side. The white men seemed undecided. They looked over the heavily armed Paiute hunting party. Regardless of who won, it would be a costly contest for one pinto pony. The leader shook his head, and the white topped wagons began to rumble out through the dust.

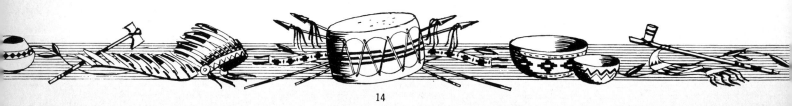

Fremont named it "Pyramid Lake"

LITTLE OVER 100 years ago in January 1844, Captain John Fremont and a small band of scouts and adventurers discovered a beautiful inland sea in the western desert, and named it for the sharp pyramid-like island. This deep blue sheet of water with its dramatic and weird setting was a traditionally sacred ground for the Paiutes.

Later at the mouth of the lake, the Indians trapped and massacred the flower of Nevada's militia and on the western shores, the Paiutes were in turn met and defeated by regulars from the coast. It has been a scene of battle, mystic rites, violence, and serene enchanting loveliness for centuries.

Today the lake is unspoiled, for it lies within an Indian reservation. The fishing in bygone years has been fabulous but has now faded. The beaches are among the best for swimming in the world, and the water is mildly salt and invigorating. Artists favor it for the stark beauty, writers for the peace and quiet.

The islands are noted as one of the largest pelican-breeding grounds in the world and the "needles" at the northern end of the lake are famous for the cormorants, endlessly wheeling and diving for fish. During the war the navy used the lake for torpedo plane training and departed leaving wharfs, airport, and improvements at Sutcliffs.

This entire area of brightly colored desert and lake, has long been the scene of Indian tradition and legends. Ancient Indian burial grounds are said to lie east of the lake. Indian petroglyphs are found in several locations. Caves have produced artifacts and relics of an early Indian culture of lake shore dwellers, fish eaters, and hunters of wild fowl.

The region is closely linked geographically and in culture with nearby Winnemucca Lake, which is dry, the vast dry lakes comprising the Smoke Creek Desert and Black Rock Desert to the north, and the Humboldt and Carson Sinks directly to the east. Through these areas roamed bands of Indians for centuries, adapting their methods of living to a country which was slowly drying into desert.

Here the Paiutes met and clashed with invading bands of Bannocks, Modocs, and Nez Perce from the north. Generations of such warfare produced an aggressive spirit among the Paiutes who inhabited this country and from here came many of the warriors who tamed and subjugated the neighboring tribes. From here too, came the most warlike and skilled leaders of the Paiutes. Black Rock Tom and Smoke Creek Sam outgeneraled the professional officers of the whites at least once, and the amateur Indian fighters many times. From here these renegades kept up an unrelenting warfare against the white invaders to the very end.

Lost Blue Bucket Mine

Paul Mylland

O F THE THOUSANDS of fanciful stories of "lost mines" there are few which appear to be authenticated and still waiting for some lucky prospector. One of these, however in northwestern Nevada, is the famous Blue Bucket Mine.

In 1845 a large wagon train bound for Oregon split up at Gravelly Ford (Beowawe) with half coming south down the Humboldt River, and about 45 wagons striking out west, through Black Rock into California and Oregon. About four days past Black Rock they entered a steep canyon, so rough as to be almost impassable, and off the main trail. Here the wagon tires left ruts in "shiny brass" but the exhausting work of getting through the canyon took all attention. The children had a game, however, tossing pebbles into the blue buckets hanging outside some of the covered wagons. Later some of these pebbles were dumped inside the wagons and were carried on into Oregon, and eventually south to Sutter's Fort.

Here everybody was extremely gold-conscious and the pebbles were immediately recognized to be gold nuggets! Letters to other companions of the trip West brought answers and more nuggets. A party of 90 was organized and went back in the face of a hostile Indian uprising, into the district, but they were attacked and nearly 50 killed. This ended the search with only two survivors who had been at the original site of the "brass ruts." They gave some nuggets and a careful description of the area to a "Doctor Dane" at Yreka. Later this doctor was placer mining, as a Hudson Bay trapper watched him retrieve nuggets. "If that's gold," remarked the trapper, "I know

where there's any amount of it. It's a place where I left my horses last winter, in a canyon where the emigrant road comes by High Rock. There's lots of these pebbles in the creek." His description convinced Dr. Dane it was the lost Blue Bucket, and they set out following a series of the trapper's dead campfires. At Goose Lake Valley, the trapper is said to have pointed to two peaks about 70 miles northward, claiming the canyon was "on this side of the right-hand peak."

Two days' travel took them there, but a huge cloudburst had washed and torn the canyon. The creek banks were piled high with uprooted sagebrush. Fresh cut gullies were everywhere. They searched and searched in vain, finally returning without a single nugget. Although many parties have searched no one has found the Blue Bucket unless the story told in 1907 by a man running a store in the small boom camp of Rosebud, 12 to 15 miles northeast of Humboldt on the Central Pacific is true.

He claimed two young greenhorns, great-grandsons of one of the discoverers of the Lost Blue Bucket, arrived from San Francisco on a two week vacation. They had read up on the district, and were very secretive.

But, at the end of their vacation, they stopped at his store and displayed a chunk of fabulously rich ore they had found by an old camp which had been destroyed by fire.

They were so "fed-up" with the desert and the rigors of prospecting, however, that they refused to go back into the district, or to lead anyone else to it. The Blue Bucket is still waiting to be found.

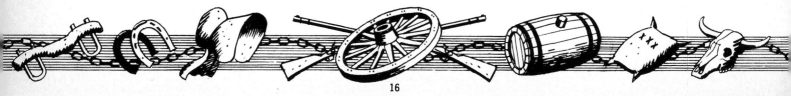

Enroute to Starvation Camp

FROM Springfield, Illinois, to Starvation Camp at the base of the bleak Donner Summit was an arduous trip in 1846, when only the faintest of trails led the way westward over plains and rugged mountains. But the Donner party was a happy and prosperous one when it set out in April of that year for California.

Two brothers, George and Jacob Donner, and their families numbering 16 persons, together with James F. Reed and a family of seven persons, and another family of twelve formed the original group that left Sangamon County, Illinois.

At Independence, Missouri, they were joined by additional recruits to the wagon train. The party in all then numbered 90 persons, but by the first week in May after they had reached Independence the train increased to over 200 wagons, all well provisioned and extremely well outfitted for the long journey westward.

At Fort Bridger in Wyoming, a portion of the immigrants decided to try a new route to California by the way of Salt Lake, known as the Hastings Cutoff; the remaining members of the party took the longer but better known route by which they eventually safely reached the point of their destination.

Those who chose the Salt Lake route were the ones whose tragic fate lead them to Starvation Camp—a place of horror and hardship that has become one of the darkest pages in the history of the westward expansion. The great desert beyond Salt Lake was a trackless, barren and foreboding place. From that point misfortunes laid hand heavily upon the wagon train whose supplies were rapidly diminishing.

When their plight became apparent, and it looked like starvation, a party of volunteers was called upon to ride ahead 700 miles to Sutters Fort on the Sacramento, a mission which would bring back supplies to save the lives of those in the wagon train. When the weary travelers reached Gravelly Ford on the Humboldt in Nevada, the worn-out cattle and travelers were subsisting on short rations.

It was here at the Ford that tragic event occurred which was to increase the misfortune of these travelers who were eventually to meet death on the shores of Donner Lake. Here John Snyder, who was driving one of the teams became involved in a quarrel with James F. Reed. During the fight, Snyder lashed at Reed with the front end of a whip, and Mrs. Reed, who was rushing in to separate the two combatants, received the cruel blow intended for her husband.

Enraged at this incident, Reed stabbed Snyder, who died a short time later. For this murder, Reed was banished from the wagon train without food or a gun. At that time he was well over 700 miles from the nearest settlement which was over the Sierras in California.

During the first night after his banishment, a friend, accompanied by Reed's little daughter, stole away from the wagon train and provided him with a few crackers, and other provisions. But for these supplies, he would have perished on the desert. However, the food was enough to enable him to make his way westward and over the Sierras before the heavy winter snows set in.

The banishment of Reed from the Donner party left it without one of its best leaders and was one of the main reasons that the party tarried too long in the Truckee Meadows and was unable to get over Donner Pass before the winter snows set in.

Strange it was, that Reed, who was banished from the wagon train, was one of those that reached safety and eventually became one of the leaders of the rescue parties to come back and relieve the suffering of the Donner party.

They call it the "Big Meadows"

AFTER THREE WEARY WEEKS of following the twisting course of the Humboldt River from its headwaters near Wells, the Pioneer Golden Army bound for California's placer grounds, paused near the present site of Lovelock on the edge of the Humboldt Sink to condition its travel-weary stock, gather wild hay, and fill every available receptacle with water before attempting the mad forty-mile dash across desert wasteland to Ragtown on the Carson River.

Oregon-bound pioneers who travelled the Humboldt Trail also tarried here in the big natural meadows where the muddy river waters sink into the ground, giving growth to abundant grasses—a feeding paradise for gaunt oxen and horses.

On this crossroads farmers turned north over the Black Rock desert toward the Willamette Valley, and gold seekers chose one of three trails, Truckee, Carson or Walker Pass to the golden land of California. Some authorities say that Peter Lassen established a trading post here for a time. It is known for sure that he erected a sign-post directing traffic along the "Lassen Road" along much of the Applegate Cut-Off to his Deer Creek Ranch in California. The oasis became known as the Big "Lassen's" Meadows. Far-sighted men like James Blake, who settled in the valley in 1861 and George Lovelock, who came a year later, began

cultivation of the fertile sink-land soil. Their move was followed by many westbound emigrants who saw the possibility of turning the desert into the garden spot it is today. The Rye Patch dam now checks run-off waters of the Humboldt River, assuring year around irrigation and the main line Southern Pacific Railroad makes principal stops in this valley town to carry its grains and grasses to world markets.

The Lovelock area has long been of interest to archeologists, who have found remnants of several early cultures and many unusual artifacts. Nevada's prehistoric "Lakeshore Civilization" reached a high point in the Lovelock area, as indicated by many caves containing ancient relics.

Geologists and mining men have found the region one of great promise. Since early days, there have been several active mining districts, and currently they appear to be on the increase in many interesting respects.

Harvest time is tuned to the chatter of machinery as modern buck rakes, binders and balers prepare produce for shipping. Recent developments may soon transform winter cattle and sheep range into a source for fresh dairy products that can be whisked in ten hours to ready markets in the bay area.

The Big Drink!

RAGTOWN ON THE Carson River remembers few tales of bloodshed or strife that would mark it as a notorious spot on the Overland Trail. Its memory stems from a deeper source—prayers of thankfulness from men and women of the Golden Army, the pitiful lowing of thirst-crazed cattle and the shrill whinnies of gaunt horses as they plunged down its muddy banks to wallow belly deep in swirling waters for the Big Drink.

Ragtown was a resting place, an oasis that marked escape from the sun-burned Forty Mile desert of alkali sink land; a preparation point for the rugged climb over the last great obstacle on the westward journey, the towering, snow-capped Sierra Nevadas.

Origin of its name seems lost to the past. Some say it was because the emigrant house-wives, advantaging themselves of the clear river water, turned out long overdue family laundries and used acres of sagebrush for spreading the clothes to dry; others claim the camp was so named because of the discarded mattresses and other household goods which littered the river banks as pioneers sought to lighten their wagon loads for the long pull over the mountains.

At any rate Ragtown was a well-remembered oasis.

It meant the end of stifling desert heat and dust where oxen died in harness on the last leg of the tortuous journey down the Humboldt, where broken wagons were abandoned as whole families set out afoot to reach fresh water. Ragtown was accustomed to the sight of stampeding oxen sliding down the banks of the Carson River for a gulp of precious water, of seeing men, women, and children splash into the stream and pour water over the dust-caked clothes as if they couldn't believe their eyes.

There was a cemetery at Ragtown too. Over two hundred members of emigrant trains who couldn't endure the last long march to water lie here. Sometimes as many as five or six wagon trains camped at Ragtown to recover their strength for the final great effort. Wagon wheels were mended. A smithy set up shop to repair broken spokes and sweat rims onto the shrunken, heat-cracked wheels. Camps spread up and down the banks of the Carson, and at night the music of fiddles, mouth organs, and accordions floated over the camp fires among the willows. It was a rest, and then a brief recreation time but eventually the trains moved on and over the Sierras. Today Ragtown is known as Leeteville, but its green trees and grass-covered soil still make distinct contrast to the barren sink land on the north where pioneers beat a groping path.

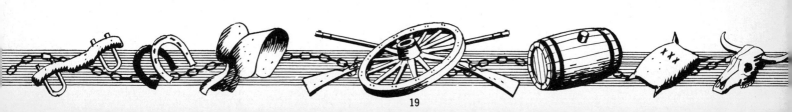

19

The Jayhawkers

Paul Wyland

TRAGIC TALES of the Donner Party's fate in the snow-choked Sierras during the winter of '46-'47 had a telling effect on westbound wagon trains for the following three years. As the winter season approached, travel through Nevada by the Hastings cutoff and Truckee River routes showed sharp decline as California-bound pioneers veered sharply south from Salt Lake over new and sometimes untried trails.

Exactly three winters after the icy grip of the Sierra Nevada mountains had taken its toll of Donnerites, the Jayhawkers, the Wades and the Bennett-Arcane parties met with a fate almost equally as terrible on the burning sands of Death Valley.

Years before white men appeared, native Indians had named Death Valley, Tomesha, meaning Ground Afire, and had the Jayhawkers attempted to negotiate this weird abyss in the heat of summer, it is likely that none would have lived to tell the tale. As it was the Jayhawkers, Wades and the Bennett-Arcane parties all entered the strange valley within a few days of each other during Christmas week of 1849. Because the Jayhawkers were first, and because their party originally had been excellently equipped, the tragedy of the valley crossing was more often associated with their sufferings than with those of either the Wade or Bennett-Arcane families. A full quarter century elapsed before a like number of people braved the stifling heat and forbidding terrain of the sub sea level expanse called Death Valley that stretches for 130 miles along the Nevada-California border, hemmed in by towering desert peaks that rise strangely and abruptly nearly a mile above the sweltering plain.

The Jayhawkers were a blithe band of thirty-six young men, who left Galesburg, Illinois in a well equipped train. From Salt Lake they turned southwest, but instead of striking the Old Spanish Trail, they elected to try the Williams route, a cutoff on the Salt Lake-Los Angeles Trail. They entered Death Valley through Furnace Creek Wash and immediately became aware of their predicament. Sometimes they wandered as much as three days without water. Finally, this once well equipped train, was reduced to the bare essentials of life, food and water. Their oxen were slaughtered and they burned their wagons to smoke the meat. Rather than keeping together, they split as judgment dictated, each small group attempting to find a route over the mountains toward the Pacific.

Asa Haynes, who captained one of the divisions, kept a pitiful diary of his group's wanderings. Brief entries such as "South 12 miles, no water, then southeast 8 miles, got weak. A man named Fish died. Starvation," tell the harrowing tale of the Jayhawkers' plight. Actually only one death within the valley proper is recorded, but the men were so weakened that many more fell by the wayside before some survivors negotiated the final mountain range and arrived at the hacienda San Francisquito early in February 1850, a forty-day hunger march from Death Valley.

Wagon Train Oasis

FOR 100 YEARS Wells has been an important point to the westward tide moving across the nation. In earliest days it was a green paradise to the pioneers, weary from a blistering desert crossing from Utah who rested there gathering strength for the terrible trip down the Humboldt.

At times more than a hundred covered wagons dotted the wild grass as oxen and horses grazed and dusty men, women and children refreshed themselves at the springs for which Wells was named. At night they sang around campfires while the menfolk took turns guarding the precious stock from raiding Indians.

The lush range and the deep wild grass soon made Wells the center of large cattle kingdoms and the community has prospered and suffered in direct reflection of the great cattle spreads around it. Wells is a junction of the Union Pacific, Southern Pacific, and Western Pacific Railroads. It also is a junction between east-west Highway 40 which follows the pioneer Humboldt river route, and Highway 93 which reaches north to Twin Falls and south to the Ely district.

Today finds Wells a small but modern and progressive community. Its chief activities are serving the ranches, railroads, and highway traffic. With the heavy flow of people through its center, Wells has a great potential tourist

business when it begins to exploit the incredibly fine hunting and fishing country all around it, as well as the jagged mountain scenery, hidden lakes, and literally thousands of miles of good skiing and winter sports terrain. Wells is a small town with a colorful history and a great future.

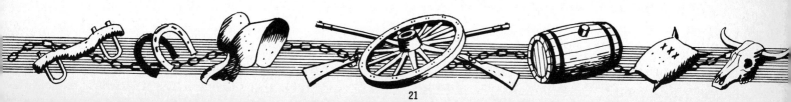

Pioneer Peddler

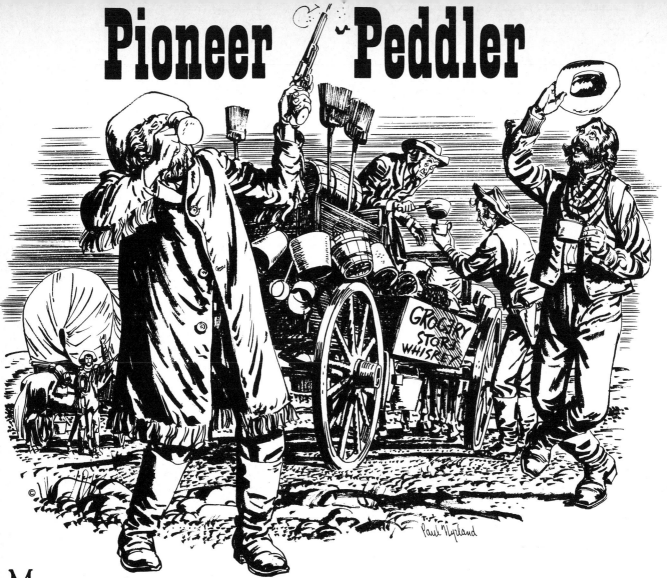

Paul Wyland

MANY TRAGEDIES and hardships along the way west could have been averted with good leadership and planning. An example of both has been left us in the diaries and log of the famous "Charleston Party Company" which was organized in February, 1849, in Charleston, Virginia. This group made a highly successful trip west, enjoying the best hunting and fishing in the world as they leisurely came across Nevada into California.

The Charleston Company was composed of 60 veterans of the Mexican war who decided to come west and mine for gold. Each contributed $300 and each was to share alike in the profits. Each agreed to a rigid set of rules and regulations, and they trained for weeks before the trip. When the group started, with good guides and excellent equipment, it had been trained for a well-planned campaign as an army trains and plans for a battle.

The party included a physician and surgeon with a stock of medicines and "a sick wagon" and was accounted to be "very free from illness and death." Two men died en route from accidents, and three died from disease, a very light casualty list by 1849 standards.

With a light load, and taking good care of their mules, they overtook many wagon trains. The men were good hunters, and soon found the long-eared "Jack Ass Rabbits" to be very good eating. Their log also tells of "deer, antelope, sagehen, duck, and streams full of big fighting trout." Minding their own business, they left the Indians alone and the Indians, in turn did not bother them. The records tell that in crossing northern Nevada they unexpectedly met a

travelling "grocery store" along the dim trail. A little peddler, with his wagon stacked high with trading goods, household items, flour, and patent medicines was shrewdly doing business. This fearless groceryman, out in the sagebrush hundreds of miles from any settlement, had a good supply of powerful whiskey and found ready customers among the Charleston Company.

The log relates that "most of us got **taught**" and it was "something" before the company could re-assemble, get to its feet, and continue down the Humboldt, with what was probably the first big hangover in Nevada history.

They made camp near Lovelock to rest their stock for the terrible dash across the Forty Mile Desert. Here they cut hay, repaired the wagons, rested the mules, and filled their water casks and barrels.

Here, too, according to their log, they found a great encampment of wagon trains. Groups were coming and going at all hours of the day and night. On the average, at least 250 wagons were spread out in the tall wild grass, and the singing, dancing, parties, prayer meetings, and activity were described in the log as "one of the liveliest places one could witness in a lifetime." They were impressed with the beauty of the Truckee River, and rode steadily up through the Truckee Meadows and over the Sierra Nevada without mishap. On September 1 they arrived at the sprawling Sacramento. Some of the party continued by riverboat to San Francisco, and the Charleston Party Company completed its casual crossing of the route west without further incident.

Pioneer Christmas

OVER ONE HUNDRED years ago, the parched and exhausted Brier family sat at the edge of Death Valley, under the winter stars, and listened to the first Christmas sermon preached in Nevada. Possibly it was just over the line in California, the records are vague; but we do know that instead of the usual "dissertation on giving" it was a simple little talk by the Reverend Brier urging his three small sons to improve themselves through education.

The Rev. J. W. Brier, his tiny wife Juliet, and their sons, aged nine, six, and four, had just walked across most of central Nevada with its rocks, lava beds, sagebrush, and alkali desert. Their route lay from Illinois to Salt Lake and Pinto Creek, Utah. There the party split, the Briers to head due west for Walkers Pass with the historic Jayhawker party. In desolate Forty Mile Canyon the Briers were forced to abandon their precious wagons and continue on foot, driving the cattle to California. They soon dropped farther and farther behind the all-male and fast-moving Jayhawkers.

The day before Christmas, 1849, found the Briers approaching Death Valley along the Amargosa Valley. Reverend Brier went ahead to scout for water, and Mrs. Brier followed, driving the stumbling cattle, and carrying the little four-year-old on her back. The mother and three children walked in this fashion all day, on into the setting sun and desert twilight.

As the stars came out, Mrs. Brier would sink to her knees every few hundred yards and feel for the ox tracks and wheel marks of the Jayhawker party ahead. The smallest child cried at times, for water, but the six and nine year old boys were as brave and uncomplaining as their mother.

At midnight they met their father at a tiny campfire and he picked up the smallest boy. Together the little family made the last six miles to camp and water. In hot and cold springs, they scrubbed off the white alkali dust and lay down to rest. Soon they were joined by two teamsters who had been with the Jayhawkers, and the little party killed one of the scrawny oxen for Christmas dinner. It was so thin, the slimy meat was almost gone but they made stew and served it with black coffee and biscuit. Too utterly tired to sing carols, and more to take their minds off the dangers ahead and their condition, the Reverend Brier preached his little Christmas sermon.

He was just finishing when William Lewis Manley arrived, scouting ahead of his wagon train, and the group soon caught up with the Jayhawkers again. But the Briers, according to the record, walked most of the 400 miles from Forty Mile Canyon in Nevada to Los Angeles, after still more adventures even more arduous than those of Christmas Eve. The tiny, five-foot Juliet Brier was indomitable.

During the three final weeks she lifted her big athletic husband to his feet each morning, steadying him a moment so he could stay on his feet all day. To the very end, she was an inspiration to the exhausted and discouraged men of the party, but she arrived safely in southern California where she bore several more children and lived to a happy old age.

Down the Humboldt to "Frenchman's"

DOWN THE HUMBOLDT to Frenchman's Ford," was the route followed by early wagon trains, trappers, cattlemen, and colorful Basque sheep outfits. The crossing was dignified by the name of Winnemucca in 1868, for the celebrated Paiute chief, when the Central Pacific Railroad tracks reached the community.

From then on Winnemucca grew rapidly, taking the county seat away from Unionville. The back country was rich in range land and supported many large cattle and sheep outfits, as it does today. It was also rich in mineral resources and Winnemucca became an important freighting center.

The town had the usual periods of excitement common to all Nevada communities, including holdups, stage robberies, violent cattle and sheep wars, gun battles over precious water, and feuds over mines and claims. Winnemucca's important position astride the natural routes across Nevada and north into Oregon have made it a key point in northern Nevada history since 1850.

The site of Winnemucca had always been a somewhat central crossroad for the various districts and communities which rose and fell throughout the years. Stage and freighter traffic to and from Paradise, the Quinn River country, the Black Rock, Unionville, the Star Mining District, many regions up and down the river and countless stations, ranches, and small communities in other areas all passed near or through Winnemucca, or affected trade there.

The ever-increasing volume of business coming south from Idaho found Winnemucca at the junction on the river, and this travel has steadily increased down until modern times with paved highways, railways, airways, and bus terminals.

Winnemucca has seen mining excitement, strikes and booms in almost every direction, and any citizen in town can show you specimens of good rock. Many families maintain winter homes in Winnemucca, but spend the summers out on large ranches nearby. Huge cattle and sheep spreads fan out from the area in almost every direction, and some of the sheep and cattle wars, and water wars left scars and feeling which only now are beginning to heal. It has been said that of all communities in Nevada, Winnemucca is probably the most typical in all catagories for those of the entire state.

Today finds Winnemucca the financial and cultural capital of some 10,000 square miles of rich ranching and mining resources and the scene of many attractive homes, fine schools, and enterprising business establishments. Served by main lines of both Western Pacific and Southern Pacific railroads and U. S. Highway 40 along the waterlevel route, Winnemucca is growing and prosperous.

Massacre Lakes

FEW TRAILS leading the emigrants westward are more replete with tragedies than the Applegate Cut-Off, which branched north from the Humboldt near Lassen's Meadows to guide travelers through northwestern Nevada into the fertile Willamette Valley of Oregon.

As early as 1844 when Captain Levi Scott, Captain Lindsay Applegate and a scout named Garrison were attacked by marauding Indians on their exploratory trip through the High Rock Canyon country, tragedy seemed to stalk the Applegate Cut-Off. On that occasion Garrison was killed and Scott wounded. Later skirmishes with the Indians at Soldier Meadows and Forty-Nine Canyon gave rise to the establishment of Fort McGarry near Summit Lake to guard the trail. Most tragic of all, however, was the battle at Massacre Lakes where a common grave holds the bodies of forty pioneers who fell there in a fearful struggle.

In the summer of 1850 a large and particularly well equipped wagon train, bound for Oregon, left the winding Humboldt and struck out for Oregon over the Applegate Cut-Off. During their trek they had been bothered by Indians and in one incident several redmen were killed. Painted warriors stalked the train in ever increasing numbers until the emigrants decided upon a united attack. It was a fatal mistake.

The white men left their wagon train and succeeded in driving the war party well to the rear of the caravan. Apparently victorious they returned to their encampment, but the redmen were upon them instantly. Unprepared for

defense they again left the train and rode out of the wagon circle to give battle. After a terrific struggle the Indians were driven off but forty men of the original company lay dead on the alkali battleground.

Widows and fatherless children joined the few remaining able-bodied men of the group in making a common grave for their dead. Fearful lest the redmen return to disinter and desecrate the bodies, oxen of the wagon train were then driven over the fresh mound to obliterate its location.

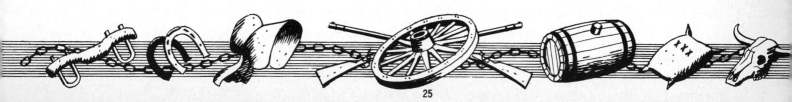

The First "Tenderfeet"

T HE SUMMER of 1849 found the dust billowing all along Nevada's Humboldt River, as little groups of gold seekers made the trip to the gold fields in California. Easily the most feared section of the entire route was the desert extending from where Lovelock is today, to Leeteville and the Carson River; or to Fernley and the Truckee.

Pioneer diaries reveal it took ox-drawn covered wagons about two days and two nights to cross the infamous Forty Mile Desert. The trail was littered with the rotting carcasses of dead animals and the desert air was foul for miles.

About midway across this bleak expanse of soft sand and alkali, the oxen, their mouths parched, their eyes bloodshot, and their steps faltering, would scent moisture in the breeze. Pawing, and bellowing, they rushed frantically ahead to a rocky slope of stunted brush with patches of swamp grass, greasewood, and tules. Here were the "Hot Springs."

Heedless of the warning clouds of steam from the great springs, the frantic animals plunged into boiling water, often dying from the terrible scalding.

Thoughtful pioneers put out barrels of hot water, which would cool for the following emigrant trains. Others dug ditches and pools to chill the water for livestock. Emigrant families learned to cook in the hot springs, setting pans of dried fruit and vegetables to float on the boiling surface.

And anyone could still see the bodies of a large ox and a small dog, their hair scalded off, still lying in the bubbling depths of the big hot spring.

The next year (1850) an emigrant named "Pop" Haver, camped at Hot Springs. His oxen had barely made it, so he decided to let them rest and regain strength in the tules and swamp grass. But just as he had his oxen back in shape and prepared to pull up stakes, a party of gold seekers arrived in a big rush to be up and over the Sierras "before all the mines were exhausted." In their haste, they offered to swap "Pop" their 70 head of sore footed oxen, five wagons, and their spare goods, for his 22 head of trail-ready fresh stock.

"Pop" couldn't resist a deal like that, so he stayed through the winter. He made four similar transactions in as many weeks. By the spring of 1851 he had over 200 head of stock, 20 wagons, and more property than he could haul. So he decided to stay, and it is probable that he later hauled in feed from the Truckee.

His camp became a fixture along the emigrant trail, and was widely known as "The Tenderfeet Station." Here tender-footed animals were traded for fresh oxen to make the final trip up over the Sierra Nevadas to California. And as new caravans approached it was often asked, "I wonder how many tenderfeet in that outfit?" So the word came to be applied first to trail-weary oxen, and then to inexperienced travelers in the frontier west. Today, nearly 100 years later, Webster defines the word and says it is of "western U. S. origin." Undoubtedly, it originated out on the alkali flats along our own U. S. Highway 40.

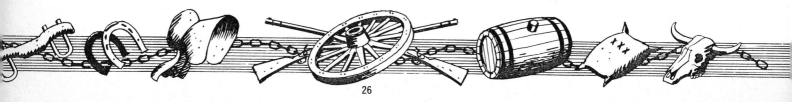

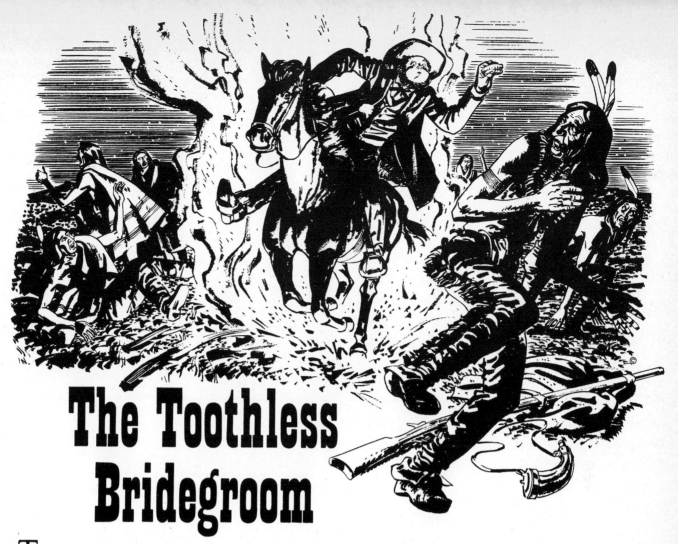

The Toothless Bridegroom

THE REST of the covered wagon train joshed quiet Harmanus Van Vleck. They accused the nervous young bridegroom of being unduly concerned about the Indians and other hazards.

It was just about 100 years ago, where the city of Reno now stands, that the little wagon train made camp for the night. The oxen made the best of the lush wild grass along the river banks, and the cattle guards watched with curiosity at the Indian fires twinkling on the foothills. The wagons were circled for the night, but cooking was still unfinished. Harmanus looked at his bride, working with the other women and worried.

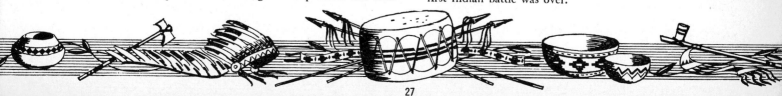

Although he knew the rest of the party were amused at his concern, he caught up his best mare, saddled, and rode out into the desert night to scout the Indian camp fires. He reflected, as his horse picked her way through the sagebrush and rocks, that if the Paiutes were hostile, the wagon camp would be almost defenseless.

He took his time, circling down wind to avoid the Indian dogs. Here he dismounted and hobbled his horse. By now he felt a trifle foolish, but he resolved to go through with it so he capped and primed his hand guns, tied his boots up on the saddle, and slipped into soft Indian moccasins. Here, low on the foothills, began the virgin pine forests reaching unbroken for miles, clear over the Sierras to the distant valleys of California.

A mile lower down the hill, he worked himself into heavy sagebrush until he was quite close to the largest of the Indian camp fires. As he edged into position and took a good look at the proceedings, his heart sank. There were many more Indians than he had suspected, they were wearing war paint, and were working themselves up to the usual frenzy preceding an attack.

Bitterly, Harmanus crept back through the buckbrush and rocks to his horse. No time, he reflected, to warn the wagon train, and little they could do if he succeeded. He cursed the lack of an armed party with him. A sudden unexpected attack in the night might rout the Indians.

Then **the idea** took form. He dismounted, kept close to his horse's head to keep her quiet, and lead her back toward the Indian fires. Finally, just out of earshot, he swung up into the saddle, took a deep breath, dug his spurs into his startled and indignant mare, and charged down through the mob of dancing, chanting savages.

Yelling, screaming, yodelling, like a dozen men . . . shouting commands and answering himself, Harmanus saw the dancers stop, stiffen, and turn with horror in their eyes to the noisy attack. And as he swept into the light of the camp fires, his horse plunging and slipping, Harmanus had an inspiration to rank with the best military tactics of the century. He pulled out his false teeth, thrust them in front of him, and made them gnash, and click, and grimace as he thundered down upon the paralyzed Paiutes.

It was too much for flesh and blood. The Paiutes had never dreamed of such a horrible creature. One look . . . and they broke into a panic-stricken mob and ran. Reno's first Indian battle was over.

Gold Canyon Jig

THREE-FOURTHS of all the women in western Utah territory, nine, to be exact, attended Nevada's first dance on New Year's Eve, 1853, when Spafford Hall's log store at the mouth of Gold Canyon was gayly lighted for the celebration to officially welcome in the New Year.

Little girls and grandmothers alike could claim the honor of "belle of the ball" because there were 150 men to ask for each dance from the nine representatives of the fair sex. Miners, ranchers and station keepers from a radius of fifty miles descended upon Gold Canyon and Spafford Hall's store for the event and only three women stayed away or else the dance committee could have claimed one hundred percent representation.

Swishing calico skirts and hobnailed miners' boots beat out a rhythm on the rough log floor until the small hours of the morning as a makeshift orchestra scraped out tunes like "Oh Suzanna" and other popular ditties for the square dances and Virginia reels. Not only was it Nevada's first dance, but a New Year's celebration, too.

Not quite used to "white men's fandango's," a band of Washoe Indians ventured close to the store and seeing that all was merriment inside, they proceeded to drive off the horses to their own meeting place near the present site of Mound House where they enjoyed a barbecue of fresh horsemeat. When the "first dance" finally broke up, tired miners and ranchers, some of whom had to ride many miles to their homes, were astounded to find that no horses awaited them. Wagon tongues stood empty, and cut ropes dangled in the chill breeze where saddle horses had been tethered the night before. A corral gate swung open and tracks in the soft alkali soil told the story.

In the chill wintry dawn most of the merrymakers had to set off on the trail of the missing animals. Late the next day they succeeded in rounding up the stock. Nursing headaches, chilled with the cold, and bitter against the simple Washoes, it was a lucky thing for all that a party of searchers did not run across any of the simple tribesmen.

A brand new series of Indian wars could easily have been touched off on the flat benches above the Carson River. Two of the animals were missing and the searchers concurred in the assumption that these had been barbecued by the Washoes. After the feast, the Indians had disappeared, letting the horses wander.

It was late in the day of the New Year, 1854, when all the celebrants were again provided with their horses and set off for their homes, but no one seemed to mind greatly, for Western Utah Territory had staged a successful dance.

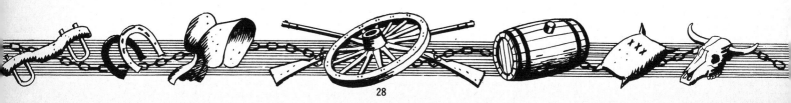

Naming the Ruby Mountains

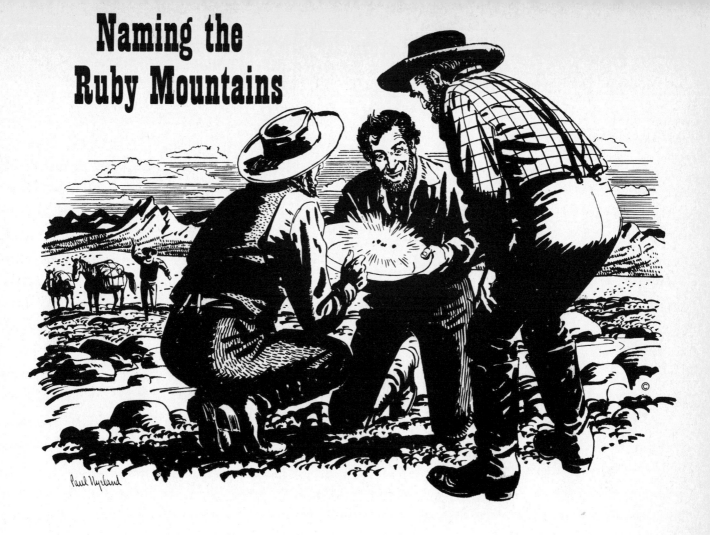

Paul Nyland

THE ARMY was seeking new routes west in 1854, and Brigham Young sent out scouts to study the land in central Nevada. So the Huntingtons, Reese, and some teamsters had worked their way as far as southern Elko County.

During a noon halt, at the foot of towering and magnificent mountains, a man named Davis killed time by panning for gold. He got colors a plenty, but instead of metal, he found rubies (red garnet) and nearly broke up the expedition! Time was short, rations were scarce, and Indians were hostile, so the party made a record, named the great range "Ruby Mountains" and hurried on to the west without further mining. They also met a band of Indians led by a chief wearing a white man's Panama hat, who was directed in eastern Nevada, by a legendary white renegade named "Hawes."

The exploration party talked its way out of a fight with the "Panama Hat Chief," and again struggled westward, killing its horses for food before reaching Mormon Station (Genoa) where Reese later made his home. On the return trip to Salt Lake, with reports on a new route avoiding the Humboldt trail, the party rode to Ragtown and then went due east into the unknown central Nevada.

They were riding through the most dreaded parts of "The Great American Desert," a land of mystery, brutal renegades and savage Indians.

This time they camped near the Toiyabe Mountains and discovered a little river meandering through the valley which they named for Reese. It is still called the "Reese River."

Again the group had a terrible ordeal, without sufficient food and water. By November they again came up Ruby Valley and met a band of Indians. Again the Huntingtons tried to talk their way out of a clash. This time they staged a "shooting match" and by sleight of hand, slipped up a target already hit in the bullseye. This was manipulated so the simple Indians believed they saw the white man shoot out the center spot at a third of a mile!

Impressed by such incredible shooting they became friendly and warned the party of another Indian ambush now set up by their former friend of the Panama hat. Alarmed, the party staged an elaborate departure, made a big campfire that night, and quietly rode for dear life in the dark across the desert to safety and Salt Lake. They arrived, starved into a state of skin and bones, their clothing in tatters, their skins sunburned to blackness.

They made it, and although the army changed its mind and later used another route, the Huntingtons reported a new way across Nevada, free from alkali water, shorter than the Humboldt trail, and destined to become famous as the way west for pony express, telegraph and stage coach.

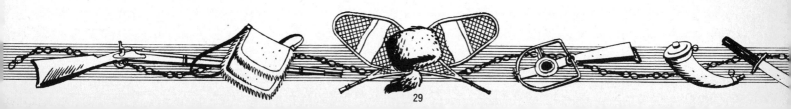

Madame Moustache

MANY OF THE fabulous and colorful characters crossing the Nevada pioneer scene came from far corners of the earth, but none of them was more appealing or more fascinating than beautiful Madame Moustache, the first "lady gambler."

First record of her appears in 1854, when she stepped off the stage at Nevada City, California, a dark-eyed, fresh-faced girl of twenty, dressed in the best of taste and the height of fashion. She promptly opened her own gambling establishment, dealing vingt et un (twenty-one) and became an immediate success. The miners liked the way she paid off bets with a friendly smile and the town approved the manner in which she kept peace and order in her establishment. She commanded admiration and respect, and her virtue was unquestioned.

After a year in Nevada City, she wandered from California mining camps to Nevada, always gambling and always a favorite. She was generous to the unfortunate, and it was said no luckless miner ever failed in asking her for a stake. She exercised considerable influence over the rough miners, and it was told that at Pioche, on a wild and riotous payday night, she broke up a pistol-flourishing mob by joking and laughing with the men.

She is said to have driven a smallpox-laden river boat away from Fort Benton at the point of her revolvers, to save the town from epidemic. It was widely told of her, and probably with truth, that she kept a watchful eye on the young and inexperienced; and protected more than one youthful miner from a fleecing at the hands of unscrupulous barkeeps, dance hall girls, and their associates. It is told how she served champagne instead of corn whiskey and had an orchestra instead of the customary lone fiddler. Whether these stories are true or not, there is sufficient evidence to show that this remarkable woman enjoyed the friendship, admiration and respect of thousands of miners throughout the raw, wild, mining camps of the west in the late fifties, sixties, and seventies.

The closing years of her life were sheer tragedy. She had amassed a considerable fortune in gambling and purchased a beautiful ranch in eastern Nevada. There she married and settled down with her husband to a quiet life of pleasant rural activity. She turned her property and all her money over to her husband but he proved to be a worthless rascal who soon squandered everything, and after he had wasted her entire fortune, he deserted her. From the profound emotional shock, a change took place in the fortunes and the appearance of Madame Moustache. Until then the records indicate she had a fresh, girl-like beauty and vivacity. Now her features coarsened, and a growth of dark hair, previously absent or virtually invisible, appeared on her upper lip, from which she derived the name "Madame Moustache."

Her old, light touch, and her skill as a gambler seemed to desert her and she failed to rise from a grinding poverty that followed her from mining camp to camp. Hairy-faced, her features coarsened, and now in her late forties, she was an outstanding object of pity. She drifted from camp to camp and into obscurity, until finally she sought the only escape left to her. The pioneer day Thompson & West history tells "on the morning of September 8, 1879, her dead body was found about two miles south of Bodie, a bottle of poison lying near. Let her many good qualities invoke leniency in criticising her failings."

Dutch Nick's

DUTCH NICK'S was a landmark on the Overland-Emigrant stage route where the dusty trail touched the banks of the Carson River, just three and a half miles north of the present location of Carson City. Although it was later surveyed as a townsite and officially named Empire City, it continued to bear the name of Dutch Nick's in honor of the original owner, Nicholas Ambrosia, who recorded his claim to the property in 1855.

With the rise of the Comstock and the building of the Virginia and Truckee Railway, Dutch Nick's became one of the most important settlements along the east fork of the Carson. Here it was that the Mexican, Morgan and Brunswick mills flourished. They ground out rich ores under pressure of water power supplied by the Carson River as it raced through a high walled canyon.

But milling was a minor activity at Empire compared with the logging industry. The river makes a sweeping curve at Dutch Nick's, basking lazily in the flatland sun before plunging the mad rapids of Brunswick canyon. The quiet water provided a perfect setting for log booms, especially after completion of the Virginia and Truckee Railway, because here the huge timbers could be guided shoreward and loaded into waiting flat cars to supply the Comstock.

Pine was cut in the Sierra Nevadas above Alpine in California, near the headwaters of the Carson, and rafted for eighty miles along the sometimes turbulent stream to

Dutch Nick's, depot of the wood business. The rafting was a source of never ending amazement in desert country as millions of board feet of pine, spruce and cedar rolled and bobbled along the river for forty days in the journey from the Carson headwaters to Dutch Nick's. In 1850 fifty thousand cords of wood reached the log booms at Empire and the major portion of it eventually reached the Comstock for timbering the deep mines. Lumbermen, like miners enjoyed the end of the ride at Dutch Nick's

and the station became widely known, retaining the name of its owner long after it was officially called Empire City.

Today it is hard to imagine that the river was once alive with logging activity. The Carson is hardly more than a trickle in the hot fall months, yet many of the buildings of the Comstock and even of Carson itself were constructed from the timber that found its way down the Carson from Alpine to Dutch Nick's.

The Old Potosi Mine

NEVADA'S OLDEST "lode" mine is generally accepted to be the old Potosi, near Goodsprings in southern Nevada. Certainly the history of the old workings which started in 1855 show it to be an early producer of lead and silver, and later a successful source for zinc.

Old Potosi was found by a party of Mormons returning to Las Vegas Ranch over the old Spanish or Mule Trail from San Bernardino. A Mormon mission had been established at Las Vegas that year, when Brigham Young sent out William Bringhurst and 30 young men to build a fort to protect the mail, and "to teach and convert the Indians."

Congress had appropriated $25,000 in 1852 to build a military road from Salt Lake City over Cajon Pass to San Bernardino. Much of the road followed the old Mexican trade trail, in use since 1830, for large caravans containing thousands of jacks, jennets, and mules en route to Sante Fe. The return trip brought valuable merchandise to California, and escorts often consisted of 300 heavily armed and mounted men.

So the Las Vegas Mission became an important point to the Mormon settlers of the pioneer southwest, and when lead was found at the Old Potosi, Brigham Young sent out Nathaniel Jones to "mine and manufacture." It was part of the church self-sufficiency program and an iron mission near Cedar City was already reported in production of nails.

Smelting at the mine was a failure, so the ore was hauled to Las Vegas where Dudd Leavitt and Isaac Grundy built a fireplace furnace and smelted from 9,000 to 10,000 pounds of lead. There was a local tradition that the Indians themselves had worked the Old Potosi, smelting it crudely and casting themselves lead bullets. At any rate it was too flaky and brittle for the Mormons, and the project failed. In 1857 when the Mormons were called back to Salt Lake City, the Old Potosi was abandoned. Isolated parties later tried to cast a few bullets at times and many of them succeeded. But it was not until Nevada became "silver conscious" in 1861 that the lead was found to be rich SILVER-BEARING GALENA! It was written that "nobody knows how many elk, bear, deer, coyotes, and Indians got their quietus with a silver bullet."

Even this discovery did not bring great mining activity to the district, however, until gold was found nearby in the '90's. But in 1905 the San Pedro, Los Angeles, and Salt Lake Railway was built, and at the same time it was found that the Old Potosi was also rich in zinc. It became the largest zinc producer at that time in Nevada and a 100-ton zinc-lead separating mill was built in 1910 at Goodsprings. A narrow-gauge was also built to connect with the railroad at Jean at the same time. So the Old Potosi with its fabulous Silver Bullets finally became a modern mine with one of the longest production records in southern Nevada.

Lucky Bill

LUCKY BILL THORRINGTON was lucky, it seemed, at everything . . . lucky at faro, lucky at roulette, and very lucky at rustling and tricky deals with livestock. He lived with his family in the early '50's at the head of Carson Valley, and had such a friendly personality that he was well liked in spite of his shady reputation.

Lucky Bill soon picked up a partner, a man named Edwards, who was popularly believed to have committed murder for which an innocent man had been hanged. He reported to Lucky Bill that a Frenchman was driving a fine-looking herd of cattle down the Truckee River from California, and that he wanted much too fancy a price for them.

Lucky Bill suggested to Edwards that he murder the Frenchman, hide his body, forge a bill of sale and spread the report that the victim had returned to California. This plan Edwards promptly carried out, without a hitch. That is, until friends of the missing Frenchman became alarmed over his absence, and instituted such a vigorous search that they recovered his body and the entire affair was brought to light.

Lucky Bill was immediately arrested by a Vigilante Committee, found guilty and sentenced to be hanged. But Edwards was in hiding. Finally the Vigilantes hinted to Lucky Bill's 16-year-old son that if he would deliver Edwards, his father would be treated leniently. The boy agreed on condition that his father's life would be saved.

It was known that Edwards was heavily armed and desperate, so the lad was to decoy him to a meeting place. That night, the boy went to Edwards, hidden in a secluded place in the Sierras near Genoa, and urged him to meet Lucky Bill, who had a plan for their escape.

Concealing the facts of his father's arrest, the boy was so earnest that Edwards' suspicions of a trap were somewhat lulled. Finally he warned the lad that if he were betrayed, he would kill the boy first; and Lucky Bill's son agreed to those terms. He then led Edwards to a lonely ranch owned by Lucky Bill which was situated near the forks of the Carson River. Here, elaborately concealed lay the Vigilantes in ambush.

Shortly after midnight Edwards reached the place. He paused at the door, listened, levelled his shotgun, and walked into the dark. A powerful man standing behind the door felled him with a club, and the Vigilantes immediately sat in a trial hearing.

Edwards was found guilty and sentenced to be hanged; but there was a great commotion in western Nevada as people believed Lucky Bill should have been released to keep the promises made to his son. Many folks felt the matter should be turned over to the regular authorities, but a majority insisted on the hanging without delay.

They gathered at the old Clear Creek Ranch at the junction of Carson and Eagle Valleys. Most of the inhabitants of western Utah Territory (Nevada) were present, and saw the rope tossed over the cottonwood limb. Lucky Bill stood up and in a powerful, clear voice, sang "The Last Rose of Summer" until the wagon was driven from under his feet. Most witnesses agree that Edwards met his death bravely too, but some accounts claim he was returned to the Honey Lake country where he was hanged for a previous crime. But all records agree that both men were hanged.

Muleback Champion

IN 1855 most immigrants viewed a crossing of Nevada Territory with dread, if not terror. So, when Major Howard Egan, a virile, bearded, iron-willed Mormon pioneer offered to bet he could go mule-back from Salt Lake to Sacramento in ten days, it looked like a fool-hardy proposition. But the fact was that the shrewd Major had made a cinch bet.

Egan had just driven a band of livestock across the route, and on the return trip had mapped carefully every foot of the way for a road which today is known as Highway 50. He was interested with partners in forming an overland stage route along this trail. And so, on September 19, 1855, Egan mounted a big mule at Salt Lake, and keeping a careful diary, again checked his proposed route, making a speed that has never been equalled on a single horse or mule to this day.

Some nights he took as much as three hours rest, and his average daytime halt on the hot blistering desert average an hour. He had listed every stream, water-hole, and creek. He was lucky in avoiding unfriendly Indians, and his choice of the best pass or canyon was invariably the easiest. So, when he came down out of the Sierra foothills into California and rode into Sacramento, his wager was forgotten, overshadowed by the amazing speed across the most difficult portion of the hazardous "way west." And his feat encouraged hundreds of wagon trains to take the central route across Nevada. The stage line followed this route, and when the pony express started in 1860, Major Egan was in charge of the Salt Lake Division. His trail knowledge was invaluable, and he had the honor of riding out with the first packet of mail from the Mormon Capital. On this ride, the record shows that at Mill Creek, Egan's fast horse slipped off the plank bridge, soaking both animal and rider, but he was instantly up and away, setting a record for that part of the trail.

It is difficult to realize that at this time Major Egan was 45 years old, square in build and face, with a luxurious beard. Respected from the Rockies to the Coast, he had two sons who carried Pony Express mail and drove stage. It was one of the Egan boys who took over the stage after the Indians murdered "Happy Harry" and Nevada's aged Congressman-elect took the stage safely into Deep Creek Station just ahead of a howling band of marauding savages.

Major Egan was born in Ireland, and came to America with Mormon-convert parents. He came west with Brigham Young and was soon known as a guide and mountaineer in the Great Basin area. He was one of the "Captains of Ten" for the protection of early Mormon settlements, but ranged farther afield than most of his faith, taking an interest in mining, ranching, store-keeping, cattle-driving and missionary work among the Paiutes.

The effect of Egan's fast, mule-back crossing on the wagon trains is hard to realize today. The horrible fate of the early Donner Party had frightened hundreds of groups to take southern routes, or north along the Oregon Trail. Egan's nonchalant trip demonstrated the directness and practical nature of a route which nearly a century later is one of the best and most colorful of the trails across the "Great Desert." It is significant that the Major made little of his trip except for his enthusiasm over the "Egan Trail."

Nevada Exodus

THE SUMMER OF 1857 found the valleys of western Nevada a rich green, under the industrious care of Mormon ranchers, with lush crops, orchards, fine barns, and fat livestock. These happy and prosperous people received a rude shock September 4, 1857, with the arrival of three nearly starved messengers from Brigham Young in Salt Lake City.

Open warfare threatened Utah, and the Mormon Church sent messengers racing across the deserts, through hostile Indian country, to bring all people back to Salt Lake City for the common defense.

Without a whimper, and without question, the Mormon families in western Nevada (then Carson County of Utah) abandoned the rich fields they had won from sagebrush, left their homes, furniture, barns, fences, and property. Some they sold to "Gentiles" who snatched up incredible bargains at sacrifice prices. Other property was simply abandoned and taken over by squatters. Funds were subscribed and the original messengers continued over the Sierra for wagon loads of ammunition. They wired for arms over the new telegraph, constructed then as far as Angel's Camp.

The "Gentiles" of the mining camps were not happy over the wagons loaded with ammunition to be used against American troops, and they harassed the party, tried to stampede the horses at night, but without success.

Arriving back in Carson Valley the messengers found the entire settlement organized in a vast wagon train and on the move! Joined by other groups from Eagle and Washoe valleys the wagon train contained nearly 1,000 people, about 150 wagons, and huge herds of stock. It wound down along the Emigrant trail, reversing the westward tide of gold and fortune seekers. Between Dayton and the Forty Mile Desert, the great wagon train halted and all persons were ordered to pay their debts and settle all accounts before leaving the country.

With one or two possible exceptions every claim was settled, some with the aid of "boards of arbitration" set up among the wagon camps.

Out on the Humboldt Sink the train was again bothered by bands of "Gentiles" who tried to stampede the stock and capture the ammunition wagons. Mormon patrols finally put some of the most persistent under guard for a night, treated them to a round of drinks in the morning, shook hands, and all departed peacefully.

The huge wagon train continued on its way across northern Nevada in late October. Three children died en route and six were born. And on November 1, 1857, the train arrived with much excitement and rejoicing in Salt Lake City. Usually viewed as a chapter in Utah history, it had an equally profound effect in Nevada.

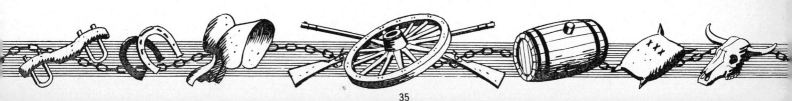

Invasion on the Colorado

TROUBLE WAS BREWING in the Mormon settlements, in March, 1858, and a Federal army under General Johnson threatened all Utah. So, when Jacob Hamblin, Mormon scout and missionary, saw a Yankee gunboat near the present site of Boulder Dam, he surmised it presaged an invasion of Zion! His men peered through the willows at a strange craft, flying the flag, and armed with a four-pound howitzer. She carried soldiers, too!

Hamblin and companions had confirmed the Indian rumor of "Americats" on the Colorado and they rushed to the tiny colony at Las Vegas, warning them to return to safety. This was the true reason for the 1858 abandonment of the Mormon mission at Las Vegas.

If this famous scout had been as wise in the ways of the War Department bureaucrats as he was in the lore of the trail, he might have realized the good ship "Explorer" was a monumental piece of red tape and folly. Anxious to learn how far up the river was navigable, it never occurred to the brass hats to ask the steamboat man who had been sailing it every day for five years! Captain Johnson knew the river well and had made his living on it.

Instead, the War Department built a new steamer at Philadelphia, tested it on the placid Delaware River, took it apart, and shipped it over the Panama Isthmus in sections, and brought it by schooner to the mouth of the Colorado.

Even testing on the calm eastern waters had damaged the fragile little steamer, and she had to be patched with makeshift sections for her journey on one of the most dangerous river on the face of the globe.

Lt. J. C. Ives and a party including scientists were sent out to make the exploration, and after putting all the pieces together, they launched the Explorer almost on New Year's Eve of 1857. She burned mesquite wood, and was continuously grounded on sand bars and rocks. And the Indians were contemptuous, having seen Captain Johnson's larger steamers. Ives had a good pilot, and despite weeks spent in getting off innumerable sand bars, they eventually reached Black Canyon. Here, stuck on a rock and making repairs when Scout Jacob Hamblin saw them, Ives suffered further embarrassment. He was supposed to be "exploring an unknown river," when down the coffee-colored flood came the big and beautiful steamer commanded by Captain Johnson. With paddlewheels churning, smoke billowing, Johnson waved from the wheelhouse, and blew a courteous salute. So chagrined was Ives he couldn't bear to whistle an answer, and Johnson went chugging down the river fuming at the discourtesy.

The crash of the Explorer on the rocks below Black Canyon threw men overboard, jammed the boiler, and tore loose the wheelhouse. After three months, this was as far up as she would sail. While she was beached on a sand bar for repairs, Lt. Ives went by row boat as far as Vegas Wash, which he mistook for the Virgin River.

The Explorer was repaired and returned downriver to Fort Yuma, where she served many years hauling freight and supplies for the army. Lt. Ives, and some members of the party, including a famous Indian guide, were ordered to do further investigating and Ives eventually became a respected and outstanding explorer of the great Southwest. His name appears on many maps and in many histories.

Robbers' Roost

TRAVELERS who followed the Overland Mail route through the West in the Sixties became accustomed to many weird sights, not the least of which were some of the change stations along the trail. Most picturesque of these little out of the way settlements between Salt Lake and the Pacific slope was Robbers' Roost near Camp Ruby in Nevada.

Origination of the name is lost in the welter of swift moving events of the period, but suffice it to say, that, though misleading, it was none-the-less intriguing, and scarcely a traveler stopped without carrying away a rather distinct impression of "western life in the raw."

The floor of the Roost was rough, uneven earth never tamped nor swept and the fine end of a spring oozed through the western wall to keep that vicinity in an eternal state of mud. The length of the interior was divided by a halfway canvas partition behind which were bunks for four men. These were covered with a litter of ragged bed-clothing while underneath the framework were heaps of rubbish, saddles, clothes, harness, sacks of wheat, oats, meal and potatoes, defended from the ground by underlying logs. A redeeming feature of the main quarters was a large fire-place that might have come from a feudal castle.

Chairs were represented in crude pioneer fashion by three-legged stools with an occasional four-legged base type. Tables were rough-dressed planks held together by rickety trestles which served for seats. They were normally adorned with a tin coffee pot, rough knives and pewter spoons. The entire inside walls of the habitation were pegged to support spurs, pistols, knives, whips and leggings.

Soap for cleaning purposes was represented by a handy supply of sandy gravel with the process of evaporation serving as the only available towel. En revanche weapons of the flesh: rifles, guns and pistols were scattered about the four corners of the house well mixed with tools such as axes, saws and chisels.

Invariably a cross-legged Indian squatted uncomfortably close to the fire if he could find room among the mongrel dogs which appeared to be part and parcel of the Roost.

Inhabitants of this strange station seemed to delight in methodically increasing the state of disorder, probably because of the apparent reactions of visitors, and somehow all this show of rough, carefree life seemed to fit strangely into the pattern of the frontier where existence was a matter of day to day concern.

Land Adjustment at Genoa

THE RICH LAND of the western valleys in Nevada could be had for the taking in 1858. Men "squatted" without question on all the land they could reasonably farm. But when a man laid claim on more ground than he could handle, that "surplus" ground was often snatched by other men resolute enough to hold it.

In 1851 Colonel Reese had purchased Genoa from previous owners, and laid claim to all the land for miles around. When Warren Wasson arrived from California, he found much land that Reese and his colony couldn't handle. So, much to their displeasure, Wasson calmly took over some of this ground and proceeded to fence it.

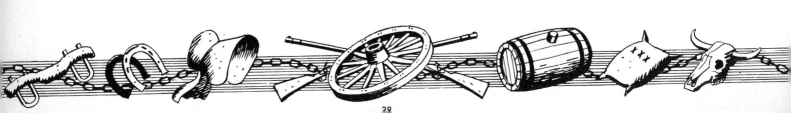

While hauling fence lumber one day, Wasson was suddenly confronted by John Trumbo, a son-in-law of Reese, and his 16-year-old son. The two of them were armed, and threatened Wasson, attempting to run him off the land.

Wasson was a cool and courageous man, later destined to become one of pioneer Nevada's outstanding heroes during Indian troubles. He knew his rights and paid no attention to the threats and gun flourishing of the Trumbos. Finally Trumbo raised his gun and fired several shots at Wasson. All missed their mark, but the bullets were coming closer and closer until Wasson drew his six gun and fired at Trumbo, wounding him in the thigh.

Trumbo fell to the ground and Wasson walked over and gave him first aid. The 16-year-old Trumbo son rushed up but Wasson wanted no quarrel with the youngster and devoted his attention to stopping the flow of blood from Trumbo's wound. The boy, however, ran over to Wasson, thrust an ancient revolver in his face and yanked the trigger.

Luckily the gun was muzzle loaded with light birdshot, which missed his eyes and did no damage other than discoloring his face for life. Wasson had five shots still in his pistol but magnanimously did not fire at the lad. Instead he picked up Trumbo, carried him to a wagon, and took him home where he was months recovering. Public sentiment was all for Wasson and the incident did much to stop "land hogging."

Such adjustments to land titles were then important, for Genoa was the first settlement in Nevada to become permanent. It had been established in 1849 by H. S. Beattie and companions who had a trading post there with a 20x60 foot log house. They sold out to a man named Moore, and Beattie returned to Salt Lake where he worked as a clerk for the Reese Brothers.

Beattie persuaded Colonel Reese to move to Genoa where the passing wagon trains offered a fantastically profitable market. And so Reese and his party purchased Genoa from Moore, sent gifts to the Indians, and laid claim to miles of nearby land.

Man for Breakfast

BODIE WAS TOUGH! It ranked with Panamint, Tombstone, and Butte in early day lawlessness and became so famous as a raw western mining camp that the expression "Bad Man From Bodie" was a commonplace description of its citizenry who managed to stay in the land of the living.

Bodie's cemetery in the shadow of Potato Peak was well marked with fresh tombstones each week as outlaws and quick-tempered miners settled differences in a blaze of hot lead. Killings became so common in the roistering gold camp that residents themselves took no offense to the fable that a "man for breakfast" was a daily occurrence.

The richness of this forbidding region, just over the line from Nevada, north of Mono Lake, was discovered in the same year as the Comstock (1859), but some twenty years elapsed before production reached its pinnacle. Meanwhile, the notoriety of the camp spread through the western diggin's. So impressive was its reputation for wickedness that once when an Aurora family considered moving to the thriving town, the young daughter of the family finished her evening prayers with a tearful "Goodbye, God, we're going to Bodie." Residents of the Mono town took up Aurora's challenge, charging that the child

had been deliberately misquoted, that what she had actually said was "Good! By God we're goin' to Bodie."

Colorful as its reputation, was the town itself, a typical mining settlement of hodge-podge false front buildings, saloons and dance halls all doing a bang-up business. Highlight of the town's entertainment was the thrice weekly arrival of the jerk line freighters from Carson City, carrying fifteen to twenty tons of supplies from the Nevada capital.

The Carson-Bodie fast freight was considered the best mountain route ever established. Experts at jerk line driving guided twenty horse teams night and day through tortuous passes between the two towns. Like the trucks and trailers of today, the articulated wagon train consisted of a large "lead wagon" and three "back action" wagons to allow for negotiating the turns. Every other span of horses throughout the twenty animal team was harnessed with high wooden hames from which lanterns were hung to enable night driving over the mountain and desert roads. Arrival of the fast freight in Bodie was much more of an incident than any tale of the previous night's "shootin'," and the saloons and other buildings of the town would empty huge crowds to the walks to view the arriving teams.

Territorial Legislature

TEN DAYS BEFORE Christmas in the year 1859 Nevada's first Territorial Legislature met in the home of J. B. Blake at Genoa, thus culminating two years of effort toward organization that eventually led to the creation of Nevada Territory in 1861 and Statehood in 1864.

Despite a lack of pretentious surroundings the first legislature got down to business by drafting a memorial to Congress seeking territorial recognition, using as a leverage the feeling of unfriendliness that still existed between the Mormons and the other residents of western Utah.

The organization movement, set on foot in 1857, fell short of achieving the desired result, and the question was again opened in June 1859 when a mass meeting was called in Carson City. Citizens gathered just a week before discovery of the fabulous Comstock Lode and when election was held on the fourteenth of July it was still not known that silver was to be a major portion of the Comstock's wealth.

Four days after the July election delegates assembled in Genoa for a nine-day session drafting the nucleus of a constitution and announcing a declaration of cause for separation from Utah Territory.

This document set forth a long series of abuses and usurpations on the part of the residents of eastern Utah and concluded with a pledge securing future protection "to erect for ourselves a Territorial Government founded upon the Republican principles of the Constitution of the United States, and that we will maintain and defend it to the best of our ability. . . . And we look to the support and protection of the Federal Government, and our fellow citizens in every part of the Union.'

Actually the declaration was the preliminary step toward provisional government with a trust to the future for recognition by Congress. Acceptance of the constitution by the voters was also attended by the election of Governor Roop and the naming of a representative to carry the plea for a Nevada territorial government to Washington.

Congress paid little heed to the matter for a year, but the increasing rush of population to the Comstock coupled with the outbreak of the Civil War brought fulfillment of dreams on March 2, 1861, when the Territory of Nevada was created by Congress. The pressures of national scope which brought about the establishment of a territory and later a state held the attention of the Federal government and the local scene was not too closely studied. Boundaries and territory were often vague and based more on contemporary politics than on economic practicability.

"Blasted Blue Stuff"

JOHNTOWNERS WERE slightly chagrined at the discovery of silver on the Comstock Lode. They realized more attention should have been given to the expressions of a Mexican miner who had been employed in Gold Canyon during the year 1853. Many miners had watched him resting on his shovel while he waved toward the brown outcroppings along the mountain peaks. "Bueno," he would say, "Mucho plata, mucho plata." They couldn't understand Mexican and the word plata meant nothing to them. The Mexican, they thought, was referring to gold buried in the mountains.

As long as the weather held out they worked the placer gravel, ekeing out two dollars a day, all the while damning the "blasted blue stuff" that covered up the quick in their rockers and interferred with amalgamation.

By the year 1858 they were working along Six Mile Canyon, but values were lessening as workers approached the upper levels and the gravel color appeared to be slightly altered. No one gave a thought to lode mining, but they refused to give up the placer search. Early in '59 Old Virginia, Pancake Comstock and others struck the surface diggings at Gold Hill. They claimed the ground for placer, blissfully ignorant of the fact that under a thin crust lay the rich vein of gold and silver-bearing quartz that was so soon to produce the fabulous wealth of Crown Point, Yellow Jacket and Kentuck.

Meanwhile, two Irishmen, Peter O'Riley and Pat McLaughlin, were trenching a ravine to follow the placer rock. It was apparent that they would have to impound the small trickle of water for their rockers and they set about digging a tiny reservoir. At four feet they struck the amazing stratum of the Ophir and were astounded at the results showing up in the pannings. From this odd looking blue-black dirt, a singular change from the clay-gravel in which they had been working, they now found gold by the pound in their rockers. Down they dug into that "blasted blue stuff," washing out the yellow metal and cussing the bluish sand that settled on the quick in the rocker bottoms.

Actually it remained for a rancher, not a miner, to explore the possibilities of the blue stuff. Augustus Harrison of Truckee Meadows took a chunk of this strange ore over the Sierras to a friend, Judge James Walsh in Grass Valley. An assay proved the ore ran to thousands of dollars per ton in gold and silver. The answer was plain . . . that "blasted blue stuff" which lay in waste dumps on the Comstock Lode was fabulously rich in silver. Harrison and his friend agreed to keep it a secret, but each had a few personal friends who gleaned the news. The assay had been run late at night, but by nine o'clock the next morning Grass Valley knew about silver in Washoe and the rush was on.

The Rush to Washoe

CALIFORNIA'S GOLD lured them West in '49. They came in great slow-moving columns, led by the dream of riches. It was the country's first great mass migration, a pioneering epic in suffering and hardship! But the quest for wealth was a burning fever! Lessons learned in crossing the plains and rugged mountains were almost forgotten, bitter disappointments faded in the intervening decade. When silver was discovered in Nevada there was a stampede of humanity back across the Sierras that made the gold rush look like a Sunday school picnic.

The rush to Washoe was anything but slow moving, no plodding oxen and lumbering covered wagons here . . . men travelled light and fast. A frying pan, a bedroll, a horse, if he could manage it, and a strong determination to strike it rich were the only requirements. The silver stampede was a backwash of the gold rush and it drew to Nevada the pick of the Californians.

News of immense wealth along the Comstock Lode spread through California in the summer of 1859 and the rush started, slowly at first, drawing fortune seekers mainly from the Western foothill towns. Men were skeptical on arriving but soon they too were afire with the fever. Many of them returned home with intention of loading supplies and returning to the fabulous lode. But winter came early that year and Washoe was snowbound, playing havoc with the plans of those who saw fortunes within their grasp.

The big storm started on November 2, 1859, and that winter turned out to be the most severe ever experienced in the West. Snow on the trails over the Sierras was waist deep while drifts piled up as high as 60 feet. Even the small settlements dotting the Comstock were isolated from each other for weeks as storms spent their fury over Sun Mountain.

Animals died for lack of feed; flour sold for $80 a sack, buzzards hovered in the air to pick the frozen carcasses of cattle gathered in the valleys for mutual warmth. Starvation was rampant, yet just over the hills in California food was abundant, but men refused to risk their lives in the tortuous crossing.

Meanwhile thousands jammed the pass near Placerville, waiting for the first break in the weather. March 1860, finally arrived and the snow turned to slush. It was the signal for one of the greatest mineral rushes ever recorded.

The silver fever had engulfed California. By foot and horseback, by sleigh and light wagon, fortune seekers swarmed over the pass, floundering in the snowbanks, wading in the mud, scarcely stopping to eat in their eagerness to get to Washoe.

Tiny way stations were jam-packed with humanity and the trail over the mountains looked like a crawling snake as the ceaseless column gained the summit and dropped down toward Nevada's desert. The rush to Washoe's riches was actually a race for wealth. In a year's time the little hamlets near Sun Mountain swelled to overflowing with humanity and still they kept coming for the Comstock's riches proved even more fabulous than the wild stories that had circulated while men waited for the snow to release its icy grip on the Sierras.

First Comstock Hotel

ALL THE FORTUNES made on the Comstock were not made in mining. In March of 1860 shrewd John L. Moore loaded up $1,600 worth of whiskey and left San Francisco for Hangtown. Arriving there he found the mountains still almost impassable with the deep snows of a late winter, but luckily he secured a pack train at a rate of 50 cents a pound to Virginia City.

He started across the Sierras with 200 blankets, tin plates, brandy, gin, whiskey, rum, and wine, totalling 2,100 pounds. And 25 days later he and his gaunt, starved mules staggered out of the snow drifts into Virginia City. Miserable, half frozen miners cheered all up and down Mt. Davidson and along the streets. They cursed and grumbled impatiently while Moore unloaded his mules, set up a 15x52 tent, spread the first carpet in Virginia City, and stuck up a flag over the top of the ridge pole.

Inside, a canvas partition divided the tent into a hotel, and a saloon. The battered sideboard of an emigrant wagon was mounted on stakes, and served as a bar. Lanterns, and candles gave some light, and the stock of liquors was arranged, opened, and placed on the back bar, in readiness. At a signal "the doors" opened.

With a loud hurrah, the mob of thirsty miners rushed into the bar and drank faster than they could be served. It was already twilight, yet $200 in liquor was sold before dark, and the bar-room enjoyed a brisk business for some time later.

The "hotel" was heavily patronized too, with 36 guests paying a dollar each for a pair of blankets to spread on the ground. A few luxurious customers slept on hay ticks, with the stuffing at 50 cents a pound and very limited at that. Shavings were collected from a Gold Hill construction job to be added to the hay, but the bundle was carelessly left outside a moment, and was devoured by the starving mules.

Other supplies soon arrived . . . flour and nails at a dollar a pound, shovels at nine dollars. Moore, when his pack train was one day out from Virginia City, had refused an offer of $8,000 for his load, just five times what it had cost him some three weeks earlier.

Liquor continued to be the most popular cargo among the early settlers. At one time Carson City was on the brink of starvation, when a pack train of liquor and flour arrived in the nick of time. The population was aroused and indignant that space on mule back had been wasted to bring the food when it could have all been used for whiskey! As usual the customers were believed right, and shrewd traders soon realized that liquor brought the greatest profit. It made fortunes in almost every early mining camp, where normal recreations were scarce and miners lived in constant excitement.

Gay Galena

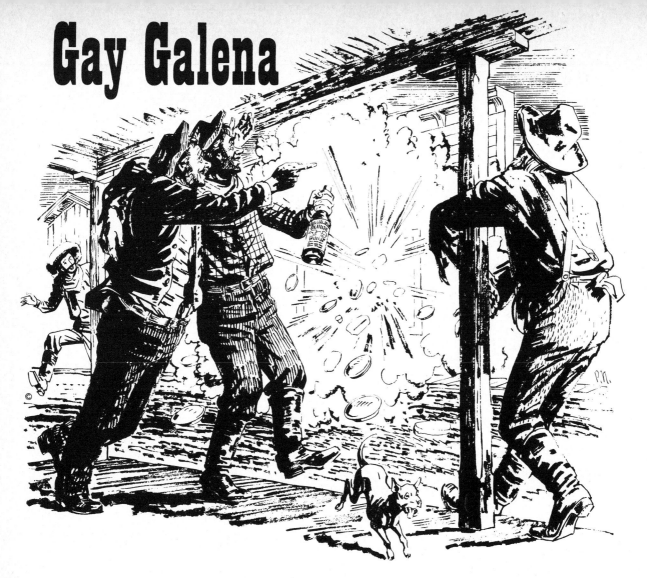

GALENA DISTRICT was organized in 1860 just west of Washoe City, and by 1864 rated the reputation of being the "gayest" town in the whole Territory, if not the coast. Both smelting and milling were failures at Galena, but the place was a howling success as a lumber town. Saw mills were strung up and down Galena Creek, Thomas Creek, and White Creek and the freighting business boomed.

One kind of freight seldom reached Galena intact. When storms or snake bite threatened, teamsters would broach cargoes of whiskey, refilling with water. Galena bartenders strengthened the weak whiskey with "mighty powerful substitutes" and Galena whiskey had a flavor all its own and a reputation among bullwhackers throughout the West. Many folks thought the State capital, or anyhow the Washoe County seat should be moved to Galena, and civic spirit was always high.

When business sagged, the town planned to hold a gigantic banquet for leading mining men, thinking to get them drunk and so to get big contracts. The affair was a terrific success, but the chairman suffered delirium tremens! In 1865 a man named Hollingsworth opened a store in Galena to sell bakery goods and candies. A very temperate man, he did not patronize the Galena saloons and a mass meeting was held to find means of protecting the saloon industry from such a deplorable example. A resolution passed that he should not remain in business unless he supported local bars, and a collection was taken for the purchase of two kegs of gun powder. These were placed

under the front of the bakery some time after midnight and covered. Most of the town was on hand around two o'clock when there was a big explosion which blew most of the pies and cakes into the street but did not harm the proprietor. He took the hint, however, and left town that day.

Mail came to Washoe City by stage, and thence to Galena in saddle bags. A small boy carried the mail and was paid by popular subscription. He would read the names on the letters, and the individuals would step up and claim their mail.

In 1865 the town was swept by a terrible fire, but promptly rebuilt. Later that year most of the timber had been stripped from the foothills for miles around, and even the Sierras were bare and clean. Flumes brought logs for miles to the Galena saw mills, but eventually the distances became too great for efficient use of this mode of transportation. Until a few years ago, many sections of these old flumes could still be seen along the upper and middle reaches of Galena canyon.

It was a town without peer for hard drinking and exciting combination! Nearby Washoe City was relieved to see Galena go, and breathed easier with the threat of competition "over." But Washoe City suffered the same fate, and soon lost the courthouse and most of its population to an upstart little railroad town a few miles north in the middle of the Truckee Meadows which had been named for a rather obscure Civil War general by the name of Reno.

Genoa's Buried Treasure

IN 1860 the boldness and perseverance of highway robbers became so pronounced the stage companies resorted to all manner of tricks to protect valuable cargoes. Some coaches had boiler iron boxes built into the rear seat. One gold dust buyer locked three rattlesnakes with his treasure. And a common method was to conceal the gold or silver in some innocent appearing container. But the robbers were seldom fooled.

One day the stagecoach making its regular run from Placerville to Genoa carried a valuable shipment of gold coins to meet the mine and mill payrolls of the Comstock. As the huge stage thundered down the narrow road it was suddenly blockaded and stopped by two daring bandits, who went along with their business with the cool thoroughness of experienced professionals.

One "heft" of the innocent looking little wooden keg proved it to be startlingly heavy, and it was promptly rolled from the stage and carried away through the pine forest. The stage rolled down the steep grade to Genoa, lighter by $20,000 in gold! Investigations by the sheriff and stage line detectives were fruitless and the golden eagles were never recovered. Eventually the excitement died down, and the incident was all but forgotten in the light of other robberies, more dramatic and exciting.

Nearly twenty years later, however, a rugged old-timer lay dying in Montana. He was such a "hard case" that those present were surprised to find he had troubles on his conscience and he was finally moved to make a deathbed confession. He called his friends together, and when he mentioned "buried treasure" their interest was intense.

The old man admitted he had been one of the two stagecoach robbers back in 1860 who had hoisted $20,000 in gold from the stage on the way to Genoa, Nevada. And he related enough details of the crime to indicate he was thoroughly familiar with it. He explained he and his partner had taken $2,000 for immediate needs and buried $18,000 at the foot of a large pine tree in Genoa. They felt it wise to leave soon after, and the treasure was still buried in the original spot.

By this time Genoa had shifted somewhat, and there were many trees which answered the description. Treasure hunting fever swept Carson Valley and much of the town was promptly dug up by excited citizenry, but to no avail. Then in 1882 the great avalanche moved many trees and landmarks, making the hunt still more difficult. But most historians agree, a treasure in gold is still waiting somewhere in Genoa! All that remains is "to find the correct pine tree!"

Lander's Engineers

IT WAS THE summer of 1860, and many of the bodies from the ghastly Ormsby Massacre still lay out in the sagebrush. The victorious Paiutes had been driven away by Federal troops, and were drifting westward toward Honey Lake Valley. A few settlers were killed and panic swept "Roop County."

"Governor" Roop and the Honey Lake Rangers frantically appealed to Col. Frederick W. Lander and his heavily armed civilian engineering party then surveying a road from Idaho to Tutt's Meadows near Honey Lake. And Lander agreed to parley with the Indians in an effort for peace.

Lander knew the Indians, and realized the many wrongs inflicted upon the Paiutes by the white settlers. Most of his stay in Nevada found him in the role of both engineer and peace-maker. Every time he took the field against the Indians, it was after sincere efforts to bring peace had failed, and lives appeared in danger.

On June 19th Lander's men and the Rangers were fired on in a canyon and one man was killed. Lander sought a parley under a flag of truce but was also fired on. A five hour battle then followed and accounts told of it still conflict strongly! One version has it that a Spaniard under Lander chased an Indian on horseback, dodged when the Indian fired at him, tossed his lasso, wheeled his horse, and snatched the astonished warrior to the ground where he was dragged to death. Other accounts deny this, but claim Lander parleyed with old Chief Winnemucca, who was present in white man's clothes, urging Lander to come ahead if he wanted to fight, or to go home if he wanted peace.

After the battle, in which Lander's men drove the Indians into the Smoke Creek Desert, Lander and his engineers returned to their work, building reservoirs for emigrant trains. Troops arrived in three days and real peace was restored. Later the engineers captured and disarmed four Paiutes near Rabbit Springs, treating them kindly and freeing them. Through them, Lander obtained an interview with Young Winnemucca, whom he promised aid for better treatment of the Paiutes. Lander kept his promise and assisted Major Dodge, the Indian Agent in keeping the settlers at peace with the Indians. For a time at least, Lander brought peace to northern Nevada, but it was a most uneasy truce with great mistrust on both sides.

Indian Outpost

PANIC SWEPT the Comstock in the spring of 1860 and spread rapidly through the Washoe country for the Paiutes were on the warpath. Williams' Station on the Carson River went up in flames and five white men died at the hands of a marauding party. Major Ormsby mustered a little band of undisciplined volunteers to avenge the redmen's assault, but his party was ambushed on the Truckee and Ormsby was fatally wounded. Survivors straggling back from the battleground quickened the fears of the frontier populace already preparing defense corps and posting sentries to ward off possible attack and pillage. The call went out for volunteers.

Along the Pony Express trail so many stations were burned and stock losses so great that mail service was discontinued for a ten day period. Alarmed at the sudden turn of events the federal government authorized construction of an Indian outpost along the Carson River. In July of 1860 Fort Churchill began to take form along the east-west trail, and a series of adobe buildings were constructed in the canyon of the Carson River.

In eleven years of activity, first as a military outpost of the California military district and later as Nevada headquarters, Fort Churchill played a prominent role in development of the west. Its garrison patrolled the trail eastward to Austin and well into the Sierras on the western leg. With the advent of the telegraph, the fort served as eastern terminus of the line from San Francisco where the pony riders picked up dispatches, rushing them to ever-changing destinations as the telegraph line forged westward from St. Jo. The Comstock nervously expecting a "secesh" movement, heard of Lincoln's election as Pony Bob brought the returns to Fort Churchill.

With the advent of the Civil War, the fort's seven hundred man garrison was rapidly depleted. Volunteers took over most of the duties as the fort became a Union recruitment station for Nevada. Completion of the telegraph, conclusion of the war and diminishing Indian troubles brought an end to Churchill as a fort. Today its adobe buildings still mark the site of this western outpost.

Bee's Grapevine Line

JUST AS the Pony Express had been an important stride in western expansion, it in turn was swallowed by an even more rapid means of communication in the early Sixties. It wasn't better horseflesh or steam locomotion that spelled "finis" for the west's most daring enterprise!!

A thin coil of wire and a small telegrapher's key unlocked the isolated frontier, and though people joshingly called the first link "Bee's Grapevine Line," they lived to see the day when this singing wire connected two oceans and cemented America into one strong nation.

Fred A. Bee and his partners, Lovell, Bishop, Jones and Randall, were farseeing men. It was their project, the Placerville, Humboldt and Salt Lake Telegraph Company, that pioneered western communication.

Fred Bee was a resident of Virginia City and consequently manager of the telegraph company there. On July 4, 1858, his company set the first pole on the line which was ultimately to become the transcontinental telegraph. Carson Valley residents had voted $1,200 toward the project and offered to take more stock if needed. By early autumn of the same year the first wire reached Genoa thus connecting Placerville with Nevada. Six months later it was extended to Carson City, and the next year Virginia City became the Nevada terminus.

Freezing high Sierra temperatures coupled with strong winds and stubborn granite formations led promoters to make the best possible use of natural facilities, hence the original line over the mountains was supported by rugged pine trees firmly entrenched in the earth. The sight of a thin wire reaching from treetop to treetop across the mountain fastness led jokesters to refer to the telegraph as "Bee's Grapevine Line," but they didn't laugh at its magic speed of communication.

In 1860 Congress authorized the construction of a telegraph line from Missouri to San Francisco and the Overland Telegraph Company was organized with a capital of one and a quarter million dollars. East and west terminals were Fort Kearney, Nebraska, and Fort Churchill, Nevada, and, as work progressed, the distance of the Pony Express run was lessened with the erection of each new station.

Pony riders carried messages to telegraph operators, who in turn relayed them over the wires. From Fort Churchill, dispatches were relayed to the Carson operator, again relayed by Carson to Placerville and once again copied and relayed by Placerville to San Francisco. It was slow telegraphy, yet hours and days faster than the Pony Express.

In 1861 the Nevada line was completed from Fort Churchill through Austin and Ruby Valley to Salt Lake, thus spanning the nation with a transcontinental telegraph. Bee's jerry-built grapevine line, flimsy as it was, had replaced the horse and rider and become a major link in winning the West.

The Spanish Bandit

WITTY, DASHING, handsome, Nickanor Rodrigues led his band of Mexican outlaws in Nevada during the booming '60's with such brilliance that not once did a jail hold him. Yet "everyone knew" he was robbing stage coaches regularly, and Wells Fargo even paid him a retainer finally to keep his band away from their bullion shipments.

Rodrigues was a polished man of the world. Born in Spain, he had lived in Rome, Paris, and Mexico City. As a host, his hospitality was fabulous. As a leader of desperadoes, he was followed with a loyalty and fanaticism by his Mexicans, that made his band almost irresistible. And, when he finally left Nevada, laden with stolen treasures, he rode for old Mexico where he and his retainers lived in lavish splendor.

Old Nevada settlers insisted that every mill in Nevada was looted at one time or another by Rodrigues or his men. At Gold Hill he snaked out precious amalgam from the hot retorts of the Imperial Mill. And when he stole a wheelbarrow load of rich amalgam from the Pacific Mill, he cached it under the fence of the Silver City cemetery 'til things cooled off a bit. He later melted it down and sold the bullion bars.

It is believed his nerviest robbery was made on a dare. At any rate he rode with Baldy Green, the stage driver who was robbed so often that people sang a popular ballad about "Baldy handing down his express box." Rodrigues rode with Baldy up on the box, and as they neared Steamboat Springs on the way to Reno, the bandit would divert Baldy's attention to something in the dark night. Again and again he snaked bullion bricks out of the boot, until he had quietly dropped three in the soft dust along the road. Later he came back and picked them up. But suspicion pointed so strongly to Rodrigues that when he tried to sell them, they were identified and held. He avoided arrest narrowly and moved operations for a time over to White Pine County. He was suspected of many stage robberies that suddenly took place in that area, but no charges would hold up in court. His band robbed Wells Fargo so regularly that the company kept people constantly chasing him. Finally Rodrigues offered to leave their stages alone for $2,000 a month, and the company gladly paid it.

This pleasant arrangement continued for some time. When the company sent out a new agent, however, the bored Rodrigues had had enough. He notified Wells Fargo the "truce was off."

He was promptly arrested, but he broke jail, and with companions started for Mexico. En route they held up at least one more stage, killing the driver, and took a band of horses from the C. H. Light ranch. Their trip to Mexico was a leisurely sojourn during which they carefully inspected and then stole the best horses along the route. In Mexico he purchased a beautiful estate, and reportedly spent the remainder of his life in elaborate luxury.

End of the Paiute Treaty

Paul Nyland

CHIEF WINNEMUCCA, great leader of all the Paiutes and son of Chief Truckee, friend of the white men, was anxious to keep peace in his territory. In 1858 he signed a treaty with Honey Lake settlers by which whites and Indians were punished for acts of aggression against each other. He took his warriors into battle on the side of the whites against the skulking Pit River tribes, rescued a wagon train near Goose Lake, and drove the Pit River Indians out of the area.

Some whites and redmen, however, seemed unable to resist the temptation to kill each other. When the Washoes raided Roop County potato fields, Winnemucca's Paiute braves rode with the whites in a battle of retaliation against the Washoes. The whites shot one of the Paiutes in the battle and Winnemucca believed it to have been deliberate. Despite gifts of appeasement, he grew increasingly cool and distrustful of the white men. Later the murder of Peter Lassen, charged first to whites and then to Paiutes (and still a mystery to this day) did not help the situation.

In January 1860, a band of Paiutes killed Dexter Demming who was infamous for his abuse of Indians, and Governor Roop sent Captain Weatherlow's rangers under Captain Tutt to trail them. They claimed the atrocity was done by the renegade Paiute band of Smoke Creek Sam.

But so many prospectors and ranchers were exposed to the Indians the Governor sought to negotiate a peaceful settlement.

His representatives finally got an audience with Winnemucca who was very cool and refused to send his men to catch the killers. The delegates, Captain Weatherlow and Thomas Harvey, finally reported on February 11, 1860, "The Paiutes are determined to rob and murder as many citizens as they can. . . . "

Governor Roop immediately asked the Military Department of the Pacific for arms, ammunition, and artillery, and some troops were sent to Honey Lake. The situation between the whites and their former Paiute friends rapidly deteriorated. Both Smoke Creek Sam and Black Rock Tom led renegade bands on raids in the back country. Chief Winnemucca became almost inaccessible to whites.

Three months later came the atrocities by whites against Indians, and the returning atrocities by Indians against whites at Williams Station. Factions of both whites and Indians excitedly clamored for war. And Major Ormsby raised his volunteers, destined for final disaster and death at Pyramid Lake, at the hands of Winnemucca's skillful war chiefs. It was the end of the Paiute Treaty and the beginning of the end of Paiute power.

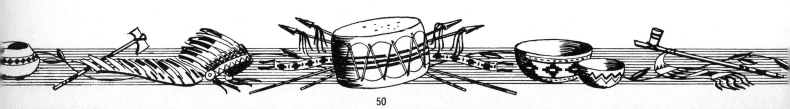

Paiute Passport

ALL NORTHERN Nevada verged on the ragged edge of panic, during the bloody Indian troubles of the early '60's. It was during this period of shocking massacres and cruelty that two wide-eyed, greenhorn, German immigrant lads were prospecting their leisurely way down the Humboldt River. Heading for a stage station, they found it a smoking ruin. And a short while later, an Indian met them, insisting they accompany him, saying, "Paiute kill many white men at Pyramid, got heap gun, many pony."

They were led through the hills to an encampment of about 500 warriors, and were presented to Chief Winnemucca himself.

That night both boys awoke in terror! An old squaw had seized one lad by the hair, and was trying to kill him with a huge knife. But before they could cry out for help, a Paiute warrior dashed up, hurled back the old Mahala, and drove her off into the shadows. Then their rescuer told them in flawless English to say nothing of the incident. "I used to be a countryman of yours," he said.

The next morning, Chief Winnemucca sent his young men to catch up the boys' horses, help them with their saddling and loading. The old man gave them some serious advice. The country was in uproar, he told them, so cease their prospecting, and get to the larger cities of western Nevada as quickly as possible.

And he gave them a string of sinew tied in a series of knots. He ordered them to show it to every Indian they met along the way, and gave them careful instructions on how to follow the trail across alkali flats, through narrow canyons and broad desert valleys to the meadows of western Nevada.

Thankfully the two boys rode off. Several times that morning, and again that afternoon, they were stopped along the trail by Indians. Each time, they obediently produced the string of sinew. And each time the Indians took the string, untied a knot, and then let them go in peace.

Once, riding up a rocky canyon, they heard shots, and rifle bullets buzzed through the air. Hastily they reined up their horses, stood up in the stirrups and yelled, while they frantically waved the string of sinew to show their "good conduct certificate." Two Indians rose up from the canyon edge, mounted ponies and rode down to them through the rocks. These warriors took the string, untied a knot, and as they handed it back, urged the boys in broken English not to tell Chief Winnemucca about the shooting.

"We good friends," they insisted, and gravely shook hands with both boys. The "magic" string seemed to solve all their problems, and they now became so cocky they rode right through a small Indian encampment. But a few miles farther on they were terrified to hear the drumming of Indian pony hoofs on the dry desert trail. A band of painted warriors raced behind them. Ashen faced, the boys reined up and waited. Roughly demanding "why the lads had failed to stop and show the string of sinew" one warrior rode up and seized the string. He untied the last knot, and waving it gayly trotted off. As he rode, the boys heard him singing an old German folk song! Ahead at last, lay safety.

Paiute Council

Aₙ OMINOUS CLOUD was gathering over western Utah territory in the spring of 1860, but newly discovered wealth of the Comstock and the mad rush to share in its riches blinded eager fortune seekers to the sullen watchfulness of the Paiutes.

Trouble with the Indians had been confined to brief wagon train conflicts, isolated stage station attacks and running fights with marauding parties. On the whole, fear of conflict with the Indians was only a remote possibility in the minds of the thousands who clambered over the Sierra summits that spring to seek their fortunes in Washoe . . . but the Paiutes sensed calamity in this sudden usurpation of their domain!

Through means of communication known only to those native sons of the plains, all the tribes were called together for a council on the shores of Pyramid Lake. Quickly they assembled, the Bannocks, the Shoshones, the Paiutes, all the tribes which roamed the land from Honey Lake to Mason and from the Humboldt flatlands to the swift flowing Truckee. Tepees were pitched on Pyramid's shores and the chiefs talked among themselves, repeated tales of how the white men were driving them from their hunting lands, felling the pinon trees which provided their winter store of food, and of how they were laughed at when they objected to such practices. With each new arrival these tales of white men's injustices increased until the camp seethed with an undercurrent of hate.

Only one chief among those assembled held a different view. He was Numaga, a young man who had always been friendly with the whites. He attempted to persuade the others that a war could only mean the eventual destruction of the Indian tribes, but his words fell upon deaf ears; so he adopted a different means. Lying upon the ground in mourner's style, he fasted three days, hoping that his sorrow would sway the other chieftains. On the third night when all the chiefs were called into final council, Numaga appeared before the dimly burning fire to make his last plea for peace. In a stirring talk he warned how a war must end, how the whites would keep coming, how their rifles would drive the Paiutes and their kinsmen into the rocky reaches of the desert to be stalked by starvation. The older chiefs listened intently, realizing that Numaga spoke with wisdom, but his words had come too late. Just as he finished talking a weary Indian rider drew up before the council fire to announce that one of the Paiute chiefs, missing from the council, had attacked Williams' Station, and killed five white men.

Knowing the futility of further argument, realizing that the white men would now seek vengeance, Numaga turned to the old chief, sorrowfully indicating that he knew the decision was already made, the Paiutes must fight!

Ormsby's Defeat

THE SOFT SPRING wind blowing over Sun Peak and through Carson Valley brought a strange chill in May, 1860, for news had just been received throughout Washoe that Indians had burned Williams' Station and murdered five white men.

For a moment men forgot the lure of wealth so near at hand in the rich Comstock Lode and indignation was rife. Here was an act of violence that called for swift and complete vengeance. No one thought to inquire as to whether the incident had been brought on by the whites themselves, although it was later reliably reported that two squaws had been stolen by the men at Williams' Station and that some Bannock braves had made up the marauding party which attacked the outpost.

Virginia City, Carson, Silver City, and Genoa all felt the impact of this sudden trouble, and determined to quell any thought of an uprising . . . each town sent volunteers to march against the Indians. Brave and experienced though they were, the four companies which marshalled under Major Ormsby, were untrained, and no time was afforded to plan a maneuver. One hundred and five men under Major Ormsby set off down the Carson River, pausing at Williams' Station to bury the murdered whites and to pick up the trail of the Indians who had fled northward toward Pyramid Lake.

In a swift march they reached the Truckee and pushed on toward Pyramid Lake hoping to catch the war party unaware, but they didn't know that all the Paiute tribes had been assembled in council at Pyramid Lake when the burning of Williams' Station took place, and that the Paiutes were prepared to meet them. As Ormsby's men advanced they suddenly saw a thin line of braves riding along a mesa just out of rifle range.

Marshalling his men, Major Ormsby ordered a charge, and almost immediately realized that he had been lured into an ambush. From all sides Paiutes rose from their hiding places, closing in on Ormsby's men. Hundreds of yelling demons armed with rifles, arrows and tomahawks sought to close off every possible avenue of escape.

As the yelling redmen closed in, Major Ormsby's practiced eye saw his only chance was to rally his men and beat a slow retreat. Making a small knoll which could be defended by the untrained band, Ormsby sought to signal his panic-stricken men, but just as he reached the knoll, his saddle turned and threw him.

Close on his heels were a horde of shouting Paiute braves. Trying to rise, Ormsby attempted to plead with them in an effort to save his men, but before he could reach his feet an arrow struck his heart. Leaderless, the volunteers now sought escape as best they could, fleeing from their pursuers in wild disorder. Shrewdly the Indians from the Black Rock country exploited the rout. With astute and cold-blooded generalship, they slaughtered the panic-stricken white men in one of the Indians' greatest military victories. The white men's first attempt to avenge an Indian outrage had met with utter failure.

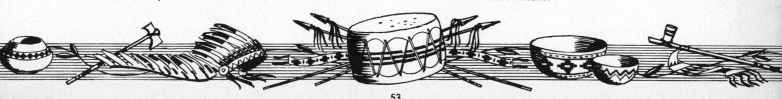

Battle of the Truckee

FIVE DAYS AFTER Major Ormsby's party had set out to chastise the Paiutes for the burning of Williams' Station, panic swept Washoe and the valley settlements.

Survivors of the awful ambush were beginning to straggle into Buckland's Station, and their tales of the massacre spread like wildfire through Virginia City, Carson, Dayton and Genoa. In five days' time a seemingly small event had thrown the west into panic. With each re-telling of how Ormsby's little band had been trapped along the Truckee, fear was heightened for the safety of all the whites in western Utah and along the California mountain fringes.

Women and children were hastened to the strongest stone buildings in each town, sentinels were stationed at vantage points and urgent requests were swiftly flashed by messenger to California towns asking aid, and warning settlers that the Paiutes might attack. Major Warren Wasson volunteered to run the Indian gauntlet alone from Carson City to Honey Lake Valley to deliver an order commanding a company of cavalry stationed there to proceed at once to Carson City. Without changing mounts Major Wasson rode the distance of 110 miles in fourteen hours to deliver his message, and immediately the cavalry from Honey Lake rode south to join the expedition against the Paiutes.

Meanwhile forces were marshalled! The Washoe regiment of eight infantry and six cavalry companies was placed under command of Colonel Jack Hays, an old Indian fighter. Major Daniel Hungerford and Captain Edward Storey, who headed the Virginia Rifles, were placed on the staff. The Third Artillery from Fort Alcatraz and the Sixth Infantry from Benicia Barracks, were ordered from the coast to join the volunteers. The well disciplined, thoroughly organized forces met at the Big Bend of the Truckee on the last day of May. The expedition was underway and there was no doubt as to its outcome.

On June 2, a scouting party found the ghastly remains of the Ormsby massacre and a short distance further north they spied an advancing band of Indians. The scouts were ordered back to the main detachment, but when they perceived Colonel Hays advancing with the regulars, they made a stand. Under Storey they stormed the Indian command post on a promontory where Chief Numaga was giving Paiute battle orders. On gaining the vantage point, they found themselves flanked by redmen, but the approaching regulars, deployed as skirmishers, passed under the low butte, driving the Paiutes before them.

For three hours the battle lasted with the Indians yielding each rock and tree only after all hope was gone. To conceal their casualties from the whites the Paiutes carried bodies of their dead and wounded, concealing them in rock piles. Hard pressed by the mile long line of white regulars and volunteers, the Paiutes fled the field at sundown. The battle of the Truckee was over, and never again did the redmen prove a serious menace.

Nevada Camel Caravans

WINNING OF the Western empire was assured late in the '60's when the Central Pacific Railroad spanned the nation with a steel ribbon, but in the years preceding its construction, pioneers who first saw the possibilities of this frontier land, had not been asleep on the transportation job. The Pony Express provided a fleet mail service while Overland Stages and Wells Fargo opened the avenues of passenger and freight transportation. Most interesting of all the early modes of freight shipment, however, was Nevada's camel experiment.

As early as 1855 the war department had experimented with the use of camels in New Mexico and California, but most of the attempts had been unsuccessful. In 1860 Captain Hancock started a camel express known as the "Dromedary Line" between Los Angeles and Fort Mojave, but this venture also petered out after a few trips, and in 1863, Secretary of War Stanton ordered the army camels sold at public auction.

Sam McLeneghan bought a number of these beasts of burden and selected ten of the best to carry freight between Sacramento and points in Nevada territory. His original idea never developed, but McLeneghan did succeed in selling his camels to a mining company in Austin and they were immediately put to work ferrying salt across desert wastes from the marshes near Walker Lake to Austin's quartz mills.

Meanwhile, another enterprising merchant of San Francisco, Otto Esche, went into Mongolia to purchase thirty-two head of Bactrian camels for use in the Nevada deserts. His dream of great profits dwindled when only fifteen of his original herd lived out the voyage to San Francisco. The survivors were auctioned for use as pack animals between Placerville and the Nevada mining camps, but they eventually came to serve the Virginia City and Carson River mills, transporting salt from the Esmeralda marshes. Carrying loads upwards of 500 pounds, the animals proved capable to the job, but when salt was discovered near the Carson River only 60 miles from the mills, the long trek from the central Nevada marshes proved to be a needless expense and the camels were turned out to roam an unfamiliar desert.

The camels had provided a lot of color and hazard to traffic along the roads and trails, for most teams of horses went completely hysterical at the sight of the ungainly beasts. The advent of a camel string was the signal for teamsters and passengers to alight and stand to their horses' heads until the camels had passed.

Once these strange animals were turned loose on the open range they provided a source for generations of real and imaginary stories. Camel adventures were a stock in trade for every bartender, pan-handler, and prospector.

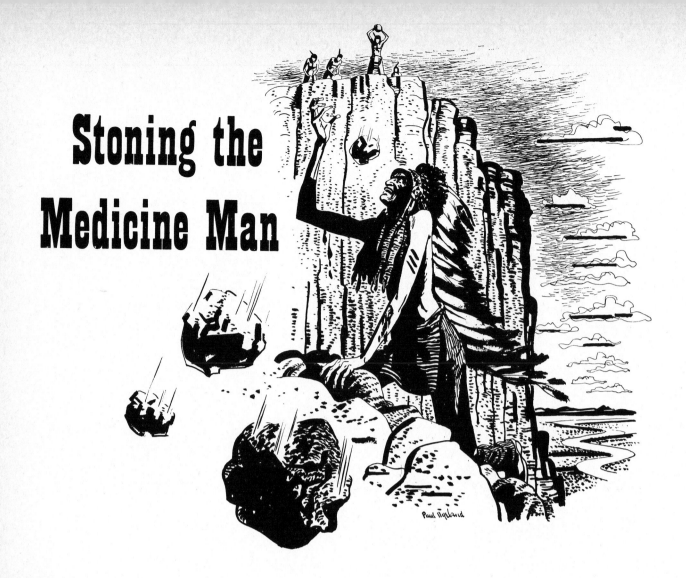

Stoning the Medicine Man

WHEN the "white death" of winter, pogonip, mantled the valleys of western Nevada, Paiute medicine men shivered inwardly, recognizing the harbinger of a plague which could sweep through a tribe leaving death in its wake.

There was reason behind this fear! Reason nurtured by generations of council law. A medicine man was chosen by lot. Seldom did he seek the honor. But, once selected he must act, administering herbs to the ailing, chanting weird rhythms by firelight outside lonely wickiups for those seriously ill. His was an honor fragilely supported by the measure of his success. Should three or more patients die under his ministrations, his life was the forfeit. Seldom did the council disregard this custom.

Wisps of damp fog were the first frightening sign! Rolling up from secluded canyons suddenly to be caught in the first frigid blasts of winter, they clung to bare tree branches freezing in lacy patterns or forming frosty scalloping along unprotected edges of sage and buckbrush. Such a sight chilled the hearts of medicine men! Their herbs and chanting had long been resisted by this delicate yet stubborn enemy that created fire in the lungs of their tribesmen. At such warning signs these tribal doctors contemplated fleeing or waiting out the slow but sure decision of the council.

Paiute tribesmen were easy prey for a quick and devastating form of pneumonia which usually followed a pogonip freeze. Medicine men had found no cure. They only knew that herbs failed to check the sweeping plague.

In the early sixties a Mason Valley farmer witnessed tribal law at work soon after pogonip had stretched its frozen fingers along the Walker River.

He was startled one morning to see a partially clad medicine man fleeing toward the hills beyond the ranch. Abandoning his spent mount, the Indian clambered toward the protection afforded by high cliffs. Following closely on his heels was a small band of braves. They, however, took a longer route and soon emerged on a higher level above the shelf where the medicine man huddled in fear.

Methodically they began tipping huge boulders over the rim, at the same time hurling smaller stones at the lone form on the ledge. No sound other than the thud of the rocks accompanied the grim business, but within an hour, apparently satisfied, the braves returned to their camp.

As an afternoon sun warmed the valley, buzzards began paying their respects to another one of the unlucky medicine men whose singing magic failed to halt the "white death." The clash between the traditions of the stone age medicine men and their rewards and punishment met little acceptance from the new laws and customs of the white men. Pioneer day courts were accustomed to such cases on down well past the turn of the century.

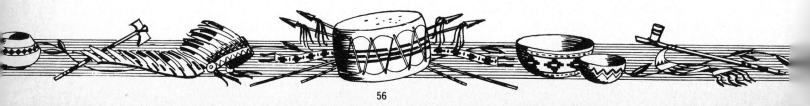

Bower's Mansion

Paul Nyland

STATELY POPLARS from the province of Lombardy and tangled Scotch broom, dear to the heart of a native highlander, guard the grandeur of Bower's Mansion from chill Washoe zephyrs sweeping off the Sierra. Could they speak, their story would be of the fabulous '60's when Lemuel "Sandy" Bower vaulted from teamster to millionaire on pyramiding silver from the Ophir shaft—when Eilley Orrum, his wife, was Queen of the Comstock and Seeress of Washoe. Despite her Scotch instincts Eilley coveted a show of wealth and the Mansion in Washoe Valley, within sight of the desert hills that belched forth millions, became Sandy's and Eilley's monument to their vanity.

Ivy from England's Windsor palace, a memento of the Bower's Grand Tour, climbed the ornate two-story sandstone structure; marble from European quarries shipped around the Horn and freighted over the mountains by bullwhackers, embellished the building; Spanish tile lined fountains in the courtyard; Venetian mirrors greeted crinolined visitors and Moroccan bound books graced the library, though Sandy could scarcely read.

Bower's Mansion was a combination of Mediterranean villa and highlander castle shadowed by towering mountains. Even gay San Francisco, flooded with Comstock millions, was awed by this spectacle where Eilley presided like a queen. But wealth disappeared almost as rapidly as it had come. Sandy Bower died in '68 and his wife was immediately involved in litigation over the Ophir mine.

Her Scotch thrift seemed suddenly to desert her and Eilley's last years were spent eking out a living by reading fortunes in the crystal ball that had predicted her own rise to riches. Her remains lie beside those of Sandy and their youthful children in a small plot on the steeply rising hill beside their once great palace.

Today the legend of Bower's Mansion, the hot springs and the cool shade lure picnickers, many of whom formerly travelled to Franktown on the V and T following the route of many early day visitors. Recently Washoe County purchased Bower's Mansion to preserve it as a recreation area.

The FISH with the EVIL EYE

HIGH IN THE Ruby Mountains overlooking the rolling plateau land far below are a series of crystal clear glacial lakes abounding with game fish. Long ago a legend developed among Indian hunters concerning one of these ice-cold glacial lakes, and in the early '60's the superstition was brought forcibly to the attention of Uncle Billie Rogers. It happened when Sho-kup, chief of the Ruby Valley tribe, died after seeing the "fish with the evil eye."

Uncle Billie was a seasoned scout who had been sent to the valley in the late '50's to investigate the land for a possible Indian reservation. He made a favorable report on the area and was so disgruntled when the government failed to follow his recommendation, that he stayed to cultivate the land and prove the fertility of the soil. Coincident with the taking up of his homestead, the Goshutes and Paiutes of the region went on the warpath, burning stage stations and creating mild havoc along the Overland Trail. The Ruby Indians were not hostile, however, and Uncle Billie cultivated their friendship as a shield against their more warlike brothers.

One day Sho-kup, chief of the valley Indians, summoned Uncle Billie to his camp. Upon arrival, the scout listened to a halting tale from the old chief, who seemed extremely ill. Sho-kup told him that he had visited the mountain lake where there was ice on the water even in summer. "Here lives a big fish," he said, "who is very evil spirit. When he rises from water and looks at Indian, Indian dies. I was at lake. I saw evil spirit. Now I am sick man." Then the old chief told Uncle Billie that he was going to die and that Buck was to succeed him as leader of the tribe. The next morning Sho-kup was dead.

To honor him the braves killed his horses to bury beside him and then sought out his wife, whom they felt should also accompany his spirit to the Happy Hunting Grounds. The wife, however, objected and fled to Uncle Billie for protection. The new chief, Buck, informed Uncle Billie that unless the old chief's wife was returned the Indians would make war on all the whites in the valley.

Uncle Billie didn't scare easily, but it was only a lucky incident that forestalled a possible massacre. While the Indians were preparing for war the medicine man was accidentally killed by a stray bullet and the braves agreed that his exalted tribal position made him a fit sacrificial substitute. The threat was sufficient to firmly impress Uncle Billie with the legend of the "Fish With The Evil Eye."

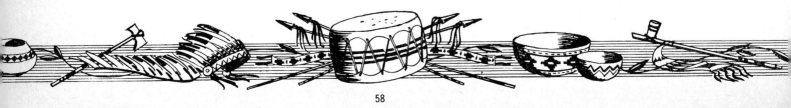

Attack at Egan

REDMEN roamed eastern Nevada's wilderness in the early '60's and often showed displeasure at the white men's encroachment upon their domain by burning Pony Express outposts and killing the station keepers. Such events were common in 1860, initial year of the frontier fast mail, when tiny change stations dotted the danger fraught trail of westward expansion. But, when the outpost at Egan was attacked, demands made upon the station keepers by the Indian were as strange as any recorded in the fabulous history of the Pony Express.

Egan was one of the loneliest change stations along the sagebrush route through eastern Nevada; the only high point of interest being arrival and departure of mail riders. Two men kept the Egan station which was well provisioned and stocked with ammunition to discourage Indian marauders.

One morning as the two station keepers were cleaning their cabin after breakfast, they heard a low, moaning sound, and upon peering out saw the station practically surrounded by a large Indian war party. The Redmen were nude except for loin cloths and their bodies were greased and paint-streaked. As the station keepers gazed in fright and amazement, an arrow whizzed into the wall near the window. It broke the spell of fear and the two men grabbed their rifles and began firing at random into the ranks of the war party.

The Indians possessed no guns, and though they wavered at the rifle volleys, they nonetheless continued to advance until the station keepers were out of ammunition. Then, they broke through the door, and expecting to make a last stand the cabin defenders were surprised to hear the chief demand, "bread."

Hoping for respite, all the bread in the cabin was piled on the table, but the chief remained unsatisfied. He surveyed the sacks of flour and commanded the white men to build a fire and begin baking bread. Through the long, hot day the station keepers continued to bake, being urged to greater effort by continued pokes in the ribs from the old chief. Meanwhile the braves ate bread and continued their yelling and noise.

Near sundown the chief had the two hostages seized by his warriors. With obvious enjoyment he told them their work was now done and they would be put to death. The men were dragged out into the yard. They were bound tightly with blanket strips to a wagon tongue which had been driven into the ground. Tribesmen began placing dry sagebrush around the men and just as it was ignited the two victims heard a crash and saw the Indians running away.

At that moment Colonel Steptoe's U. S. Cavalry had ridden into sight and begun a charge on the Indians. The intended victims were freed from the stake, handed weapons and ammunition, and added their rifle fire to that of the cavalry in dispersing the war party.

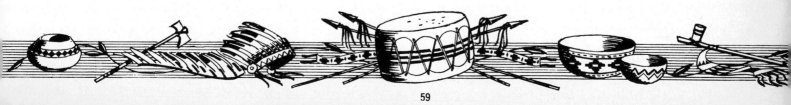

Pony Bob

THE RANKS of the dauntless pony express riders were filled with heroes, but none was more famous, or dashing than "Pony Bob" Haslam. As early as the spring of 1860, Pony Bob had raced with death across the alkali flats of Nevada, from Friday Station to Smith Creek while the Paiute tribes in all directions were rising for battle. In 36 hours he made the round-trip alone while the stations burned, keepers were killed, and ranchers fled to safety.

Pony Bob was idolized by the entire West and that year he was chosen to carry two historic messages. War and secession hinged on the election, and all Nevada Territory was excited over Lincoln's campaign. The election returns were carried by pony between the gap in the telegraph at Fort Kearny and Fort Churchill, and the best horses and men in the nation were assembled for the task. Election was November 7 and by the 12th the entire Territory had stopped work to listen for the coming of Pony Bob, and the election returns. And a little after midnight on the 14th the sentinels at Fort Churchill heard the thudding of hoofs far out on the flats. Quickly the guard was called, the whole fort turned out, and in a moment Pony Bob, powdered with alkali, his horse bathed in lather, thundered through the gates. Bob shouted as he passed, "Lincoln's Elected!" and the whole fort cheered 'till the hills echoed. Frantically the telegraph operator cleared

his wire and pounded out the great news to Sacramento and San Francisco, where waiting newspapers rolled out extras bearing the incredible banner: "ONLY SEVEN DAYS FROM THE EAST!" A great record had then been set.

The November ride was magnificent, but by March the entire nation awaited Lincoln's inaugural address and its message on the approaching war. Terrible storms lashed the country and the pony mail was running late, taking 11 to 17 days from Fort Kearny to Fort Churchill. Again the plans were elaborate for horses and men, and again Pony Bob raced across the desert, through a blizzard of sleet, mud, and flood-swollen creeks.

This time he made the 120 miles from Smith Creek (near Austin) to Churchill in eight hours, ten minutes, averaging nearly 15 miles an hour, and ruining several horses. Flood waters on the Platte smeared some of the manuscript, making it unreadable, but most of the historic document was clear and intelligible. The entire Territory read the news with enthusiasm. Cannon were fired, bells rung, and the Comstockers lugged a great pole on camel-back to the peak of Mt. Davidson, and lashed a thirty-foot flag to the tip. On the way down they chanted "John Brown's Body," and pledged bullion "to squelch the rebellion."

Hands Up Sir!

THERE WERE many ways of making a lucrative living in the boom days of the Comstock! To many men, digging in the hard brown earth for a probable treasure was slightly distasteful, especially when other avenues promising quick wealth were evident. Virginia City was no different from other camps of the Sixties; her fabulous riches drew a motley assortment of humanity.

Stage robberies were prevalent. Investigation proved that many of these were planned and conducted by a group of prominent residents who operated a mill in Six Mile Canyon as a blind for their endless shipments of bullion. In Virginia itself stock trading was as much a business as mining and many of the deals appeared to be more than slightly "off color." Flourishing as these extra-legal enterprises proved to be, there was another means of making a good living that had many devotees.

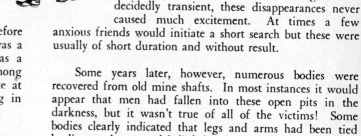

On the southern extremity of Virginia where C street's gradual rise comes to an abrupt end before plunging down the steep canyon to Gold Hill there was a rocky, sagebrush shelf, known as the Divide. It was a favorite haunt for footpads who found easy pickings among revelers as they made their way toward Gold Hill late at night or in the early morning hours after celebrating in Virginia City.

In '61 and '62 before the row of homes and business establishments stretched in an unbroken line between the two towns, night prowlers found the Divide a perfect place to carry on their business of robbery. Flickering candles and lamplight, were far away and darkness completely covered their operations, while stacks of lumber and mine dumps made convenient hiding places.

Favorite salutation of the robbers when they accosted an unwary reveler was "Hands Up, Sir!" Then at pistol point, the masked footpad or his accomplice would relieve the frightened and unhappy victim of whatever cash he had on his person and release him with the curt order "move on!"

Victims weren't always this lucky! During the years of '61 and '62, when the business of robbery was flourishing along the Divide, a few residents of both Gold Hill and Virginia City disappeared overnight, but acquaintances were too busy to check on their whereabouts, and since the population of a boom mining town is decidedly transient, these disappearances never caused much excitement. At times a few anxious friends would initiate a short search but these were usually of short duration and without result.

Some years later, however, numerous bodies were recovered from old mine shafts. In most instances it would appear that men had fallen into these open pits in the darkness, but it wasn't true of all of the victims! Some bodies clearly indicated that legs and arms had been tied leading to the general belief that footpads along the Divide might have run into trouble and were forced to dispose of their victims as quickly and quietly as possible.

Battle Mountain

INCENSED EMIGRANTS, whose wagon train had been attacked at Gravelly Ford on the Humboldt River, were actually responsible for the naming of Battle Mountain though the central Nevada mining supply point and rail head did not spring into existence for some years after the occurrence which brought its name.

Marauding redmen in full paint and war bonnets waylaid a large wagon train at Gravelly Ford in 1861, slaying several whites and fleeing westward with their loot. Entrenching themselves in the low hills south of the present site of Battle Mountain they awaited arrival of the emigrants' posse, hoping to ambush their pursuers. Wily plainsmen, who by this time had learned how to cope with their Indian adversaries, circled the hills to the south and attacked the marauders from the rear, turning the planned ambush into a complete rout for the redmen. The brief battle marked the last serious Indian threat to overland travel along Nevada's Humboldt Trail. A full year before completion of the Central Pacific Railroad, Battle Mountain had become

an important supply point for the rich mineral area of northern Lander County.

Completion of the transcontinental rail route enhanced its prosperity as silver, gold and copper from the sagebrush hills flowed into Battle Mountain for shipment over the Central Pacific Railroad. Austin's wealth found outlet in the '70's when the Nevada Central connected that famous camp and the upper Reese River with the Central Pacific Railroad at Battle Mountain.

Situated astride important U. S. Highway 40 and directly on the transcontinental path of both the Southern Pacific and Western Pacific railroads, Battle Mountain today ranks as one of the state's major mineral shipping points.

The community is also situated on the transcontinental airway, and has a major airport capable of serving the largest commercial air liners. It is the center of a rich ranching area, and serves as headquarters and supply point for many of the state's most important sheep and cattle outfits.

Farmer Peel

PERHAPS IT WAS his soft blonde beard and rosy cheeks that made Farmer Peel look like such a peaceful individual when he arrived on the Comstock from Salt Lake City, but folks soon learned he was a man to reckon with despite his rather pleasant features.

El Dorado Johnny came to town about the same time, and being anxious to establish a reputation for himself, walked into Pat Lynch's saloon one morning inquiring if any "chiefs" were about. Farmer Peel, lounging at the bar, glanced at Johnny and casually questioned, "I guess you mean that remark for me?"

"Anyone can take it that likes," scoffed Johnny.

"Very well, let's settle it right now," said Peel, "come out into the street."

Johnny walked out of the door with a smile on his face, but when he reached the middle of the street and turned to meet Peel, he saw only the quick flame of the latter's pistol, and he dropped in his tracks.

Peel hadn't bothered to go any further than the saloon door, deeming El Dorado Johnny as rather "small fry" competition. Soon afterward it was learned that Peel had five notches in his gun from Utah shootings, and, of course, he was immediately regarded as one of the Comstock Chiefs, a dubious title reserved for gunmen with itchy fingers.

The law didn't bother Farmer Peel since his shootings were reserved for the type of citizenry that Virginia City could well do without. But once in a while Peel imbibed too freely and then he became a real menace. On one of these occasions he was so obstreperous that the combined police force and a number of indignant citizens subdued him and took him before Police Judge Davenport.

The judge was a mild-mannered man exceedingly proud of his long flowing beard which he believed added to the dignity of his office. At great length he lectured Farmer Peel and wound up by fining the "chief" one hundred dollars. Apparently filled with remorse for his actions, Farmer Peel asked the judge to release him on his own recognizance until he could raise the fine money.

Being granted his request, Peel proceeded to his favorite spot and within thirty minutes was well filled with "firewater" again.

Stomping back to the courtroom, Farmer Peel caused quite a commotion by knocking down several chairs and benches that impeded his progress. Halting in front of the magistrate, Peel announced, "Judge, I've come to settle that fine."

"Very good of you, Mr. Peel," Judge Davenport replied, reaching to receive the money.

Farmer Peel failed to notice the motion. Already he had firmly grasped two fists full of the judge's luxuriant beard. With this firm purchase he unmercifully pounded the magistrate's head against the wall, giving him such a "wooling" that the poor jurist was knocked almost senseless. Apparently satisfied with his work, Farmer Peel strode from the courtroom without anyone so much as attempting to lay a hand on him.

Calling a Bluff

FIGHTING SAM BROWN was known up and down the Pacific Coast as "big chief," a title gained by those of the desperado class who boasted enough murders to fill a good-sized section in any mining cemetery. Sam's mistake, however, was his trip to the Comstock region in 1861 where the desire to magnify his reputation proved fatal.

Big and slouchy, Sam's loathsome appearance was emphasized by a coarse, dirty beard which had been allowed to grow so long and unruly that he parted and tied it under his chin rather than going to the trouble of trimming it. Immediately following his arrival on the booming Comstock, Sam set about proving his "big chief" title was not idle gossip.

On his first night in Virginia he picked a fight with a rather tipsy reveler in one of the crowded saloons, and scarcely had there been an exchange of words, when Sam whipped out his bowie knife and ripped his defenseless adversary, killing him immediately. Casually wiping the blood from his weapon, Sam stretched out on a bench and went to sleep. The incident had telling effects, Sam Brown had established his reputation on the Comstock, but the success of this and a half dozen other killings went to his head.

Hearing that one of his cronies was to stand court trial in Genoa, Sam vowed he would ride down, terrorize the court and succeed in having his fellow desperado released.

Arriving on the scene, Sam strode into the makeshift court-room, throwing the assembled spectators into consternation. Some sought refuge under benches, others dived out of windows, but while Sam was enjoying the scene, Senator William Stewart, who had been assisting in prosecuting the case, covered the "big chief" with two Colt pistols.

"Now, Mr. Brown," said Stewart, "you've bragged that you would come down here and swear the defendant free. I'm here to tell you that if you attempt any of your gun play or give false testimony, I'll blow your fool brains out." Then proceeding with cross examination Senator Stewart succeeded in making Brown admit that the defendant had a bad reputation. Before the court session was over, Brown had retained Stewart as his own attorney to defend him in a Plumas County action.

Somewhat chagrined by the way his bluff had been called, Sam mounted his horse and started again for Virginia City. On the way he took a pot shot at one of the persons in the yard as he passed Van Sickles' Station. Van Sickle himself, irked by the free gun play and disgusted by the obnoxious chief and his everlasting bullying, made an instant decision that he "had had enough." He reached for his shotgun and ammunition, and with the aid of a fast horse, overtook the fleeing rider and riddled him with a load of buckshot. It was the end of fighting Sam Brown, "big chief" of the Comstock.

Eagle Valley Railway

ABE CURRY was the type of man who planned ahead! When he first arrived in Western Utah Territory in 1858 he tried to purchase some property at Genoa, but found the price too high and resolved to "build a town of his own."

A short time later, together with three associates, F. M. Proctor, B. F. Green, and J. J. Musser, Abe Curry purchased the Eagle Valley ranch, destined to become the site of Nevada's capitol within three years.

On the east boundary, the original Curry purchase included Warm Springs, present site of the State penitentiary. On this spot Curry constructed a stone building known as Curry's Hot Springs Hotel. Meanwhile Major Ormsby had built a hostelry in Carson City named Ormsby House. These two men, along with many another far-seeing individual, were already planning that Carson would become headquarters of the territory. Ormsby, prior to his death in 1860, was often heard to remark that his Ormsby House would be a fine place to house the legislators when the territory was organized . . . and, such was the case since Governor Nye set up headquarters there.

When the territorial legislators assembled, it became evident that no place with sufficient room was available for the group's sessions. Then it was that Abe Curry's planning showed real foresight. Mr. Curry offered the vacant third story of his Warm Springs Hotel, rent free. His offer was seized upon immediately, but a major problem . . . one of transportation . . . . still remained to be solved.

Undaunted by this apparently minor difficulty, Abe Curry made the additional offer of free transportation for the legislators from Carson to Warm Springs, a distance of nearly two miles. In order to make good his offer, Mr. Curry immediately set about building the first Nevada streetcar. The sandy roadway between Carson and Warm Springs was graded and scantlings were used to bolster the track. When this was completed, Mr. Curry placed his rolling stock in service. It consisted of a flat car and a window-less passenger car with benches for seats.

When the session convened the legislators were hauled each morning from Ormsby House in Carson City to Curry's Warm Springs, and each evening when the sessions recessed, the legislators were transported back to Carson over the rough railway. Motive power for the first streetcar consisted of two rather ragged-appearing mules.

Although the Eagle Valley Railroad appeared to be born of benevolence, it was not entirely unprofitable. The legislators rode on free passes, but Abe Curry had thoughtfully added a flat car for freight purposes. Stone from the Warm Springs quarry was in demand for building in Carson City, and it was seldom that the horsecar started the trip to the capital without a pay load.

Fort Churchill Fifth Column

EXACTLY A YEAR after the final battle at Pyramid Lake there came rumors of more trouble with the Indians in western Nevada. During April of 1861 about 1,500 Paiutes assembled at the fisheries near the mouth of Walker River. Their brush wickiups extended along the banks of the river and near the beaches of the lake for miles in one huge encampment, near where Schurz stands today. Along with the trapping of fish in willow wicker "corrals" was much conversation in whispers. Wahe, the cruel "spirit chief," half-brother to Winnemucca, was back, and he had a plan.

Wahe's plan called for the murder of the new Indian Agent, Warren Wasson. With Wasson dead, the Paiutes planned to seize the rifles and powder at the agency, and concealing the weapons under blankets and rabbit robes, filter into Fort Churchill in small groups. It was known that only 40 officers and men comprised the garrison at the adobe fort. At a signal, the Paiutes would slaughter the garrison, and with powder, bullets and guns from the arsenal there were arms enough for the entire Paiute nation!

But Wasson, the Indian Agent, was a kindly man who had won real friendship among the Paiutes. A young interpreter told the plan to the agent, who listened tight-lipped. There was no time to send for help or to alert the little garrison at Fort Churchill. Wasson had to meet the situation alone and unarmed. And alone, he met it. Taking his life in his hands, he strode down to the great crowds of Indians at the fisheries and called the chiefs and sub-chiefs together.

Boldly he told them why the plan would fail. He recognized Bannocks from Idaho and Oregon, and delegates from Paiute bands from far and wide in the Territory. There was a very real and very large war in the making. He also noticed, as he told of the white man's power for vengeance, and repeated the tale of the final victory at Pyramid a year before, that the Indians were listening to him and restraining Wahe from interrupting him. They admired him for his courage, and nodded when he called on individuals who had been to California and seen the white man's armies, ships, and magic. Wahe saw the agent winning over his warriors with unanswerable logic, and suddenly panic stricken, he mounted his pony and rode off across the desert. Wasson kept talking, smoked the pipe, and the peace parley was over without bloodshed.

Wahe fled on and on in terror, until he reached Oregon. His power and the fear of his magic were gone forever. The Bannocks quietly rode away to the north, and the Paiute emmissaries drifted back to their own bands. Peace returned to the Territory and security to Fort Churchill. It had been stripped of men by the needs of the grim Civil War. Wasson was greatly respected by Paiute and whites.

Many months later Wahe decided to return to Nevada, and he appeared again at the mouth of the Walker. But this time the Paiutes were unimpressed, and two chiefs promptly beat him to death with war clubs.

They were still a little afraid of Wahe's once vaunted magic, however, and just to be safe, they chopped his body up into tiny pieces, and then rode far out of camp, scattering the bloody fragments over the vast reaches of the desert.

Death at Gravelly Ford

THE WESTWARD trail was well marked with scenes of death and privation in the early gold rush years, and not the least of these hardships were encountered along the winding Humboldt in Nevada. But by 1861 possibility of Indian attack was slight, and the trail was considered a main travel arterial where lack of abundant food and water were the only major obstacles in the way of slow moving wagon trains. It was, therefore, reason for great alarm when a Shoshone war party attacked and massacred thirteen persons near Gravelly Ford in the fall of '61.

The emigrants with their oxen drawn wagons had stopped at the Stebbins trading post in Ruby Valley after negotiating the salt desert, and during the time they waited for their travel-weary stock to regain strength, Mr. and Mrs. Stebbins became attached to a little blonde haired ten year old girl, one of four children making the overland journey with the tiny wagon train. The Stebbins' tried to persuade her parents to let the little girl remain with them but were unsuccessful in their plea, and at length, the wagon train pulled away from the trading post to follow the river across Nevada.

An elderly Shoshone squaw, employed by the Stebbins family, had overheard some of the tribal braves mapping plans for an attack on the wagon train. Fearing for the safety of the little child, yet not daring to reveal her secret, the squaw followed the wagons for several days until they reached a stopping place at Yago canyon near Gravelly Ford on the Humboldt. There they were suddenly attacked by a small band of Shoshones. The squaw rushed into the melee and rescued the little girl. Her flight was noted by some of the Shoshone warriors, but they did not immediately give chase, being too occupied with the attack.

For a day and a night the squaw sped back toward the Stebbins ranch in Ruby, carrying the little child, not daring to hesitate even for a rest, knowing that pursuers were close on her heels. On the second evening she was overtaken by two fleet-footed braves, and despite a struggle, she was knocked senseless. When she recovered consciousness, the little child had been killed. The war party had thus accounted for all thirteen persons of the train. Twelve others lay dead among the burning embers of their wagons on the banks of the Humboldt at Gravelly Ford.

Almost a year later, when the massacre was nearly forgotten, the two Shoshone braves who had followed the squaw and killed the little girl, put in an appearance at the Stebbins ranch in Ruby Valley. They were immediately recognized since the old squaw had described them. They were seized by the irate station residents. One was shot as he attempted to escape and the other was hung.

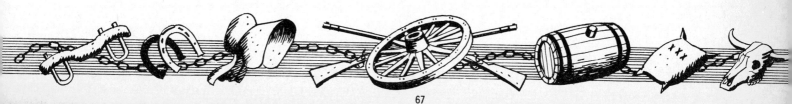

Incredible Austin !

NEVER AS widely publicized as Virginia City, Austin had the same fantastic boom, with a population of 10,000 and a dazzling flood of millions in bullion pouring from her mills. Austin set the pace for most of Nevada and many a Lander county incident is today mistakenly attributed to the Comstock area.

Of nationwide scope was the stock promotion bubble of the Reese River Navigation Company . . . when thousands of credulous souls bought shares in a company "to freight rich ores from mines to mill on barges floating down the Reese River." Little could they tell that the impressive river on the maps was (like most Nevada rivers) only a few inches deep!

Today's Red Cross and recent war bond drives are still patterned after the idea originated by the famous Gridley sack of flour which was auctioned over and over again for

relief and welfare funds in Austin first and then the rest of the state and San Francisco.

Camels were used to haul salt near Austin, and the community produced $50,000,000 in rich ores. Austin was

the childhood home of Emma Nevada and is the site of Stokes' Castle still reputedly an enigma of the desert. Austin was practically on the first pony express route across Nevada. It is still colorful and unspoiled, one of the most interesting places in central Nevada.

Orson Hyde's Curse

O N THE SEVENTEENTH of January, 1854, the Territorial Legislature of Utah created Carson County as the political subdivision embracing its westernmost fringes. The Act also authorized Utah's governor to appoint a Probate Judge, whose duties would primarily be concerned with the organization of this outpost area. Thus it was that Orson Hyde came to Genoa, an event that was eventually climaxed with bitter feeling and the now famous Orson Hyde's Curse.

A year and some few months after passage of the Act, Orson Hyde, a Mormon Elder, who had been selected as Probate Judge for Carson County, arrived with his retinue at Mormon Station. In a business-like manner he called for election of county officers and set the wheels of government and justice in motion. Within a year after his arrival, he had ordered the surveying of Mormon Station and the renaming of the town Genoa. It was then that numerous followers of his faith began moving from the Salt Lake area into Carson County along the Sierra watershed, where they took up agricultural and timbering pursuits.

Although Carson County was peaceful, clouds of discontent were gathering over the City of the Saints (Salt Lake). Trouble was brewing between the United States government and the followers of Brigham Young. As if in anticipation of events to follow, Orson Hyde returned to the Utah ·capital late in 1856. The following year, some eight months after Orson Hyde's departure, the Mormons answered the call of their leader, Brigham Young, to return and defend the City of the Saints. President Buchanan had sent troops to Salt Lake to re-establish the Government's supremacy.

The exodus of faithful, practically depopulated Carson County and much of the land, including buildings, sawmills and other business ventures. changed hands for a mere fraction of their worth. This was the change in the course of events that raised the wrath of Orson Hyde.

Nearly seven years after he first set foot in Carson County, the Mormon Elder addressed a lengthy letter to the people of Carson and Washoe valleys. In it he set down his claim of twenty thousand dollars for his sawmill and land holdings in Washoe Valley. Between quotations from the scriptures Orson Hyde mentioned that during the period he had been away, he had received as rent "one span of small, indifferent mules, an old worn-out harness, two yokes of oxen and an old wagon." Should his demand for twenty thousand dollars remain uncancelled, Orson Hyde said, the people of Carson and Washoe valleys shall be "visited with thunder and with earthquake and with floods, with pestilence and with famine until your names are not known amongst men."

There is no record that the account was ever settled, and despite Orson Hyde's curse, Washoe Valley has been richly productive through the years.

Murder at Schell Creek

IT WAS 1862, and two young toughs named Ransom Young and James Wabb found things getting too hot around San Jose. They stole a Jenny to carry their packs and made a desperate escape over the Sierras, and so it was they were just breathing easier at the Truckee Meadows, when they met three wealthy mining men, also traveling east. These men had sold out their claims in California, cleaned up, and were taking 150 head of horses on their way home as an investment. Little knowing the vile character of Young and Wabb, they were glad to hire the two experienced men to get the band of horses eastward. Wabb and Young could scarcely conceal their delight.

The party travelled across Nevada without incident to Egan Canyon, where Wabb delighted saloon loafers with an exhibition of his brutal but amazing skill with horses. Riding on, the party camped that night at Schell Creek, cooked supper, and went to bed. Next morning the outfit moved on east, and it was not until three day later when Indians found the shockingly battered bodies of the three prosperous miners, that people at Schell Creek Station, and other stations on east, realized the party of **five** men had diminished to **two**! In alarm a posse was sworn and started pursuit, concealing themselves by using the stagecoach instead of saddle horses. Soon they found their quarry at Riverside Station, Utah, but in the confusion

Wabb escaped on a wounded horse. A few days later, weak with hunger, Wabb was captured by a teamster and the two young men were given a speedy trial at Schell Creek by an informal Vigilante group.

Young soon broke down and confessed, blaming the murder plot on Wabb, who, he said, killed two men with a hatchet while they slept. Young admitted knocking one victim down with an axe, and "Wabb finished him off." Repeatedly Young told of wanting to get help, of wanting to prevent the ghastly killings, but was too weak-willed to oppose his older companion. Wabb remained uncowed at the trial, even when the mob decided it was too far to Austin and the courthouse, for a formal and long drawn out legal trial.

The men were given a good breakfast, handcuffed, and allowed to make a speech from the plank scaffold. All the employees of the Overland Mail and other Schell Creek Station residents appeared as witnesses, hearing Young's confession and "advice to young men." They also heard Wabb shout, revile, and curse the entire assemblage. Then flour sacks were tied over their heads, the plank snatched from beneath their feet, and pioneer justice was done. The murderers were hanged "facing the graves of their victims on a grassy hillside under a stately pine, near a beautiful spring."

Paiute "Cold War"

JAMES NYE, Territorial Governor of Nevada, was anxious to end a series of bloody wars with the Paiutes by a peace conference. In a single year the Paiutes had massacred Ormsby's expedition on the Truckee, white troops had slaughtered Winnemucca's warriors at Pyramid, and Fort Churchill troops had waged a rough campaign against the Paiutes in Owens Valley.

Indian Agent Wasson finally negotiated a meeting between Chief Winnemucca and the Governor on the lower Truckee on May 23, 1862, but the Indians were bitter and reluctant. The two parties finally gathered, each hoping to impress the other. The Governor had a plan to convince the Paiutes of the hopelessness of their cause and the wisdom of accepting the conditions of a white civilization here.

Old Chief Winnemucca understood well the resources of the white man, and knew he now had no chance in battle. But he wanted to make as powerful and as belligerent an impression as possible to gain concessions and advantages for his people. He switched from war chief to showman quickly and well.

Accordingly, when Governor Nye, Wasson, Captain Price and 100 California Volunteer Cavalrymen arrived on the lower Truckee near Nixon, they found Winnemucca and all his sub-chiefs in full regalia. Massed behind them stood 400 painted warriors in battle dress. As the whites rode up, the 400 warriors raised their voices in a wild chant, and then, before the horrified gaze of the Governor's party, they plunged into a frantic war dance on a huge bed of live coals. Eye witnesses report that hundreds of the tribesmen danced in their bare feet on the glowing red embers of a great sagebrush fire; dancing, and chanting without indicating by any sign or expression, the torture beneath their feet. The dancing continued for hours, while other warriors demonstrated feats of warlike skill. Wasson gave Winnemucca the property of his dead brother Wahe, but the old chief only grunted his displeasure. And Numaga, the great diplomat of the Paiutes, gave the Indian agent his pipe of peace, a magnificent bow and arrow, his war head-dress of otter skin and eagle feathers, and his tomahawk.

Although no formal peace treaty came from the meeting, it marked effectively the end of organized conflict between the Indians and whites of Nevada, and was a final defiant gesture on the part of the hopelessly defeated Paiutes. They had been driven from the best meadow lands, their pine nut trees cut for fuel, the deer and rabbits slaughtered for food. There was nothing to do but to try to learn the ways of the white man who had come to stay.

Old French Canal

Paul Mykland

PIONEERS who followed the twisting course of the Humboldt River through Nevada on their way to the golden land of California in the early fifties found little to praise about the muddy stream that curved snakelike through the barren desert land. True, it provided brackish water for horses and oxen and along its banks there was, at some seasons, a sparse amount of grass for feed. For purposes other than that they scorned the lazy, slow moving river.

Ten years elapsed and the Humbolt trail still bore the brunt of Overland travel, but by that time the territory of Nevada was beginning to produce undreamed of mineral wealth . . . a richness hidden under the sun-browned overburden of desert mountains that escaped notice of early travellers as they hastened toward the lush Pacific slope and the placer gold that lay in the beds of clear, singing mountain streams.

In the sixties the Star mining district became an exciting Nevada development. The towns of Unionville, Star City and Dun Glen were bustling and Mill City was established seventeen miles to the north of the new district in anticipation of becoming the milling center for all ores from the Star district. Then it was that the slow moving Humboldt was eyed in a different light. J. A. Ginacca pondered the problem of mill operation. He foresaw gigantic developments provided the right kind of power could be supplied. After studying the situation he interested the Lay brothers of Golconda in his enterprise: the construction of a canal from Preble on the river to Mill City. The canal, he believed, would provide enough power to operate forty mills of twenty stamps each even during the dry portions of the year.

Planning the canal consumed nearly a year and the Lay brothers, who were of French extraction, succeeded in raising some capital in their native country. Offices were established in San Francisco and actual work was commenced on the "Old French Canal" in 1862. It was to be ninety miles long from Preble to, or slightly beyond Mill City. Width was established at fifteen feet and the canal was to be dug to a depth of three feet. It was believed that it would provide not only motive power for the mills, but also a waterway for small barges. Irrigation of soil along the route was not an inconsiderable factor.

Indian labor using oxen-powered metal-faced wooden scrapers was employed on the project. Twenty-eight miles of the canal were completed at a cost of about one hundred thousand dollars before it was conceded that the scheme would not work.

Because of poor engineering the water did not have enough drop and the project was abandoned near the present site of Winnemucca. With the stoppage of work on the "Old French Canal" central Nevada's only projected desert waterway was given up, never to be tried again.

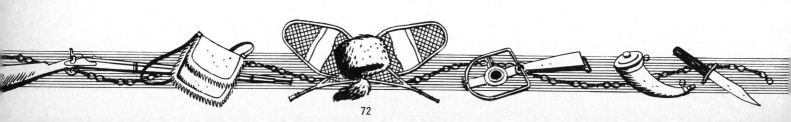

Ben Holladay's Line

Paul Nyeland

WHEN THE Pony Express, owned by Russell, Majors and Waddell failed in 1862 for $200,000 it was purchased at auction by Ben Holladay. The new owner was one of the most remarkable men of his time, and he quickly saw that the coming of the telegraph was making the Pony Express unnecessary, but, he reasoned, that a fast overland stage line was a necessity for the growing West.

Holladay, who had a great gift for organizing, with tremendous energy and drive, set up a huge overland stage organization between the Missouri and the Pacific. He had a general superintendent, attorney, paymaster; and under these officials he hired division superintendents, each with smaller divisions supervised by division agents every 200 miles. These division agents had charge of stock, bought supplies, hired employees, and kept the stations by means of lesser employees, including drivers, station keepers, stock tenders, stock buyers, carpenters, and blacksmiths.

Holladay was one of the West's outstanding men during the '60's and well known to thousands of men strung across half of the continent. While his company was officially known as "The Ben Holladay Overland Mail and Express Company" it was popularly called "Ben Holladay's Line" and its owner as "Old Ben."

Twice a year, "Old Ben" made a trip across his entire line, in his own specially constructed coach. This huge, lumbering affair was fitted up with coil springs, a bed, a writing table with oil lamp and reflector, and other comforts. Dashing across the desert and over the mountains at a fast clip both night and day, he lived and worked as he travelled. These trips created tremendous excitement along the route. Holladay was as impressive in his coach and his magnificent equipment, as any later railway magnate, steamship owner or airline executive.

At one time "Old Ben" made a fast trip from Folsom, California, to the Missouri River. At every station along the route, his agents were ready and waiting with fresh teams. The stagecoach literally "flew" over plains, mountains, and desert, beating the regular schedule by five full days. His record-breaking time was twelve days and two hours, and was the quickest trip ever made with a vehicle across this distance until the building of the railroad.

Although his equipment and its operation were considered a miracle of transportation at the time, modern travellers would have smothered in the heavy clouds of alkali dust which continually filled the interior of the stage. It took a strong stomach to roll and rock with the heavy coaches, hour after hour, in the long stretches.

The Escape of Mayfield

SO UNJUST was the conviction of William Mayfield for murder, in 1862, that when he broke jail, the sheriff had an extremely difficult time to avoid recapturing him, and half of Washoe and Ormsby counties had a hand in assisting in his escape.

Mayfield was a Southern sympathizer, a democrat, and a gambler. He was suspected of giving shelter to a notorious California desperado named Plummer, and it is probable that he actually did conceal Plummer at one time, but when Sheriff John Blackburn searched Mayfield's cabin it was empty and no trace of the bandit could be found.

Blackburn was sheriff of Ormsby County and a former U. S. Marshal in Nevada Territory. He had enjoyed a reputation as a fine peace officer for many years; but some historians claim he later became a blustering bully, a drunk and insanely cruel.

Sheriff Blackburn later met the southerner in a Carson saloon and tried to pick a fight with Mayfield. The sheriff finally flew into a towering rage, yanked his pistol from its holster, and flew at Mayfield. Half the crowd in the saloon seized the livid sheriff and tried to restrain him, but he threw them off and soon had Mayfield in a corner, fighting for his life.

At last, in desperation, Mayfield drew his bowie knife and stabbed Blackburn six times, killing him instantly. But Mayfield, the southern sympathizer, was "tried by a jury on which there wasn't a single democrat" and he was promptly found guilty of murder.

In the state prison waiting an appeal, Mayfield soon obtained tools from his friends, and in short order managed to loosen the bars on his windows. He is said to have waited, watching his guards play poker with Warden Abe Curry outside his cell. As Mayfield later told it—"I saw the old man (Warden Abe Curry) raising a hand that had just been dealt him. I waited until he got a better one. A few minutes afterward the guard got queens and sevens before the draw. He bet twenty. The old man stayed, and they took one card each. The old man caught a king, making a king full; the guard drew a queen, making a queen full. They bet and bet until they had about two hundred in the pot. Then I concluded that if I didn't go on this hand, I never could, so I went."

He slipped through the window and down to his friends, who had a fast horse and $1,000 in cash waiting for him.

He was soon up and over the Sierras, but he had a sweetheart in Carson City so he drifted back, hiding at Huffaker's Station near Reno. "All Washoe County" knew Mayfield was at Huffaker's. So many people were in on the secret that finally the new sheriff and posse were forced to search there. Later, relating the incident, members of the posse told of seeing Mayfield's feet and legs beneath a dress hanging on the wall. Deputies managed to look everywhere but in the right place, and Mayfield immediately and rapidly and gratefully left for Idaho.

The Rolling Stones of Pahranagat

THERE WERE PERIODS during the Comstock heyday, few though they were when homicide had a holiday, when no new strikes were reported, when the stock market was static. These were the times when editors scratched their heads for something of interest to fill the columns that normally were overcrowded with killings both in C street and on the San Francisco Exchange.

For editors and newsmen during such dull periods there were but two courses. One was to launch a bitter attack against the opposition. That usually brought about an equally vitriolic answer which in turn would call for rebuttal. The other was·to fabricate . . . and in this art men of the Comstock were supreme. Mark Twain began his literary career on the Territorial Enterprise in Virginia City, but actually he played second fiddle to the plodding work horse of the Bonanza Days . . . William Wright, better known as Dan DeQuille.

Dan had a label for his fabrications. He called them "Quaints," and one of his best, one that caused him no little embarrassment, was the "Rolling Stones of Pahranagat."

On one of these dull days Dan set his scene in Pahranagat Valley some four hundred miles south of the Comstock. This region, he claimed, was infested with stones which were drawn together by some mysterious power and then scattered wide apart only to be returned in a moving quivering mass to a place that appeared to be the magnetic center of the valley.

Since Dan had a couple of newspaper columns to fill on this particular day, he enlarged upon his thesis, predicting a new doctrine concerning electrical propulsion and repulsion, indicating that these rocks which would appear to be loadstone, would start off with wonderful celerity to rejoin their fellow rocks from whatever point they were released.

DeQuille was a conceded authority on mining and his articles always found access to reprint. Somewhere along the line, whether in the telling, or in additional fabrication, it came to light that the rolling stones tumbled to the valley floor at night and returned to the hills in daytime, or vice-versa.

Some months later the story found its way into reprint in Germany, whereupon DeQuille received a letter from noted German scientists demanding additional details. Slightly embarrassed over his "quaint," DeQuille replied, disclaiming veracity of the story, but his disclaimer was treated as an unprofessional attempt to keep brother scientists in ignorance about the wonderful stones.

And, as if to add insult to injury, a circus sent Dan an offer of ten thousand dollars if he could get his stones to perform under a big top.

Happy Harry

"H̲APPY" HANK HARPER, driver of the Overland Stage in eastern Nevada, had no way of knowing this particular March afternoon in 1863, that red barbaric death lurked in the shadows of the stage station at Eight-Mile near the Schell Creek range. The stage rolled in a travelling cloud of dust, the horses eager to reach water now that the station was in view.

These were tragic days in the Nevada country. Troops had been largely drawn off by Civil War needs. Indian tribes were rising on every hand and raids and attacks became more and more common. A few hours before the Gos-ute War chief, White Horse, had led a party of braves out on a raid on Eight Mile station, now a few hundred yards ahead of the galloping team. White Horse had killed the station stock tender, driven off the live stock, and tortured the cook to death, stringing his body up between two adobe buildings.

Now the Indians, seeing the high dust cloud of the approaching stage coach sensed more loot. Quickly they dropped low and hid in the shadows to ambush the stage.

But "Happy" Harry had been alert to danger all the way across Nevada. Something about the horses in the corral looked unfamiliar. Something dangled between the cabins in the breeze. A closer look and his horrified gaze made out the naked body of a dead man. The corral animals were runty Indian ponies, not the sleek, well fed stage horses. Sensing a trap, "Happy" Harry cracked his big whip like a pistol shot, wheeled his team off the road and started cross country through the sagebrush at a dead run,

the coach lurching crazily and his passengers thrown in a heap on the floor below.

Instantly the Indians opened fire, the shots hitting both "Happy" Harry, and a passenger on the seat beside him, John Liverton, who fell across the footboard. "Happy" hung on to the reins, although badly wounded and called on his passengers for help. Below, in a tangled pile on the floor of the stage were the two young sons of John Liverton, and the aged Nevada congressman, Judge Gordon Mott, who was on his way to Washington to serve as a Nevada delegate.

Opening the door, and with his white hair blowing in the wind, the Judge crawled along the side of the bouncing stage coach. Indian bullets whistled all around him, but slowly he climbed up on the seat box. He started to push Liverton's body overboard until he saw the man was still alive.

Then the old Judge took the reins, and with "Happy" Harry talking to his horses in soothing tones, the stage picked up speed at a great clip across the level desert. Runty in-bred ponies were no match for the grain-fed express horses, and the stage rapidly drew away from the shots and bloodcurdling screams.

Soon the stage drew near Deep Creek station, eight miles from the scene of the attack. The whip fell from "Happy's" hands, but he kept calling encouragement to his team. Finally, a few hundred yards from the station, "Happy" Harry called to his team one last time, and then sank across the footboard dead. But his four passengers were all saved.

Roop County War

WHEN NEVADA TERRITORY was organized in 1861 most settlers in the Susanville-Honey Lake area favored inclusion and territorial organization divided Nevada into nine counties, one of which was "Roop" County comprising the Honey Lake district.

California, however, maintained that the area was part of Plumas County, California. Nothing daunted, the new Nevada Territorial Legislature called for the election of officials in Roop County in 1862, and commissioned those selected. It also appointed John S. Ward probate judge, and precipitated open warfare!

Judge Ward (Nev.) issued an injunction restraining William Young, California justice of the peace from performing his official functions. The justice failed to heed the court order, and Judge Ward (Nev.) had the Justice of the peace (Calif.) arrested and fined for contempt of court. Then the County Court of Plumas County (Calif.) issued an order restraining Judge Ward (Nev.) or Wm. H. Naileigh, sheriff of Roop County (Nev.) from exercising any jurisdiction. They refused and were arrested by the California officials, but a crowd of citizens overtook them and rescued the Nevada authorities. The sheriff grimly went to Quincy, organized 100 heavily armed men, and returned to Susanville, occupying the upper end of town.

Naileigh, the rescued Nevada sheriff, meanwhile had proclaimed an insurrection, calling on all able-bodied citizens of Roop County to arm to keep order. These "Nevada" forces, about 75 strong, occupied a small log house in lower Susanville, since known as Fort Defiance.

Sunday morning, February 15, 1863, Pierce's California group suddenly seized a large barn 150 yards from the Nevada men and started to fortify it with huge timbers. The Nevada forces notified them to evacuate the barn. Instead the Californians sent out a party of six for more timbers, and the Nevadans opened fire. One man fell with a shattered hip.

Shooting on both sides continued for hours, and two men on the Nevada side were slightly wounded. Finally a party of citizens from the town, with white flags, effected a series of armistices. Although scores of volunteers from all parts of Honey Lake hurried to reinforce the Nevada "army" and the California authorities rushed in a small cannon, hostilities did not resume. The Nevada and California governors quickly ordered a survey of the State line by Butler Ives of Nevada and John Kidder of California, which proved Honey Lake to be in California, and Aurora with its rich mines to the south to be in Nevada. Today some authorities agree that the strip of California east of the Sierras should have been in Nevada.

Sugarfoot Jack

NO ONE seems to remember the real name of the tall, wax-faced, loose-jointed young fellow, but he did have a nickname and that was sufficient for anyone in Virginia City during the year 1863.

The rowdy toughs knew him only by the handle of Sugarfoot Jack and they recalled that he had a peculiar hankering to be counted as one of them even though the only qualification he possessed was a consuming ambition to be real tough. Sugarfoot paid the penalty of his attempted disguise when he uttered an idle threat at a crucial time.

At that period the Comstock Lode was well aware of the presence of Tom Peasley, a giant of a man, who at thirty was considered one of the real leaders of Washoe, even though he preferred the company of the more turbulent crowd. He was foreman of the first hook and ladder company and later chief engineer of the fire department as well as sheriff, but that was after he had lost some of the exuberance of youth.

From the time he arrived on Sun Mountain, he was extremely popular, and his feats of strength were a source of marvel to Sugarfoot Jack, who yearned for a life as exciting as that led by Tom Peasley. Wherever Tom showed up, Sugarfoot was to be found on the fringes of the crowd. Like as not Tom Peasley and his cronies would wind up an evening of celebration with a good street fight and Sugarfoot enjoyed the fun.

When he was in a boisterous mood Tom Peasley considered it great fun to greet a friend with a hearty slap on the back. Because of his immense strength such a blow would often knock the man down, but Tom thought it great sport, and such a show of affection seldom caused him any trouble, besides it always created a great deal of merriment.

One night Sugarfoot was awaiting the arrival of the Peasley gang at a free and easy masquerade. Quite unobtrusively Tom arrived and greeted Sugarfoot with one of his hearty back slaps. The blow sent Sugarfoot sprawling onto the dance floor, his gangling frame describing a grotesque arc before he crumpled at the feet of some dancers. After a good laugh all around, the matter was apparently forgotten, but Sugarfoot Jack felt the comic display had injured his self-evaluated stature as a tough guy. As he left the ballroom, he muttered a threat that could have meant he was going to "get" Tom Peasley.

Hearing whispers of the threat, Tom's cronies hastened to inform the strong man that Sugarfoot was armed and waiting for him to put in an appearance along Virginia City's main thoroughfare, C street. Being anything but a coward Tom Peasley, with his troupe at his heels, set out for C street. Soon he spied Sugarfoot cringing behind an awning post.

Such a position, Peasley realized, could be a vantage point, so without waiting he emptied his pistol at the target and Sugarfoot fell to the street. His threat had evidently been an empty one for he died unarmed.

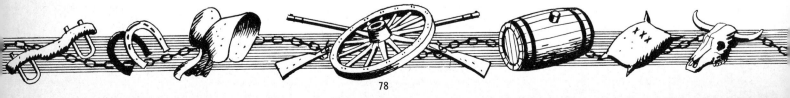

Stagecoach Racing

STAGECOACHING was a cutthroat enterprise in early day Nevada, and often the business went to the man whose coaches made the fastest time. With rival lines operating between most points and competition so keen that some outfits gave rides away free, every trip was likely to turn into a hair-raising life and death race between coaches and fast teams.

R. Gelatt, one of the Territory's leading stage coach operators who based near old Mormon Station at Genoa, recalled that his lady passengers almost always requested the driver not to participate in any racing. But when a rival stagecoach would try to pass, these same ladies were usually the most eager and excited of all passengers to race.

Gelatt learned the business as a youngster, and later worked for his brother. In those days all western Nevada was a network of stage lines; Carson City through Genoa to Wellington, and connecting there to Aurora; Folsom through Carson to Virginia City; Carson City to Huffakers where a connection was made with the Reno-Virginia City via Geiger Grade; and Virginia City to Glenbrook.

Gelatt and a rival named Johnson engaged in a struggle for the business between Placerville (Hangtown) and Carson. Johnson offered to haul some next loads with luggage free, and to supply free whiskey and cigars. When Gelatt countered with his regular fare, the passengers were so impressed they remained with him. Finally Johnson challenged Gelatt to a race, with a side bet, but Gelatt had

secretly trained his teams to start running from a standing start, and he won the race handily as his passengers cheered and waved from the rocking top of the lumbering and heavy laden stagecoach.

It was an exciting business for the owners, as new lines were always starting and often gave rides away free until they could get established. Fares were often cut and reduced until one company or another went broke or gave up. The competition, of course, gave rise to the racing and many a big stagecoach load of passengers arrived covered with dust and disheveled, exhausted, but thrilled with a breakneck ride over the Sierras or across the desert.

Betting between passengers, drivers, and owners of rival stage lines often reached astonishing figures. It became the popular thing for passengers to brag about the fast time made between various points, especially along the route from Hangtown to communities in Nevada. Here the rival coaches thundered down narrow mountain roads, and along the sides of sheer cliffs. It was said a stagecoach trip down Geiger Grade from Virginia City to Reno when the driver was "out to make fast time" was enough to restore one's faith in religion in a single trip! Less spectacular but faster trips were made across the desert, and every driver sought to hang up a new record, and every passenger to boast of it.

The railroads ended the big overland stage lines, but the connecting network of stage lines prospered for more than a third of a century after the Central Pacific was completed.

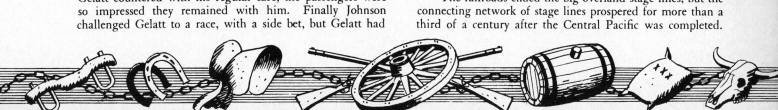

"Hurrah for Abe Linkeln"

RALLY 'ROUND THE FLAG BOYS

FEELING RAN mighty high in Nevada Territory in 1863! Sympathy with North and South in the Civil War was about evenly divided and emigrants were usually careful about revealing their true feelings whenever they struck a Nevada town in their westward journey. Like as not the camp would be a Secesh stronghold, or again, it might be sympathetic with the Union cause, thus pioneers considered it wise to keep their mouths closed and their teams moving until they were able to take the pulse of the community.

A few of these hardy westerners weren't so discreet, however, like the head of one family who staged a Union rally all his own down the main street of a little Secesh town just east of Austin. This California bound family became separated from its wagon train in central Nevada and decided to make it to the eastern base of the Sierra alone. Not wishing anyone to mistake his sympathies, the head of the family hoisted a Union flag just aft the driver's seat. On approaching a small mining town, the family was startled to see a young man come riding toward them at breakneck speed. Reaching the slow moving wagon, the young man pulled up and addressed his remark to the driver:

"Cap," he said, "take a fool's advice and haul down that dish rag, we don't tolerate your breed here. This is a Secesh camp."

The mother of the family describes the incident that followed: "Pop, he's Union to the hub," she said. "When this fancy looking fellow gave us that warning, Pop, he just stuck the flag toward the young whipper-snapper and says, 'Stranger, if you're spilin' for diffikilty, you can have it. The first man that lays a hand on that flag, I'll drop him sure!"

"The young feller looked black," Mom said, "but he changed his base and made for the camp, since Pop had his turkey duster well in hand. Then Pop cracked his blacksnake and we rid with flying colors right into town. The gals jined the chorus' and all of us, big and little, peeked out of the wagon and give 'em a chorus of 'Rally 'round the Flag 'as we bumped through the main street.

"It stirred 'em up considerable and they looked mighty hard at us, but there was a look in Pop's eye as he sot with his rifle in one hand and his blacksnake in the other. There was something in his eye didn't exactly please 'em.

"Let 'em rip," the people said as we raced through the town, and "we ripped." Just for a partin' stare as we left the town, we all sang out in a chorus, just as loud and long as you please, "Hurrah," we yells, "Hurrah for Abe Linkelin."

Let 'er Burn

IN THE MIDDLE YEARS of the Civil War the mining camp of Aurora had attained a prominent place among western mineral capitals. Her mines were producing rich ores and her citizens foresaw a bright future.

Along with Bodie and the Comstock, the town struggled for a "place in the sun" and whenever any tales of wrongdoing were attributed to her immediate vicinity, it was a good bet that the story would be subjected to modification, and upon retelling, the locale of such happenings would surely be near Bodie or somewhere along the Comstock.

In all, Aurora was a typical western boom town with aspirations to become a mining capital of the west, and in striving for such fame, it was only natural that several organizations, social, and otherwise, came into prominence within a short space of time. One of these was the famous Deluge Bucket Company, a volunteer firemen's organization that rivaled the Warrens of Carson City in its heyday.

When the town had attained the dignity of incorporation the Deluge Bucket Company was right in stride, a brand new hand pumper engine was added to the firemen's equipment.

One early morning in 1863 the volunteers were hastily summoned to extinguish a blazing frame building. Gallantly manning their positions, men of the Deluge Bucket Company hauled the heavy pumper to the scene of the blaze and immediately set about extinguishing the flames which had gained quite some headway. Whether it was the shortage of water or the extremely hard exercise afforded by the new pump, could never be correctly ascertained, but the flames kept spreading. The wonderful stream of water that the pump was guaranteed to produce, was a mere trickle, more mud than water.

After some minutes of arduous exercise, men of the Deluge Bucket Company developed a spontaneous dislike for this severe form of calisthenics and retired to the nearest likely resting spot away from the heat to regain their breath.

Emerging from the smoke and flame of the burning building, the fire company captain was ready to give his charges a severe tongue lashing, when, to his amazement, he noticed the pumper was manned by wives of the volunteers, who had assumed their husbands' posts when the menfolks "gave out."

Accompanied by shouts of encouragement from onlookers, the wives were manning the pumper with concentrated zeal. Dismayed at the first real test of the new equipment, and slightly chagrined by the behavior of his gallant fire crew, the captain took a last look at the blazing building and curtly commanded the womenfolk to cease their labors with his decision, "Let 'Er Burn."

Washoe Lake Ice Boat

Paul Nyland

FORMS OF SPORT and recreation in the new State of Nevada were few and far between in 1863, and this was particularly true during the winter months. So when a few imaginative and adventuresome souls at Washoe City designed and built an ice boat, it immediately became the center of interest for hundreds of miles around.

The ice boat was brilliantly designed and soundly constructed, and many a long winter's evening went into the building. It was said that advice and some labor were obtained from the best engineering minds on the Comstock. Certainly Washoe City itself contained some brilliant men in the late '60's. At any rate, several accounts reveal that the cold and bitter winter of 1863 found Washoe Lake frozen hard, and a beautiful ice boat ready to make the most of it.

The owner and crew soon mastered the handling of the strange craft, and became adept at loading her up with enthusiastic and unsuspecting friends and visitors. It seemed everybody in Nevada wanted a ride on the ice boat. Estimates of her speed ranged from 60 to 100 miles an hour, which seems quite possible in view of the terrific winds in Washoe Valley.

With a terrific Washoe Zephyr filling the canvas to bursting, the light ice boat would skim along Washoe Lake with the speed of an airplane. Then, without warning, her skipper would pull hard on the tiller, and whip the boat around in a tight turn that broke the grasp of every unsuspecting passenger aboard. Sports and fun in pioneer Nevada were rough and rugged, and ice boating proved no exception. The poor passengers were torn from the ice boat and hurled by centrifugal force out across the smooth ice. Many would shoot and scoot over 50 yards according to contemporary reports, but no fractured skulls or broken collar bones were listed in the records. Then the sail would be dropped and the ice boat pull up and stop. The battered passengers would pick themselves up and painfully hobble over to the boat to the accompaniment of loud guffaws by the crew.

At last all passengers would be loaded back on the boat. History fails to record a single case of a passenger whose shattered nerves and dignity prevented him from eagerly accepting more rides. And so, loaded full, the sail hoisted, the ice boat would soon be gliding over Washoe Lake again at a hundred miles or so an hour, and ready for another sharp turn and fast unloading.

Eventually the ice boat arrived at the north end of the lake and all hands would proceed to the Lake House at Washoe City (not to be confused with the Lake House in Reno) for some medication for tattered nerves and frozen arms and legs. Usual remedy at the Lake House, following an ice boat ride, according to history, was a generous series of hot toddies, in which each member of the crew toasted each passenger, and all passengers returned this courtesy. Some of the stories following the exchanges of these toasts rival the ice boat rides themselves. Perhaps the latest recorded exploits came early in this century. For a lark, ranchers Gib Douglas and Ira Winters drove across the ice in a new automobile on a bet.

Public Servant in '63

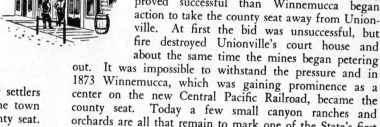

Pᴜʙʟɪᴄ SERVICE IN '63 was fraught with difficulties, not all of them political. At least such was the case in Unionville, seat of the original Humboldt County, where the elements conspired against hastily constructed adobe buildings causing public officials to be constantly vigilant in keeping the records dry.

Despite its name, Unionville was originally a stronghold of southern sympathy. It was actually divided into three settlements; Lower Town or Dixie, Centerville and Upper Town. Throughout the Civil War Centerville was like the Mason-Dixon line running between the two townsites with opposite sympathies. Approximately a year after the camp was established in 1861, an influx of Northerners, gradually took over control and the entire settlement was baptized Unionville. The southerners maintained their homes in Lower Town and the northerners stayed in Upper Town. The two distinct settlements with Centerville in between were connected by an hourly shuttle stage.

In the spring of '63 approximately twenty new settlers a day were arriving to seek silver fortunes, and the town was thriving not only from mining, but as the county seat. Troubles then began for public officials.

The elements, seemingly unimpressed by the importance of the new mining camp, began playing havoc with hasty construction. Rains concentrated with particular vigor on the court house which began to leak like a sieve. One official that year moved his records to a corner cubby-hole of the court house remarking that "at least the rain didn't come down any thicker there than it did outside." Within a few months it became necessary to rent a saloon for the court house, but when the first rain arrived, the boasted "concrete roof" of the rented structure proved to be no more than sand and lime laid on canvas.

Immigrants from Europe finally succeeded in teaching settlers how to do an expert thatching job, but hardly had the new type roofing proved successful than Winnemucca began action to take the county seat away from Unionville. At first the bid was unsuccessful, but fire destroyed Unionville's court house and about the same time the mines began petering out. It was impossible to withstand the pressure and in 1873 Winnemucca, which was gaining prominence as a center on the new Central Pacific Railroad, became the county seat. Today a few small canyon ranches and orchards are all that remain to mark one of the State's first mining camps.

Citizen's Safety Committee

AURORA'S REIGN of terror came to a sudden halt on February 9, 1864, when three hundred fifty citizens of that rip-roaring mining camp decided they had suffered overly long the indignities of a cutthroat desperado band. The decision fatally affected four of the gang and succeeded in driving the remaining outlaws out of the area for a good many months.

Like many another Nevada mining camp, Aurora's rich ores attracted all sorts of people including a plentiful representation of those who had little regard for human life and no use for the law. This gang of rowdies succeeded in running things just about as they pleased, accenting their actions with gunplay. It had become useless to resort to the court for settling any type of dispute in which the gang was concerned.

It was impossible to get a jury to convict one of them. Even the law enforcement officers and the jurists were known to close their eyes to many of the "goings on" for fear they might be among the next batch of victims.

Once started, however, events progressed rapidly. On the first day of February 1864, W. R. Johnson of Hoy's Station on the West Walker, was killed by four of the desperadoes because they felt he had been responsible in doing away with one of the gang.

Not only did they shoot him, but cut his throat and burned his clothes, leaving him lying on an Aurora street. Soon after dawn, word of the murder spread through town and some of the citizens decided the time for action had

arrived. Three of the suspects, John Daily, James Masterson, and Three-fingered Jack McDowell were arrested. The fourth, William Buckley, fled and a sheriff's posse took out after him, finally locating his hideout in an abandoned mine tunnel!

Meanwhile the newly formed Citizens' Safety Committee took complete charge. Members arrested the deputy sheriff and other law enforcement officers, took the sheriff into custody when he returned with Buckley, and proceeded to clamp a martial law on the town.

Saloons were required to close their doors at nine o'clock each evening. Under the guidance of Colonel Palmer, the Citizens' Safety Committee patrolled the streets and maintained the best order Aurora had ever witnessed in its short but hectic history.

On the ninth day following the murder, the four prisoners were marched to a quadruple gallows, surrounded by a hollow square of armed Safety Committee members. Governor Nye, fearing real trouble would result from this extra-legal justice, wired officials requesting there be no violence.

The answer was immediate "all quiet and orderly, four men will be hung in half an hour." And, the hanging was on schedule. At 1:30 o'clock in the afternoon, the four prisoners mounted the gallows, and as a small cannon boomed a signal, the traps were sprung. In the short space of nine days Aurora's outraged citizens brought an end to lawlessness through a hastily formed Citizens' Safety Committee.

Buel's Shoe Fund

FINANCIAL IMPETUS for Nevada's initial attempts to provide school facilities for its rapidly expanding population in the early Sixties was characteristic of the mining fraternity's philosophy "easy come, easy go." Ardent supporters of free public education worked long and hard while Nevada was still a territory, to set the wheels of such a system in motion. They were rewarded by such incidents as Austin's Buel Shoe Fund and Carson City's Rowdy Fund, which fanned public fancy and paved the way for better facilities when Nevada became a State in 1864.

Colonel D. E. "Dave" Buel was a prominent resident of Austin and once a candidate on the democratic ticket for mayor of the town. That was when democratic and republican party affiliations distinguished a party man as being either a southerner or a northerner. Dave Buel was prominent for many reasons, not the least of which was his prodigious stature. Of course he wore good-sized shoes. He needed them to support his giant frame.

A committee had been appointed in Austin to raise funds for a school, but money wasn't flowing in rapidly enough to please the solicitors, so one of them managed to filch Dave Buel's high button shoes. It was generally agreed that there wasn't another shoe in Austin quite that size. Setting up an auction booth in downtown Austin, Tom

Wade proceeded to accept bids on the Colonel's shoe. Over the auction block it went again and again, each time being put back in Tom Wade's hands for another sale. Before Dave Buel got his shoes back, Austin's public school fund was one hundred six dollars richer. Austin had suddenly become enthusiastic about education.

Meanwhile in Carson City an unsuspecting theatre audience was terrified one evening when two heavily-armed men entered the building and in loud voices demanded that the curtain be lowered.

When their order was not immediately obeyed, they rushed the stage and the actors fled. Then with deliberation they proceeded to slash the curtain to ribbons with their formidable bowie knives.

It was some days before all those present realized the affair was staged by a couple of public spirited citizens who cheerfully paid a one thousand dollar fine, but specified that it go to support the schools.

The incident gained publicity as Carson's Rowdy Fund. From such typically western beginnings, the cause of the common school rapidly came to be recognized and public education in Nevada was well on its way to acceptance by the time the territory became a State.

The Lost Breyfogle Mine

FOR 86 YEARS, western prospectors have been baffled and fascinated with the true story of Jacob Breyfogle, the Austin blacksmith, who staggered delirious out of the blazing Nevada desert the summer of 1864 with his arms loaded with some of the richest ore the world has ever seen. Generations of mining men have devoted their lives to finding Breyfogle's mine somewhere in the desert without success.

Breyfogle left Austin to go prospecting, although there is one version of the story which claims he really left to guide a party of Confederate sympathizers from Austin to Arizona. At any rate, somewhere in the vast wilderness south of Austin, one of his saddle horses strayed from camp, and in searching for it, Breyfogle became confused and lost.

Even today the south-central Nevada desert can be brutal, and in 1864 it was a death trap. Breyfogle wandered for days and his route has been a matter of study and conjecture ever since.

Most authorities believe he walked all over central Nevada and there are sufficient scraps of evidence to consider he might have been at points ranging from Silver Peak to Ash Meadows, and to Forty Mile Canyon. An Indian admitted trailing him for miles with the plan of murdering him for his excellent shoes, but evidently was frightened away by the heat-maddened blacksmith.

It is apparent the man staggered a tremendous distance across wide valleys, soft glaring alkali lakes, sharp and brutal lava beds; toiled up mountain ranges of solid rock, all shimmering with desert heat. He struggled through tall sagebrush and boulder strewn slopes at the mouth of every canyon, looking for the tell-tale willow green that signals "water" to the desert wanderer. While out of his head, Breyfogle came across a reddish outcrop of strange ore, laced with free gold and magnificently beautiful in its richness. With his feet cut to ribbons on the lava beds, his black tongue swollen 'til he couldn't talk, his lips cracked and bleeding, and his eyes almost swollen shut, Breyfogle still recognized his outcrop as valuable ore! Above his frantic fear of the desert, fighting off death with every step, his instinct as a prospector rose above everything else. He drew out his small pick and broke off samples of the ore, carefully wrapping and pocketing about fifteen pounds of rock.

From then on he had no known lucid moments. Nearly three generations of prospectors, engineers, and explorers have tried to retrace his steps. It is generally told that he was found while staggering toward a mirage lake, and rescued by Indians who sheltered him from the blistering sun; giving him water in small sips until he regained his reason and strength.

When Breyfogle exhibited his rich red ore in Austin, it created a terrific sensation and started a search that has never ended. He led several parties himself, but could never locate the red outcrop. Goldfield, Ellendale, Clifford, and other strikes have been hailed as the real missing Breyfogle, but in each case their ore failed to resemble the original reddish rock.

Some samples of this fabulous ore were known to be owned and displayed in Austin and the ore became familiar to many mining experts in early day Nevada. In modern times interest has slacked considerably in the search. The price of gold, the rugged nature of the country with its lack of water in summer and its sudden freezing storms in winter do not combine to make an inviting picture. And in recent years a large section of the country has been reserved by the government as a bombing range for military aircraft.

So perhaps one of the richest mines in the world is yet awaiting the man who can retrace the sun-crazed steps of delirious Jacob Breyfogle, the man who found and lost one of the greatest treasures of all time.

Virginia City Gasped

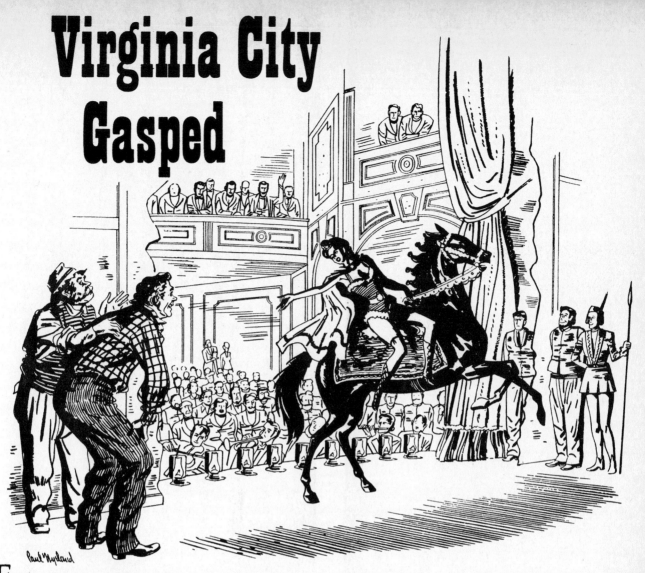

FROM THE VERY outset Virginia City displayed an eager appetite for entertainment. Hardly was the rush to the Comstock well underway before a theatre was constructed in this newly-born, raw, rough city. That was in 1860, and almost before the first one was completed, two more theatres were erected. Wthin three years the town's entertainment was as fabulous as the lode itself. At one time five different companies were playing nightly to packed houses, presenting anything and everything in drama from Shakespeare on down the list and, as if this wasn't enough, six additional variety shows were packing overflow audiences into tent pavilions with song and dance routines.

Virginia City had reached the pinnacle . . . the Comstock was the cultural capital of the west . . . a reputation that even San Francisco couldn't dispute for two decades! But, accustomed to the best the stage had to offer, even Virginia City gasped at daring Adah Menken!

Piper's Opera House was in no little way responsible for Virginia City's entertainment fame. Across its stage, managed by David Belasco, the great and near great passed in review before the appreciative eyes of Comstock theatre goers. From its flickering footlights the golden voice of Adelina Patti held listeners spellbound; down its sloping boards General Tom Thumb and his diminutive wife walked toward a thunderous roar of approval and found Virginia City at their feet. Others had their triumphs here too, Edwin Booth, Clara Morris, James O'Neill, Frank Mayo, Madame Modjeska and countless others. Such plays as "East Lynne," "Davy Crockett," "Under The Gaslight," and a long series of Shakespearian renditions were almost common diet for theatre goers. No wonder then that Adah Menken became the particular favorite!

If Adah had astounded San Francisco, she certainly succeeded in amazing Virginia City, but Virginia City loved amusement! Ladies tittered and blushed behind their fluttering fans, but men leaned forward in their seats when Adah Menken appeared in Mazeppa riding a horse across the stage of Piper's Opera House. It wasn't the horse that caused excitement, but Adah herself, for in this daring scene she was clad in pink tights! Her startling departure from the accepted mode of stage dress was comparable to the fan dance or strip tease of half a century later.

Virginia City loved it, and to show proper appreciation the camp presented Adah Menken with a bar of bullion worth two thousand dollars. Virginia City and later historians have made much of the "cultural recreation" available on the Comstock, but the intense young people on Sun Mountain were impatient for quick fortunes, and truth was, they loved the colorful and the sensational.

The Humboldt Rangers

ON THE MORNING of May 3, 1864, a party of seven prospectors awoke to see Indians driving off their stock. Giving pursuit, they found themselves ambushed at the base of Disaster Peak, and in the ensuing running fight, only three escaped, including one badly wounded.

Great excitement prevailed in the little mining towns of Star City, Unionville, Dun Glen, and Paradise. Nevadans have always been quick to raise semi-military units when needed, and in short order the Humboldt Rangers, a troop of irregular cavalry, had recruited 49 men and officers, with five Paiute scouts. The Rangers rode out on a punitive expedition to restore order in the northern part of the country.

Following the trail of the murdered prospectors, the Rangers crossed the Santa Rosa and Quinn River, and rode up to Disaster Peak where they found the mutilated bodies and many Indian tracks leading westward. With small patrols of scouts ahead, the Rangers beat to and fro through the vast country between McDermitt and the Puebla Mountains, crossing and recrossing streams, deserts, dry lakes, swamps, lava beds, and mountain ranges.

They staggered through the mire of the Quinn, lugging

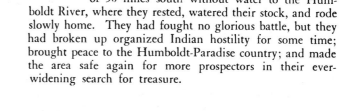

supplies by hand and wading in the muck, leading their horses. They forded the bitter cold Kings River, Trout Creek, and the headwaters of the Quinn. Torn by mahogany and brush, their horses clattered over the lava rocks and slides of the Rattlesnake Range, Puebla Range, and others.

They never closed with a large band of Indians, but their scouts and patrols exterminated three small parties, and recovered much personal property of the murdered men and some 16 head of stolen cattle. Low on food, the Rangers swung south, again engaging in a small skirmish in which they lost one man and killed three more hostile Indians.

By now most of the Indian party was believed to have broken into small groups, all fleeing the Humboldt Country. Weary, hungry, and cold, the Rangers made a final forced march of 50 miles south without water to the Humboldt River, where they rested, watered their stock, and rode slowly home. They had fought no glorious battle, but they had broken up organized Indian hostility for some time; brought peace to the Humboldt-Paradise country; and made the area safe again for more prospectors in their ever-widening search for treasure.

Washoe City

WASHOE CITY was a rip-snortin' town in '64. The air was usually blue with a special variety of the "King's English" as the bullwhackers "cussed them cattle," but its heart was kind and its politics divided between the merits of North and South as the Civil War moved gradually toward Union victory.

Galena and other lumber camps on the Sierra slopes to the west of Washoe provided an endless stream of timber for the Comstock mines and bullwhackers paused in Washoe to "wet their whistles" before tackling the long grind over Ophir grade to haul giant rough log "sets" and spiling to Sun Peak.

A particular character of the ox team days was Jim Mathews, whose bullwhacking was legendary. On his way from Thomas canyon through Galena to Washoe Jim often found his lumber load almost hopelessly bogged down in the creek as the thirsty oxen stopped for water. Jim had a speech impediment in normal conversation, but when talking to his oxen, could make a forcible, if not pleasing oration. After several unsuccessful attempts to get the yoke pulling together, he would mount a nearby stump and give vent to his pent up feeling with a volume of profanity seldom heard. He would wind up by calling

on the Apostles to come down and "help cuss them cattle." Then descending from the stump he made a final attempt at drawing the timber load from the creek bed. As if inspired the oxen answered with a steady pull which always accomplished the purpose. After each of these episodes Jim became a hero and drinks were usually "on the house," but when Jim tried to explain his feat he lapsed into stuttering and had to abandon imparting the means of his success to admiring teamsters.

Advent of the railroad spelled doom for Washoe City. Lumber could go to the mines via Carson and rich Comstock ores, some of which had previously been milled in Washoe Valley, were transported to mills along the Carson River. Reno was the Comstock supply point on the Central Pacific, and Carson the state capital. As lumbering along the Sierras began to slump, residents left Washoe City for other towns and after several unsuccessful attempts Reno succeeded in its move to wrest the county seat from Washoe City. Today some of the old stone stores and feed barns still stand, but Washoe itself, once a rollicking town of seven thousand that echoed oaths and whip snappings of the bullwhackers is now a remnant of the Comstock heyday. Perhaps the largest relic of the old town is now the cemetery.

AURORA votes 'em both

THE SUN GODDESS smiled on her Nevada namesake, Aurora. Thirty millions in bullion came from her mines, attracting ten thousand people over Luckyboy grade into the booming camp of the 1860's. But politics rather than gold brought far-flung fame to the thriving hamlet which was aggressively claimed by both the State of California and the Territory of Nevada.

Probably the only town in the nation's history to serve simultaneously as county seat for two counties in different States, Aurora solved the dispute by placing full political tickets in the election race of 1863 for Mono County, California, and Esmeralda County, Nevada. Residents trooped to the polling places and cast ballots for their respective choices in both California and Nevada. Officials for both counties were duly elected, the majority of them being citizens of Aurora.

Sometime later when the boundary dispute was settled by survey, placing Aurora within Nevada, some of the duly elected California officials took up their duties in Bridgeport, the new county seat of Mono, well within the boundaries of California. Esmeralda officials continued to

dispense justice, enforce and execute laws from the Aurora courthouse.

Scarcely a quiet community, Aurora considered itself a Union community and when a "Secesh" element became noisy in 1862 the town turned into an armed camp with the Esmeralda Rifles forcing the southern ringleaders to swear allegiance to the Union flag. During the town's heyday, a hastily organized "601" committee, composed of the more substantial element, applied the rather fatal rope treatment to gun-toters who proved a menace to law enforcement.

Mark Twain knew Aurora before he went to the Territorial Enterprise in Virginia City, but most colorful of the town's early characters was Milton Sharp, prince of Nevada's highway bandits.

A polite and handsome Robin Hood, Sharp devoted his time to preying on Wells Fargo stages. It was said his loot went to the poor. During one of a series of arrests, Sharp gained particular distinction by digging his way out of the Aurora jail in order to pursue his chosen "profession."

The Sanitary Sack of Flour

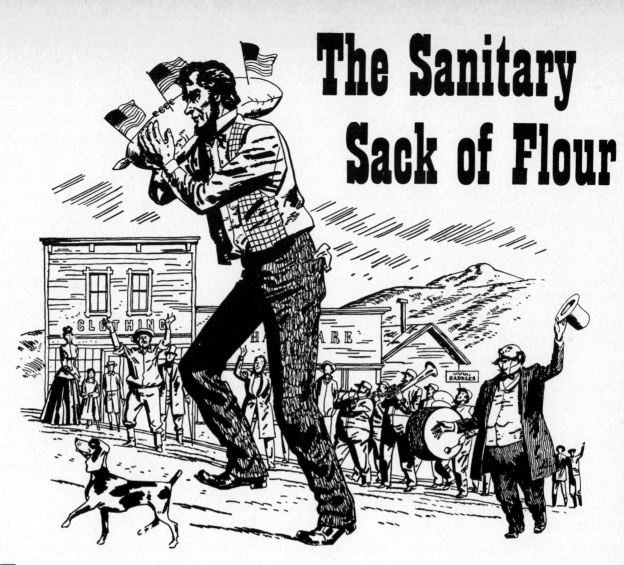

FIFTY POUNDS of flour is something of a prize package in these expensive days, but even so it couldn't hold a candle to the fabulous Gridley Sack of Flour which netted $175,000 for the Sanitary Fund in 1864. It started in the boom mining town of Austin over an election bet, but when the final take was counted cash and currency worth nearly a fifth of a million dollars had been accumulated for the Sanitary Fund and the sack of flour had travelled across the land, selling over the auction blocks of the nation's major cities.

R. C. Gridley was an Austin grocer, a native of Missouri with pronounced secessionist leanings. When the city elections of 1864 showed signs of a heated campaign between the Democratic and Republican contenders for the mayor's position, Gridley made a bet with H. S. Herrick, also of Austin, who supported the Republican candidate.

The loser was to carry a fifty-pound sack of flour from Clifton to Upper Austin. If Gridley lost the bet his march was to be accompanied by a brass band playing "John Brown's Body," while if Herrick lost, he was to do his chore to the tune of "Dixie.'

On the day following election, Herrick appeared in front of Gridley's store, for the Republican candidate had won the election. The Austin brass band struck up the opening bars of "John Brown's Body," and Gridley, shouldering the sack of flour, started his march at the head of a parade which featured a crepe-draped broom (the insignia of democracy). The flour sack was completely decorated with red, white and blue ribbons and numerous Union flags.

The parade soon drew attention of the entire population of Austin and when the march was completed the flour was returned to Central Austin and placed upon the auction block with the announcement that proceeds would be turned over to the Sanitary Fund, a Charity which sought to relieve suffering created by the Civil War.

So spirited was the bidding that the day's sale netted more than six thousand dollars. Each time it was bid in over the auction block, cash was paid and the flour was returned to be auctioned again. Such was the success of the venture that Gridley took the sack of flour to the Comstock where twenty-five thousand dollars went into the coffers of the Sanitary Fund from the auction proceeds.

From Virginia City the flour travelled with Gridley to San Francisco and the principal Pacific Coast cities and then eastward across the nation. Nevada and California alone raised $175,000, and a great deal more was added to the fund in the eastward journey.

So great was the fame of the Sanitary Sack of Flour that Austin adopted its replica for the city seal and coat of arms, and Gridley, who had been a staunch secessionist, became an ardent Unionist.

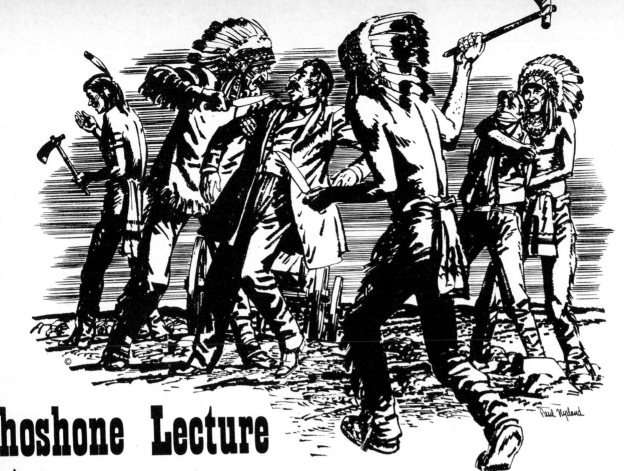

Shoshone Lecture

A GENERATION OF Nevadans with ideas about radio and television might have difficulty realizing the position held a century ago by popular lecturers. These men travelled the nation, had tremendous followings, and were much sought over for speaking dates. Some had an equivalent of Hooper ratings that would be respected today. In 1864 one of the most famous humorists and lecturers in America was Artemus Ward, and during his famous tour through the Far West, he arrived in the town of Austin at the time of the Reese River "Rush."

Austin was a colorful spot. On one day the traffic to Reese River included 274 freight teams, 19 passenger wagons or coaches, three pack trains, 69 horsemen, and 31 on foot. On a trip from Virginia City to Austin, one traveller counted 400 teams en route.

A new stone building opposite the court-house was the largest spot in town, but was unlighted. Ward walked from his hotel to this new building, carrying a lighted lamp in his hand, with hundreds of miners streaming after him. The hall instantly filled and jammed to overflowing, and the lecture was received with tremendous shouts of laughter. It was a huge success!

A few miles out of Austin was the tiny settlement of Big Creek and a delegation from this rapidly growing camp collared the great Artemus Ward and urged him to give his lecture in their "city." Hingston, the manager, was dubious about the trip as there had been a lot of Indian trouble in the district.

Finally Ward and his manager accepted. The lecture was held in the largest building, a saloon "Young America." Some 150 miners paid $2.00 each to sit on kegs, boxes, and the floor. Ward said the floor was dirt and the roof of sagebrush. A wood fire blazed at one end of the room,

and Ward spoke from behind the bar. It was said the barkeep continued sales throughout the lecture, which was an overwhelming and hilarious success!

It's a lonely home road today, and 80 years ago with wild Indians on the loose, it was anything but re-assuring. Just as they had feared, a band of Shoshones suddenly materialized out of the night and completely surrounded them. Hingston was grabbed before he could draw his new pistol. Both men were brutally dragged from the buggy and forced to their knees while the savages debated their fate in Shoshone harangues.

Finally one warrior, in broken English, put a knife to Ward's scalp, and asked his name. "Artemus Ward," came the answer through chattering teeth. "Ugh . . . talkee man!" exclaimed the Indian and brandishing his knife he commanded . . . "talkee **now** . . . talkee."

To appease the blood-thirsty gang, Ward began one of his lectures, but got little attention. At random points the Indians howled with glee. They made so much noise he had to talk louder and louder to be heard. Desperate, he put everything into his talk he could think up, but the Indians remained unmoved and unappreciative.

At last he reached the climax of his talk, and as he did so the warriors fell strangely silent. One of them turned and quite clearly said in disgust . . . "Oh, Bosh!"

It was only then the great lecturer realized he was the victim of a practical joke and the "Indians" were white men who had come out from Austin to scare him and his manager. So home they all went, with much joshing and laughing, to tell and re-tell the story of Artemus Ward's lecture to the Shoshones. It is said that Ward did not relish his part in the story too keenly, for his later versions varied somewhat from Austin's.

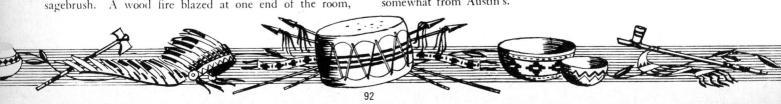

Nevada's First Seaport

CONVERTS TO THE Mormon faith were coming by the hundreds from Europe in the 1850's and by any route it was a long, arduous and dangerous trip. The leaders in Salt Lake City sought a way to bring in the converts which would avoid the hostile sections of the United States.

A plan was adopted to bring the converts across the Atlantic to Panama, then up the Gulf to the Colorado, and up that river to the head of navigation, and then by road to Salt Lake City. Accordingly, Elder Anson Call was given the task to establish a port and colony on the Colorado River and build a road to Pahranagat Valley!

The doughty Elder took this assignment in his stride. On December 17, 1864, he had his men digging the foundations for a stone building at "Callville" a short distance above Black Canyon and now under Lake Mead. They also erected a landing, corrals, and other buildings.

Within the next two years he built 140 miles of road to Pahranagat and there linked it to Salt Lake City. The flow of emigrants to Utah commenced. Steamboats Esmeralda and the Nina Tilden made regular trips between Yuma and Callville. For nearly five years the little colony was a busy place. The tiny port not only served the traffic to Salt Lake City but it also was a shipping point for the Mormon farms to the north and the ranch and trail at the present site of Las Vegas.

In five years, however, the news of the new transcontinental railroad had a dampening effect on Callville, and trade dropped off. In June of 1864 the landing was abandoned.

By the middle of June, 1869, the community was so far gone that a passing mail carrier from St. George noted that three desperate horse thieves had been pursued by a posse as far as Callville and found the little town abandoned. Their pursuers were only a few hours behind them and capture meant death. With horses exhausted and the dry desert surrounding them for miles, their predicament was desperate, until one robber with a flash of inspiration, pried the giant wooden doors from the stone walls of the old church warehouse. Leaving their starved horses to the posse, they piled saddles and baggage on the huge wooden doors which they improvised into a large and heavy raft. And to this day, no word has been heard of the Church warehouse doors, or the desperate men who sailed them into oblivion.

The Hanging at Dayton

Paul Nyeland

THE LITTLE TOWN of Dayton was very proud of its early day reputation as a law-abiding camp. So when James Linn plunged his dagger into the heart of John Doyle on the main street, in 1864, the respectable citizens of the town all moved quickly to punish the murderer.

Dayton started in '49 with the first house built in Nevada east of Carson. Traders and emigrants had panned a few colors at the mouth of gold canyon, known as Hall's Station or McMarlin's. In 1861 it was renamed for John Day, the county surveyor, and in 1864 John Reese imported hundreds of Chinese to build a ditch to run some mills. Locally the place was then called "Chinatown," and many of the Orientals remained to pan around the countryside.

John Doyle ran a saloon and dance hall, and the girls lived above the saloon. He got in an argument with Linn, who was a customer, and the argument soon moved to the street, on a hot August night, and then flared into a fight. In the struggle, Linn stabbed Doyle and was then promptly seized by the citizens of the town.

While one committee guarded him in his jail cell, another group quietly built a gallows, and hid it under the little church. Another committee went about the town advising everyone to go home quietly, without further question. A group of masked men were quietly patrolling the streets, and soon all of Dayton was as quite as a grave.

The next morning the sheriff was "astonished" to find Linn dead in his cell! It was soon reported that the vigilantes had taken Linn to the gallows late at night. When he tried to cry out for help, they had gagged him, filling his mouth with dirt; and the hanging had been quick and efficient. The body was then returned to the jail, the gallows taken apart, and the committees returned to bed.

An unexpected result was the immediate clearing the town of many undesirables, these worthies all departing before the early dawn of the next day. The news was received at nearby Fort Churchill with great excitement, and a detachment of troops dispatched at a gallop to "restore order to Dayton." These soldiers were soon patrolling the town. And in Carson City, Governor Nye was equally disturbed and came post-haste with all his staff, having heard Dayton was filled with a disorderly mob.

When the Governor arrived he found all quiet and orderly, but he went upstairs to the balcony of Odeon Hall and there, for the first time in Nevada history, read the riot act. He read to a deserted street and then drove back to Carson. Dayton gradually resumed a normal air as the troops also departed. It had punished its own violence according to its own mining camp code.

Caliente and Panaca

ALONG THE DEEP flood channel of Meadow Valley Wash in eastern Nevada, only a few miles from the Utah border, lie the farming town of Panaca and the railroad division point of Caliente. Though the clock jumps forward an hour here to conform with the standard of the Mountain Zone . . . time itself is captured and held still in nearby Cathedral Gorge State Park where wind and rain of countless centuries have carved spires, minarets and lofty skyscrapers from the soft, pliable clay.

Founded in the closing year of the Civil War by a little band of Mormons under the leadership of Francis Lee, Panaca today presents an excellent example of pioneering in its broad, rich farms where crops flourish in the warm summer sun and rarely feel the nipping frost of mild winters. Product finds its way to waiting markets at Caliente where the Union Pacific Railroad maintains a division point on its run between Salt Lake City and Las Vegas. This green oasis, dotted by brilliant yellow company houses is an Eden of lovely spring roses. The town lies deep in a canyon, with sheer rock walls rising on all sides to towering vivid colored and dramatic heights.

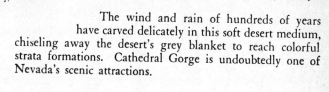

Between the two towns and only a mile from U. S. Highway 93 lies Cathedral Gorge, a fifteen hundred-acre State park that has long been the beautiful, natural backdrop for Easter morning services as the desert sun breaks through domed castles and colored recesses to provide one of nature's breathtaking spectacles.

The chasm, cut from the rolling plateau of the Highland foothills, is in reality a wasteland but the forces of erosion have done such a masterful work of sculpture that imagination needs no urging to picture massive cathedrals and ancient castles in this broad sweep of reddish grey sand and clay. Domed shrines and pinnacles, columned recesses beyond count meet the gaze in every direction. At sunset the desert shadows conspire with nature to conjure a vista of lower Manhattan or a feudal estate of far away Europe.

The wind and rain of hundreds of years have carved delicately in this soft desert medium, chiseling away the desert's grey blanket to reach colorful strata formations. Cathedral Gorge is undoubtedly one of Nevada's scenic attractions.

Hinds Hot Springs

AURORA AND BODIE beckoned gold-hungry miners in the middle sixties and one of the major pathways to the bustling camps was the Walker River route, which led fortune seekers through fertile Smith Valley. In the northern end of the valley, J. C. Hinds, an enterprising pioneer combined the business of ranching with that of milling, but soon found he had an even more important natural resource to rely upon in the medicinal springs which rose on his property.

Years before white men set foot along the Walker, these springs were a favorite gathering place of Indian tribes which realized the curative powers of the boiling waters. Signs of ancient tribal camping grounds are still evident at Old Hind's Hot Springs where flint and obsidian arrow heads and hunting implements have been found in semi-abundance.

Hinds set about developing his frontier spa into a mecca for those who sought cures from chronic pains and ailments. Since travel was bustling, it wasn't long before the name of his hot springs had become famous along the gold trail to California. Experimentation with the medicinal waters led him to offer three kinds of curative baths for clients. Each separate bath combined the various spring waters at different temperatures and the success of his venture was reflected in the popularity of the resort.

Not unmindful of other sources of revenue which his strategic location afforded, Hinds built a rock arrastre and then constructed a thirty-foot wooden water-wheel which was powered by the flowing spring waters. This mill, though crude, offered a convenient custom plant for the ores of miners operating in the near vicinity. And, since the hot springs was on a major freight road, his mill soon had all the ore it could handle and it was necessary for Hinds to employ three shifts of workers to keep the water-wheel and arrastre in full production around the clock.

Hinds Hot Springs became a somewhat noisy, but nonetheless very busy combination, spa, milling center and ranch. Freighters on their way to the booming camps put up for the night at Hinds Hot Springs, since feed was available for teams; miners brought their ore down from the hills by the wagon load, and in the midst of it all stage coaches brought semi-invalids from the far away Pacific coast for rest and treatment.

Time, fire and the elements have brought many changes through the years, since the days when the Hot Springs was a major stop on Mason pass. The coming of the railroads, and then the later advent of motor traffic brought many shifts in transportation routes. Coupled with this have been the usual rise and fall of mining communities and the growth of new irrigation projects. Bodie and Aurora have become ghost cities, and modern travel now follows a southern route through Wilson canyon.

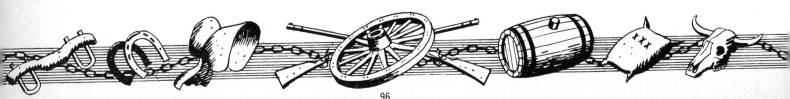

Washoe Causeway

LUXURY INCIDENT to the living of the Caliphs of Ophir mine and mill during the early sixties would have been sufficient to engulf fabulous Arabian Sheiks with green envy.

With Ophir stock bringing $4,000 a share on the market and little of it to be had at the price, tycoons of mine and mill literally rolled in wealth and their weekend gatherings in Washoe Valley at Ophir mill were as fabulous as any tale out of Arabian Nights.

Shaking the dust of the mines and the press of business worries from their collective personages each Saturday afternoon, managers, superintendents and big stockholders thundered down Ophir grade in their rubber-tired caleches, across Washoe Causeway and on to Ophir mill in the shadow of Slide Mountain for a weekend of banqueting, revelry and profit counting.

Disdaining more than casual glances at the string of lumbering ore wagons, toiling under loads of high grade ore that was amassing fortunes for them, the Caliphs of Ophir guided their gaited teams through the maze of traffic across the bright red causeway to the home of the mill superintendent. There for a night and a day at loaded banquet tables and through a haze of blue Havana cigar smoke over blue chips they forgot the weekday worries of Ophir production, and spoke of five figure profits for as many days' work.

Despite the weekend holiday mood, management of mine and mill was no haphazard operation. The flamboyant red causeway which threaded half a mile of marsh at the north end of Washoe Lake was a piece of engineering thoughtfully planned to speed up delivery of ore from mine to mill and the equally important transportation of wood and supplies from Washoe Valley back to the Comstock.

Ophir mill and the town which surrounded it grew from the necessity of milling ore closer to the point of production. Formerly high grade had gone muleback over

the Sierras to San Francisco. With the erection of Ophir mill outlet was afforded not alone for high grade, but also for the lower value ore which formerly weathered on the dumps.

With construction of the Virginia and Truckee Railway, Washoe Causeway and its neighboring bridge on the south which connected the Dall mill at Franktown with Ophir grade, gradually lapsed into disuse. In the sixties, however, the red causeways of Washoe were the freightways of western wealth.

Ring Bolt Rapids

ANSON B. CALL believed firmly that the territory of southern Nevada would one day embrace large settlements of Zionites so he was anxious to obey the church order which requested the building of a fort at the head of the Colorado river's navigable waters. Accordingly in the early Sixties Fort Callville, an adobe settlement, was established by him about seven miles up river above the present site of Hoover Dam and now covered by 400 feet of water.

Purpose of the community was to receive supplies and proselytes brought up river by steamer from Mexican and California towns. At the river port of Fort Callville converts of Zion along with precious supplies, were transported by wagon to southern Nevada and Utah settlements. It was also intended that farm products raised by the Mormons in the warm southern Nevada climate, could be shipped down river by steamer to coastal California.

Exploration of the Colorado had been attempted a few years earlier, a stern-wheeler, Explorer U. S., had made a number of trips up the Colorado, experiencing difficulty in the rapids just below the site of Fort Callville. To overcome this challenge to navigation the settlers of Fort Callville, who had already produced a steamer by the name of Esmeralda, set a huge, 12-inch iron ring in an enormous reddish-grey boulder on the Nevada side of the river just below the adobe fort. The Esmeralda was equipped with a steam winch on deck, and upon approaching Ring Bolt rapids, a heavy cable, the far end of which was attached to the ring, was winched in, helping the lumbering steamer over the swift water. Much the same procedure was followed when the Esmeralda left Fort Callville. The cable was let out easily, as the steamer made weigh down stream, thus checking her progress through the dangerous white water.

The Esmeralda plied between Callville and Mazatlan on a fairly regular schedule. Much of the freight picked up at Mazatlan and consigned to Utah settlements, had been shipped around the Horn from eastern manufacturing areas.

Though somewhat crude, navigation on the Colorado flourished until railroads put an end to the isolation of southern Nevada. Attempts to increase usage of the river failed when it became impossible to obtain federal funds for removing many navigation obstacles, and gradually steamers disappeared from the river's muddy waters, but even today Ring Bolt Rapids is a testimonial of the ingenuity employed by early-day settlers in linking Nevada's wilderness with the outside world.

Death of Col. McDermit

Paul Nyeland

INDIANS WERE "human beings," according to Col. Charles McDermit, commanding the Military Department of Nevada, and he believed in treating them with decent consideration. He even went so far as to take prisoners, feeding them at his camps.

The Colonel was a popular and very able commander and had the respect of all Nevada, in spite of some criticism of his leniency with the Indians. But ranchers, station keepers, and mail carriers were harried by hostile Indians so badly in 1865, the Colonel left his base at Fort Churchill to suppress the Paiutes. He made his northern headquarters at a camp on Quinn River and soon had a few Indian prisoners.

The troops noticed their prisoners were watching every move but laid it to curiosity. At times a prisoner or two would vanish from the camp, but it was not deemed important for the campaign was planned to pacify the Indians instead of exterminating them. It was later very evident, however, the Indians were shrewdly studying the strange ways of the white man's army to learn who was "chief." Never for a minute had they given up the idea of retaliation.

Some days later, Col. McDermit was returning from a scouting expedition and approaching his camp on the Nevada-Idaho line. A carefully prepared Indian ambush allowed the point of his column and at least one other officer to pass them before they singled out the commanding officer and opened fire. Two men were wounded and the Colonel shot in the breast, dying some four hours later, August 6, 1865.

The death of this fine man was a blow to all the settlers in northern Nevada. Within a week the War Department authorized the erection of a fort on the site of Quinn River Station, to be named for Col. McDermit (and misspelled to this day) and to be the largest in northern Nevada. It required 10,000 acres of military reserve, stone buildings for three officers' quarters, two large barracks, hospital, guard house, warehouses and stables. Food and forage for a year were to be held there at all times.

Lt. Col. Hooker, 6th Infantry, succeeded to command and opened a vigorous campaign to suppress Indian troubles, which flared all over northern Nevada for a long time. End result was the establishment in northern Nevada of Fort McGarry, Fort Scott, Fort Ruby, Fort Halleck, and many camps and stations, and the opening of a bloody and ruthless period of raids on the part of both whites and Indians.

Twenty years later, Fort McDermit was turned into a school and reservation for Indians where the original humane philosophy of Col. McDermit was successfully proven on the very site of his death.

Commotion at Como

COMO WAS A lusty mining camp in the closing days of the Civil War and despite the fact that it was reached by a twisting mountain road it was the county seat and center of activity for Lyon County.

Mining operations necessitated the cutting of numerous pinon pines which covered the hillsides, and the logging operations reached such proportions that Paiute Chief Numaga approached the mine owners and asked them to stop cutting down the trees since they were depriving the Indians of essential foodstuff. He explained that the Paiutes gathered pine nuts each fall as one of their staple crops.

Disregarding Numaga's request the tree cutting proceeded at an even more rapid rate, but there was tension in the air since the wood-cutters were well aware of the Paiutes' feelings. One day as a number of loggers were returning to Como they saw a group of Indians observing them. Perhaps it was their guilty consciences that prompted them to flee for their homes. Word spread in Como that the Paiutes were on the warpath and a

message was sent to Fort Churchill requesting troops. Meanwhile a camp password was devised and residents prepared to stand off an attack.

Quite unaware of all the commotion two miners, coming up the road from Dayton after dark were fired upon when they failed to give the password. Hearing the shots an over-anxious Como resident piled out of his cabin to help defend the town and in his rush tripped and discharged his gun. Moments later the entire male population poured volley after volley down the canyon where the two cowering miners took shelter behind a huge boulder.

By dawn the soldiers and miners had nearly exhausted their ammunition, and since there was no sign of life, they prepared to venture from the town to count dead Indians. Much to their chagrin Chief Numaga sauntered into the camp to inquire about all the shooting during the night. He said his village had been disturbed and his warriors had been caused a great deal of unnecessary worry.

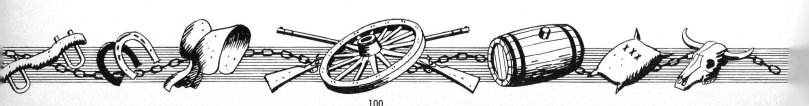

Pizen Switch

A WILLOW THATCH HUT and an uncommon brand of firewater dispensed by an enterprising businessman of the roaring '60's is responsible for the original name of the settlement that sprang up in Mason Valley on the Walker River—Pizen Switch.

Gold seekers bound for booming Aurora gave up their quest for minerals when they realized the fertility of the river loam and at the outset of the '60's a small settlement took form along the banks of the Walker.

An itinerant disciple of the white apron and glass, whose only claim to fortune was a full barrel of whiskey, realized the business possibilities of this crossroad and set about building himself a thatch hut of willow switches. Miners and cowboys spread the word when the hut opened for business and soon it became known as the Switch, a name which eventually took in the whole settlement. Trade was brisk, but transportation was slow and soon the original barrel of whiskey showed signs of giving out. Enterprising as ever, the proprietor stealthily sought to keep in business by adding now and then a couple of gallons of water and whatever flavoring was close at hand such as a plug or two of chewing tobacco.

It soon became apparent to patrons that the tonic did not deserve the name of whiskey and in their clipped western speech it became known simply as "Pizen," a prefix which attached itself to the Switch and thus for a year Mason Valley's present town of Yerington was "Pizen Switch."

It is said that a vengeance committee organized for the purpose of scalping anyone careless enough to use the name in reference to the town. At any rate within a year the settlement was Greenfield and in later years in honor of H. M. Yerington, an official of the Virginia and Truckee Railroad, the name was permanently changed to Yerington. It was rumored this name was used to entice the V. & T. to extend to the town. If so, it failed to work. Today it is one of the State's most prosperous agricultural and livestock centers, while nearby copper and other mineral deposits give promise of a bright future.

Shoshone Peace Pipe

IN THE SPRING of 1865, the aggressive Paiute and Bannock tribes gathered 80 miles north of Gravelly Ford on the Humboldt River, and sent many small bands of warriors among the peaceful Shoshones, urging them to join the other tribes on the war path. The continual propaganda work of these small bands agitated and excited the Shoshones until they gathered on the Reese River with some 300 families, near Austin.

The situation was extremely tense as the new State had been nearly stripped of troops in the final struggles of the Civil War. Isolated ranchers, miners, and settlers were in a panic as the agitated Shoshone met night after night in council, debating the idea of plunging the tribes into bloody war. Their's was the balancing decision.

Resolving to take direct action, the first governor of the new State of Nevada, Blaisdel, rode from Carson to Austin with Colonel McDermit and his interpreter S. H. Bilson. At Austin they joined local militia officers and dignitaries, and the governor donned a bright red sash of office. On June 6, 1865 the party rode out to the Shoshone camp on the Reese River and the Governor opened negotiations with the Indians in person. The little party of whites was tremendously outnumbered but the governor calmly reminded the Shoshones how they had been bullied by the Paiutes before the coming of the white men, until they had been reduced to a diet of gophers, snakes, and jackrabbits. The best hunting areas were even forbidden to

them. He told them how, under the whites, they had reached a prosperity equal to their ancient enemies and urged them not to listen to the warlike Paiutes and Bannocks.

The governor, sitting in the council and now gathering assurance, told the red men how the Great White Father had been busy with a war among his white children. His power was great, and his soldiers were as numerous as the sagebrush on the desert. The Shoshone grunted approval.

The Great White Father had been grieved to learn of bad Indians on the Reese River and he hoped his Shoshone children would have none of them, but would live in peace and happiness. More grunts of approval.

The Great White Father asked his Shoshone children not to sell powder or guns to the Paiute or Bannock, or to trade with them. The Governor then promised to aid the Shoshone with his own personal funds pending further aid from the Great White Father. The Shoshone rose with enthusiasm.

This evidently clinched it, for after a few impassioned Shoshone talks, the tribal pipe of peace was brought out and passed among the chiefs, and the Governor, and the officers of the party. Nevada's first Peace Conference was a complete success! War did not break out along the Reese River.

Black Rock Tom

ONE OF THE FEW Indians who refused to bow to the power of the white man during the exciting '60's in pioneer Nevada was the daring renegade known as Black Rock Tom. In 1865, he led a small band of Paiutes, Bannocks, and Shoshones in a series of raids and attacks that terrorized all of northern Nevada. He defied ranchers, posses, and even detachments of troops sent out from Fort Churchill and Fort McDermitt.

Black Rock Tom rode a magnificent white horse, which became a symbol to many Indians of a defiant gesture against the whites. Certainly the prestige of the whites suffered heavily when Tom would keep just on the outer edge of rifle range, and taunt the soldiers and posses to try to catch him. His white horse could outrun anything in Nevada at that time, and was believed by the Indians to be a magic animal.

Many crimes against white settlers were blamed on Black Rock Tom, possibly some without justification. Any small wagon train, or isolated ranch was fair game for Tom and his shrieking, painted warriors who descended without warning, killing, torturing, burning, stealing, and then vanishing back into the great fastness of the Black Rock Desert. Tom's warriors trapped an ox train near Rabbit Hole in 1865 and terrorized Paradise Valley. On November 9th a detachment of troops under Lieutenant Penwell attacked Tom's band but were driven off, being unable to dislodge them from their positions. On November 13th, Lieutenant Hosmer of Company B, 2nd California Cavalry, with 60 troops, four civilians, 14 Indians, located Tom's band on the Quinn River Sink at the head of the Black Rock Desert. They swept down on Tom's band, and killed all except one squaw, five warriors, and Black Rock Tom, who escaped.

Pursuit of Black Rock Tom was now relentless. The army sent part of Company B from Dun Glen and Company I from Fort McDermitt, the detachments meeting in a pincer movement at Kane Springs. It was now December, with snow on the desert, and so cold the men had to lead their horses to keep from freezing. At daybreak they surprised the remnant of Tom's band and slaughtered 40, leaving only a boy, a squaw, and an old man alive. But Tom was away, and so survived the attack.

But it meant the complete end of Tom's band, and so, with the entire group of men, women, and children exterminated, Black Rock Tom lost heart and gave up. He left his famous white horse with an Indian band in the northern tip of Nevada, and then walked in to surrender.

Tom was clapped into jail with a squad of soldiers detailed to guard him. White citizens, however, managed to talk to Tom and persuaded him that the people were going to take him away from the soldiers and hang him. They urged him to escape and make a run for it. They finally convinced him, and the soldiers carefully allowed him to get out of his cell and make a dash for it. He was then shot down while trying to escape.

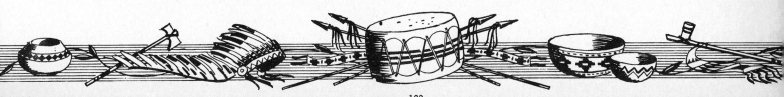

Red Devils
in Paradise

SHEER PEAKS of the towering Santa Rosas rise abruptly above Paradise Valley in northern Humboldt County, sheltering its green fields from the elements. Cattle and sheep graze contentedly. The picture it presents might easily be along the southern slope of the Pyrenees, native home of many early settlers. But it wasn't always peaceful in Paradise!!!!

In the early Sixties prospectors visited the valley and because of the quiet and apparent peace they named it Paradise Valley. Soon after small homesteads began to appear along the watercourses and industrious home-steaders started tilling the soil and planting crops. In the spring of 1865 bloodcurdling tales of horror filtered into the valley as an Indian tribe took to the warpath. Two friendly Indians warned one of the newcomers of approaching trouble, but before the alarm could be spread tell-tale columns of smoke rose from the outlying settlements along the mountain fringe as the painted Red Devils fired cabins and burned newly sewn crops.

Hoping to stand off the advancing war party, eleven men, three women and four children barricaded themselves in a corral. For several hours they stood off the circling Indian warriors. The women and children loaded guns for the men defenders who picked off yelling red targets as they circled ever closer to the frail fort. Two of the men

were killed in a hail of Indian arrows and the surrounding cabins and corrals were burned by the frenzied warriors before organized aid from a distant section of the valley drove off the Indians.

This attack was only the first in a series of raids which accounted for numerous murders as well as the burning of many habitations and the driving away of valuable stock. Cavalry from Fort Churchill, dispatched from the banks of

the Carson at the first hint of trouble, finally drove off the Redmen, but not before a great part of the valley was pillaged.

Peace returned to the valley a few years later, but even today a red carpet of Indian paintbrush which flowers every spring along the fringe of the Santa Rosas is remindful of the blood once shed in Paradise.

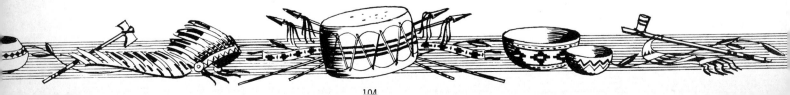

Torture at Granite Creek

LONGEST AND BITTEREST opposition to the ever-increasing hordes of white men in Nevada came from the Paiutes of the Granite Creek and Black Rock desert country in northern Washoe and Humboldt counties.

On April 1, 1865, a large cloud of smoke had been seen rising from the site of the Granite Creek Station where the roads from Susanville intersected with those from Truckee Meadows and the settlements along the Humboldt near present day Winnemucca. From the cloud of smoke it was believed the station had been attacked by Indians. Seven days later two parties of armed men left the Unionville area, 85 miles away, to investigate.

They found a scene of tragedy, and proof the three men at the Station had put up a heroic fight, firing through ten loopholes they had cut in the massive sod walls. Every bit of evidence pointed to a terrific battle to the death. The Paiutes had attacked from a nearby stone corral, the front of which was so bespattered with bullets as to "appear to be solid lead." The Indians ran low on shot and had resorted to firing nuts and bolts. Reconstructing the scene, the relief party found how the Indians had reached a storehouse, and from it fired the roof of the sod station. With the roof crashing down upon them in flames, and bullets whistling in every window and door, one man had died in the ruins, the remaining one had raced for his life,

to be pursued by three mounted Indians who brought him back, held him down with boulders, and had built a fire on his body. Pieces of his skeleton were found under ashes and piles of rock.

The other man ran a distance, but had been shot down and his body hacked to pieces. Even the dog had been skinned, the hide tanned, and staked out! Spokes had been chopped from the wagon wheels, furniture was shattered, lumber and haystacks burned, stove broken, pots chopped up, and farm tools were demolished. It was a completely "scorched earth" battle.

Everything indicated the men had put up a desperate resistance until driven out by fire, and had then been shockingly tortured and killed. The orgy of destruction which followed, told plainly what lay in store for other isolated settlements in northern Nevada, and an appeal went out to the Army. Eight months later Camp McKee, a military post, was established at Granite Creek, and with other armed outposts, helped maintain order in the always turbulent Black Rock, Quinn River, and Honey Lake areas. But even the Army was unable to maintain complete order in this vast district, and pitched battles took place here from time to time for years to come, ending with the last Indian battle in America in this same section of Nevada, as late as 1911.

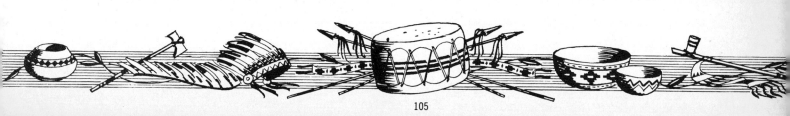

Chinese Oath

NEVADA MINING CAMPS in the '50's and '60's were thronged with thousands of Chinese, shipped in to build the railroads and do the menial work that goes into building an empire. Thousands of miles from home, bewildered by strange foreign customs, exploited, mistreated, the Chinese managed somehow to thrive and prosper.

Their own customs were a constant source of wonderment, and ridicule to the white inhabitants of the early camps. Joss houses rose in most towns, tong meeting houses, and "Chinatowns" were common. And like the Indians, the Chinese had great difficulty understanding the white man's law and courts.

It was soon found that a Chinese had no regard for an oath taken in court, with his hand on the Bible. The Book meant nothing to the "heathen Chinee," but for some reason most Chinese took an oath seriously if it was made over a freshly-killed fowl, accompanied by the burning of punk and squibs and references to "sacred ancestors."

Although the Nevada court procedure made no allowance for it, many a Chinese trial in a Nevada court featured this custom. When a Chinese witness was to be sworn, the bailiff or clerk brought in a squawking and indignant chicken, wrung its neck to the delight of the onlookers and jury, and then placed it beneath the hand of the Chinese on the stand. At the same time other attaches of the Court would burn punk, squibs, sometimes firecrackers. After a little of this mumbo-jumbo, the lawyers would then try to extract some information from the witness.

The first Chinese came to the coast in 1852 and in that first year, more than 20,000 arrived and went to work. By 1869 over 100,000 had come to California and Nevada and some 40,000 returned to China. The frugal Chinese could work a stream or a digging and prosper where a white man would starve. To this day you can pan gold where white men worked, but the streams worked by Chinese are barren in the extreme. They also drifted into other work, and Chinese restaurants and laundries are still common in Nevada towns.

The Chinese queue was sacred to these Orientals, and a source of much amusement to the whites, some of whom enjoyed tormenting and teasing the helpless foreigners. In Elko County, the sheriff cut off the pig-tails of four Chinese, and they promptly brought suit. A State law prohibiting pig-tails was proposed and debated in the State legislature, but nothing came of it. Most records of Chinese in Nevada deal with crime, or with funny stories.

When Governor Nye arrived at the Territorial Capital he was serenaded by about 50 "musicians" to the most horrible caterwauling. The committee and distinguished guests gravely applauded one number after another.

New to the far west and anxious to please his fellow citizens, the new governor suffered in silence until at the end of a particularly awful "number" the Carson folks could no longer keep a straight face and burst out laughing. The bandmaster compared his recital to a "cat fight" and the new governor realized he had been "jobbed." Guffawing at the joke on himself, he instantly won the admiration and friendship of all present, including the Chinese "musicians." The new governor was a good sport and off to a fine start in the rugged Territory of Nevada.

Murder at Cortez

A WILD, BITTER GAME of poker it was, that night of September 18, 1866, and the free and easy card rules of the raw little mining camp of Cortez irritated big Bill Broadwater! His irritation increased with every hand as he continued to lose steadily to John Llewelyn, across the green table. With the exception of mining magnates George Hearst and Simeon Wenban, it looked like Llewelyn would soon have all the cash in Cortez.

Before long he did have all Broadwater's cash. Then he won his six gun. Ruefully slapping his empty holster, Bill slammed down his prize Henry rifle on the green table, and with the very next hand he had lost that, too! It was too much for Broadwater and in a murderous red haze of fury he snatched up his lost rifle in one hand, and squeezed the trigger. With a roar it sent a bullet crashing into Llewelyn's breast and he slumped across the table, spewing chips, six gun, and money onto the plank floor.

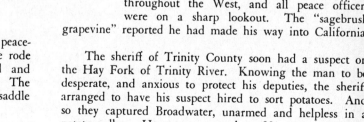

Realizing too late what he had done, Broadwater peacefully surrendered. Held under guard that night, he rode out in the morning with two guards, Glassford and Maguire, headed for the sheriff's office at Austin. The Henry rifle, as material evidence, swung in an open saddle scabbard under Glassford's stirrup.

About 20 miles south of Cortez, Glassford reined up and dismounted to inspect a defective cinch. While he was on the ground and screened by his horse from Broadwater, the prisoner leaned over, plucked the Henry rifle from the scabbard, and in an amused tone ordered his two captors to "reach fast." As both men stood with hands uplifted, the grinning Broadwater calmly took a revolver and blankets and then trotted off down the sagebrush trail. He swung around in the saddle and fired three shots which failed to hit his guards but succeeded in discouraging any ideas about recapture. Broadwater dropped from sight.

Meanwhile Llewelyn died of his wound and the little town of Cortez was boiling mad at the two careless guards. Feeling ran very high, but charges against the guards were dropped for lack of evidence, and soon the popular interest swung to the search for Broadwater. Descriptions had been broadcast throughout the West, and all peace officers were on a sharp lookout. The "sagebrush grapevine" reported he had made his way into California.

The sheriff of Trinity County soon had a suspect on the Hay Fork of Trinity River. Knowing the man to be desperate, and anxious to protect his deputies, the sheriff arranged to have his suspect hired to sort potatoes. And so they captured Broadwater, unarmed and helpless in a potato cellar. He was sentenced to 20 years in Carson prison.

Lady Cattle Rustler

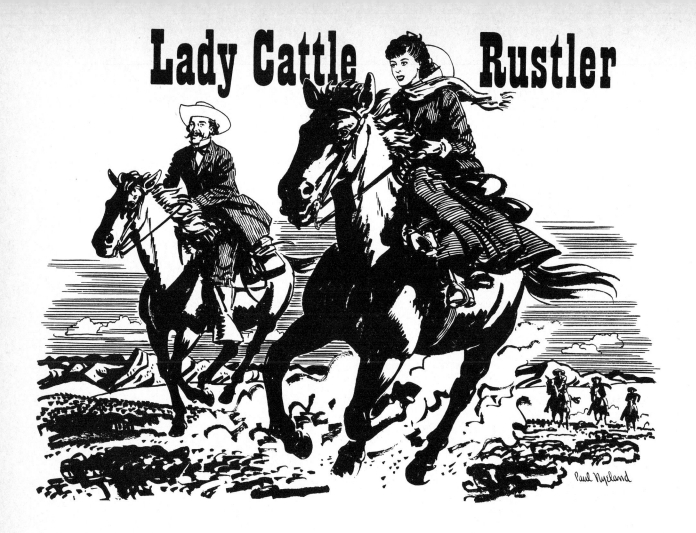

Paul Nyeland

W HEN RENEGADE bands of Indians attacked Paradise Valley, killing Susie Raper's brother and crippling her husband, they unwittingly launched one of Nevada's most charming outlaws on her career of crime.

Forced to flee Paradise Valley around 1866, Susie and her family took refuge at Dun Glen, under the protection of a detachment of the Nevada Volunteers. This protection evidently had great appeal for Susie, for she soon decided to take her family to California and leave them there. She turned her famous charm on the owner of a freighting outfit, and soon hitch-hiked a ride to California for herself and her family.

History neglects the fascinating details, except to tell that Susie left Dun Glen without a cent, but when the outfit arrived on the coast, the teamster hadn't a dime, and Susie owned all the wagons, teams, and harness! She promptly turned the new freighting outfit into spot cash, and returned to central Nevada.

She next turned up in the company of a handsome military man, Captain Payne, who left the Nevada Volunteers, to take up a career of cattle rustling in company with Susie. The pair of them worked the cattle country along the Humboldt River, centering in the Carlin area.

With happy enthusiasm they stole herds of cattle from all the big ranches, changing brands brazenly, and building up prosperous herds of their own. Finally when Elko became a county, there were some who took a cold view of these operations and Susie was arrested. She was arrested again and again, but when she turned on her charm, it seemed no jury of twelve men could be found in all of Elko County which would vote to convict her.

After she had been repeatedly acquitted, Susie and her captain increased the scope of their new activities. Overconfident, they finally became so open handed and so generous to themselves in wholesale thefts of cattle, that Elko County lost much of its enthusiasm for the beautiful cattle rustler. Her popularity suffered such a decline that she was again arrested. This time it looked like they might empanel a jury which could resist her charms and send her down to the prison at Carson City. Panic stricken, Susie turned her smile on the law officers.

Just how she got away isn't in the record, except to say she escaped custody on a magnificent horse, and with her dashing companion fled across the desert to Colorado Territory. She never came back, and finally drifted away from Captain Payne, and down into New Mexico. When last heard from she had prevailed upon a man there to deed her his property, and he had been inconsiderate enough to make it necessary for her to kill him. The record closes with her awaiting trial in New Mexico, charged with the murder of her latest friend, and with no mention of her charms or beauty.

First Colorado Voyager?

MAJOR J. W. POWELL, U. S. Corps of Engineers, and official explorer of the Colorado River in 1869, is today recognized as "the first man to descend the mighty stream," but there are many old-timers who were positive this honor belongs to James White, a simple and honest prospector. And it could be true.

September 8, 1867, Mormon residents at Callville on the lower Colorado were amazed when a raft of three cottonwood poles, bearing a nearly naked white man drifted to the bank. The man was burned raw and blistered; his entire body was bruised, and bleeding, and he was nearly dead from starvation. Delirious, half crazed from exposure, he claimed to have descended the river!

This man, (White), said his two companions had been prospecting on the San Juan River where it joins the Colorado. One man was killed in an attack by Indians and their mules, horses, and supplies stolen. The two remaining men fled to the river, built a raft, and set adrift. Three days later, one man drowned in a whirlpool, and White lashed himself to the raft for safety.

Dashed over rocks, down waterfalls, under whirlpools, White lost his flour sack, but found mesquite beans on the river bank. He met Indians and traded his pistol for the hind quarters of a dog. And sixteen days later he had arrived at Callville.

Later exploration found much of White's description of the geography of the river at fault, and his story was doubted. Many supporters sprang to his aid, claiming his condition was such he could not have made accurate observations. Books were written for and against White, who made no attempt to cash in on his story, and was obviously sincere.

He lived out his life as a blacksmith in a little Colorado town, where he was periodically sought out by sensation-seeking writers, and by scientists who were bitterly divided on the subject. White himself never took part in the "Great Debate" but remained positive to his death that he had made the complete descent, as claimed.

Major Powell's survey and carefully documented and photographed expedition was the first scientific study of the area and clearly deserves great credit. The fantastic hardships undergone by Powell's party tend to make White's feat seem impossible, but the question of "where White could have launched his raft upriver from Callville, with the vast canyon walls impassable even today" has never been answered. White either performed the "impossible descent of the river" or the "impossible descent of the canyons" and his physical and mental condition at Callville indicate he had spent much time in great suffering. He is said to have sincerely believed in his achievement all his life, and died without really being aware of the magnitude of the feat.

Riding the Rail

FROM Erin and Cornwall rough and rugged miners flocked to Nevada's gold bonanzas in the Sixties, and, whether first or third generation away from Bantry Bay or Lands End, they all nursed a long standing, deep down feud that flared into near open warfare in many Nevada camps.

Belmont in the late Sixties was prosperous and the great majority of miners traced their immediate ancestry to the Emerald Isle. In the spring of '67 orders came through from eastern directors to close down the Silver Bend Company, known as the Child and Canfield property.

Because work had been proceeding at a good pace and since there were no indications that ore bodies were petering out, the Irish miners mistakenly anticipated that the management intended only a token close down in order to hire cheaper Cornish labor. The rumor gained momentum and by nightfall a mob formed and seized Mr. Canfield.

Placing him astride a log rail which was slung from the shoulders of two burly Irish miners, the mob paraded Belmont's main street, visiting every saloon along the way, taunting and frightening Canfield. At length the mob, growing rougher by the moment, stopped at Highbridge Saloon and as they ordered a round of drinks, allowed Canfield to get down off the rail, but persisted in heckling him.

As the miners prepared to resume the march, Canfield was ordered to climb on the rail once again. At that moment, a soft spoken onlooker by the name of Lewis M. Bodrow, told Canfield "if you do not choose to get on that rail, you need not do so."

This was the first opposition the miners had encountered during their parade, and it offended Patrick Digmen, one of the leaders. He lashed out at Bodrow and struck him in the face.

Meanwhile another of the mob, sensing trouble, stepped out of the door and fired his pistol. Within a matter of seconds about twenty-five shots were fired and a rough and tumble fight was underway.

Bodrow, a former city marshal in Austin, received a number of fatal bullet wounds in addition to two deep knife cuts, but two shots were fired from his pistol, showing he had retaliated, and Patrick Digmen was the fatal target of one of those shots.

Canfield was spirited away by friends during the melee and many of the town's citizens, aroused by the incident, took up the trail of the mob leaders. Over two thousand dollars was subscribed to aid in the search which resulted in the capture and jailing of two Irish miners.

High Justice at Hiko

NOTORIOUS AMONG Nevada's outlaws of the late 1860's was L. B. Vail, horse thief and cattle-rustler, who delighted in the playful pastime of killing his associates and then sleeping on their graves.

At one time as many as three small mounds marked the final resting places of his erstwhile partners and Vail would make such a spot his campground for a number of weeks. This slight peculiarity in his mode of living was conducive to a nomadic sort of life, and Vail roamed from the upper stretches of the Reese River southward to Pahranagat Valley. He was accompanied by a stock trading partner, Robert Knox, and the two soon became a familiar sight in and around Hiko. As time went by, however, it was brought to the attention of residents that Knox no longer accompanied Vail. In fact, visits of the latter to Hiko were rare occasions.

The sudden disappearance of Knox caused some concern and the finger of guilt pointed toward Vail, whose reputation had preceded him to southern Nevada. However, it was not until some Indians passing one of

Vail's camping spots in the valley, discovered a saddle that had been buried, but dug up by coyotes, that Vail was accused. In Hiko residents identified the saddle as having been the property of Knox and returning to the camping spot with their Indian guides they exhumed and identified the body of Mr. Knox, whereupon a posse arrested Vail and took him to the jail in Hiko.

Annoyed at what seemed an interminable delay in bringing the horse-trader to justice citizens of Hiko and Pahranagat stormed the jail and took the prisoner before a court organized for that specific purpose. The accused was assured of a fair trial, but proceedings of the self-appointed court were interrupted time and again by the sound of construction as a gallows was rigged outside the window while a coffin was nailed together within the court room itself.

The grave deliberations of the court consumed nearly sixty minutes and before the hour was up the horse-trader's body swung from the new gallows as the citizens' committee dispensed its first dose of high justice.

The Hardin City Mystery

Paul Nyland

SINCE 1867 no man has solved the mystery of the "ore from Hardin City," and old timers seem to think it must have been haunted. Some believe the answer may yet bring fabulous riches from a mine now well known in northern Washoe County.

In the '40's and '50's there were many reports of lost mines, ledges, and canyons literally paved with free silver in the Black Rock Country. This is the same area thought to be the scene of the fabled "Lost Blue Bucket Mine," and here one party claimed to have seen a canyon literally paved with lead. They took some for bullets, later found it to be silver! A wagon train in 1852 passed a ravine said to be cut in volcanic ash through which protruded slabs of free silver! All these, on the return of search parties, were later found to be covered by cloudbursts, but the district soon acquired a reputation as a site of one or more great deposits of raw silver. And finally in January 1866, two Idaho men found rich-looking ore which resulted in the entire area being "staked out" in a flash boom and rush.

A load of the ore brought very poor returns, however, when it was milled in Unionville. Since the assays appeared so rich, a load of the same ore was taken to the Dall Mill near Washoe City. Here Hiskey, the foreman, a good judge of ore, declared the rock to be "worthless"; but it was run anyway and proved astonishingly rich! This brought about the prompt establishment of Hardin City with a mill near the site of the mine itself. Men flocked to the area by the thousand, and excitement was intense.

But again, when the ore was milled at Hardin City, it proved worthless! Some experts thought it was the water at Hardin City, and so other wagon loads of the same ore were milled at various places, including the Dall Mill, and again all of the results were fantastically rich! But a repeated run back at Hardin City proved worthless.

Then a new assayer was hired at Hardin City, and he believed the rock to be worthless. The controversy went on . . . one load of ore giving a rich yield, the next proving worthless. Finally the mill at Hardin City was shut down. People began to move away, and the "city" dropped to a handful.

Eventually they left, and the buildings fell apart until only a few adobe ruins remained of a once active and busy mining camp. Old mill reports still indicate that some of this mysterious ore was extremely rich. Others show it to be worthless rock. For years the argument raged. Mill foremen, assayers, and engineers were suspected, questioned, and investigated but without a single clue or result being found. It is said the man who can solve the old Hardin City mystery (and many have tried) will have his fortune made many times over.

First July Fourth

IN JULY 1868 the neighboring mining camps of Hamilton and Treasure Hill in what is now White Pine County, joined to observe their first Fourth of July. Committees were appointed (according to an account by Fred Hart) on "Flag," "Music," and "Ball of the Evening." The complacent Flag Committee awoke with horror on July 2, to the realization that the nearest flag was in Austin, 120 miles away. Music was easier, as a man named Pike could play the "Arkansas Traveller" on the violin, and parts of a quadrille. Two women were available for the Ball.

A sub-committee was appointed to follow Pike and keep him sober for the event, only three drinks per hour being allowed him on this eventful day. The Flag Committee in desperation began a search for flag materials. They located and confiscated in the public interest, a bed quilt with red calico lining. They "borrowed" white canvas tenting from a store. And finally they heard of a Mormon family camping in the gulch below town that had a blue veil, and what was more, four girls and their mother.

The committee immediately called on this family and obtained the blue veil for the flag. The five ladies increased the number of the fair sex for the Ball by 250%, but the mother explained that none of them had any shoes. A shoe committee was immediately appointed and quietly obtained several pairs of brogans borrowed from the miners. Shoes were important as the rough board floor of the

"ballroom" was splintery.

So, at the appointed time on July Fourth, the parade formed in Hamilton and marched up the hill to Treasure City. Since there was no band, a couple of good whistlers followed the flag, then the Mormon girls, then Pike and his body guard, and then the rest of the town. At Treasure Hill the procession paused for Literary Exercises, with the

speaker of the day talking from the top of the town watering trough. At the conclusion, the assemblage applauded warmly and passed a resolution that the flag, then flying from a pole, should form a part of the society's archives for the newly organized White Pine Pioneers. Sad to say, in the rush that followed to new strikes, the flag was inadvertently used as a bed sheet, and lost to posterity.

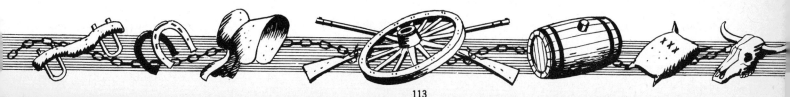

TREASURE HILL

A RICH CHUNK of silver chloride ore found by an Indian on the bleak nine thousand foot slope of Treasure Hill started a rush of twenty-five thousand people to Hamilton in 1868. Though the Monte Cristo Mining Company had operated properties on the White Pine range for three years, it was an almost solid chunk of silver from Treasure Hill that made the Hamilton district a fabulous Nevada camp of the late Sixties where a handful of crackers brought two dollars and water sold for twenty-five cents a bucket.

So rich, and seemingly so plentiful was the Treasure Hill silver that financiers actually worried lest this huge mountain of white metal might glut the world monetary market.

Two men who joined the rush to Hamilton early in '68 constructed a little rock shelter to ward off chilling winter winds and snow. When the spring thaw set in they discovered the walls of their tiny cabin contained seventy-five thousand dollars worth of high grade silver.

Thirteen thousand claims were staked out in two years while swapping, trading and selling of property vied with speculation in townsites and the stock market for primary interest. One New York company is said to have hired a seeress to telegraph instructions on where to dig next. And well they could afford it for White Pine stocks had a total list value of seventy million dollars on the market. One property alone, the Eberhardt mine on Treasure Hill, scooped 3,200 tons of ore from a shallow 70 by 28 foot glory hole and realized three million dollars

on the venture. A court house was hastily erected to shelter a recording office and Hamilton became the seat of White Pine county.

These were the riches that lured the west's most notorious highwaymen to the new camp. Freighting stages, carrying ore to the Central Pacific Railroad at Wells and Elko, were relieved of their cargo at least twice weekly by bandits.

The apparently solid silver crust of the mountains failed to hold out at any depth and men who had sunk fortunes in Hamilton trade and buildings, began to worry

over their investments. In 1873, a disgruntled businessman, hoping to collect his insurance, set fire to the rear of his store in the early morning hours. He had first taken the precaution of shutting off the valve that controlled the Hamilton water supply. Fire swept the town. A decade later the county seat was moved to Ely, and today gaunt, weatherbeaten structures and crumbling foundations are the desolate remains of one of the west's most fabulous silver camps.

Nevada's Pahute County

FEW PEOPLE TODAY realize that much of Clark County was once a sub-division of Arizona, known as Pahute County, with full representation in the Arizona Territorial Legislature which met in those days in Tucson. Octavious Gass of Callville, Nevada, was elected with Andrew Gibbon of St. Thomas, and the two men decided the easiest way to make the long trip to Tucson would be by rowboat.

Accordingly they had James Leithead whip-saw the lumber on Sheep Mountain, and build a 14-foot rowboat at St. Thomas. They hauled the boat overland to the Colorado River at Fort Callville, where they set sail down to Yuma. Gass was a desert-bred man, and very timid about boats, but Gibbons was an old hand with the oars. He delighted in terrifying his companion as they swept down the coffee colored torrent of the great Colorado on a trip that still challenges boatmen today.

Their tiny boat plunged down the great canyons at breath-taking speed, covered with huge clouds of spray. It barely survived the great thundering rapids, with vast rocks and treacherous whirlpools. They hung up on hidden sandbars, fought mosquitoes, hunger, and cold night winds. And finally, after days of rowing, drifting, and bailing, they debarked in sun-baked Yuma.

Here they found overland travel to Tucson in a state of turmoil from Indian uprisings. At least one stage driver and load of passengers, were massacred by the Indians before the roads could be opened, and the Pahute County delegation was finally seated in the legislature, six days late! After adjournment, Gibbons purchased a saddle horse and rode the 500 miles back to St. Thomas through the worst deserts of the southwest, filled with hostile Indians. Gass took the stagecoach to San Diego before returning to Las Vegas.

These were trying times for the settlers in southern Nevada. In 1868 "one degree" of Arizona was given to Nevada, establishing the present boundary, and soon another degree was taken from Utah and given to this state. Muddy Valley settlers who had paid taxes in Utah, found themselves in Arizona, then in Nevada. Having paid taxes to Utah and then Arizona, the third payment was too much! Many started to return to Salt Lake, and Brigham Young ordered them to abandon Muddy Valley. In March 1871, some 250 Mormon families left St. Thomas, Overton, St. Joseph, and Junctionville. They left their homes, farms, orchards, vineyards, and thousands of bushels of wheat. The exodus included all families with the exception of one, delaying the development of this part of Nevada by many years.

Two Gun Watchman

Paul Nyland

HISTORY FAILS to tell us much about the origin of a youthful watchman named George McIntyre in the raw young camp of Elko in 1868. He guarded huge piles of freight stacked in the center of town by the railroad, destined for teaming to the booming, brawling new camps of White Pine, Pioche, and Eureka.

Young McIntyre got his watchman's job when the railroad admired the way he defended himself in a bar room brawl against several brawny woodchoppers, known to be "bad men." But as soon as he got the new job, the woodchoppers camp sent word it was out to "get" the new Central Pacific watchman. And, as good as their threat, a big mob of them soon arrived in Elko, drunk, ugly, and yelling for McIntyre to show himself.

After an hour of this racket, the watchman suddenly appeared on the scene with a six gun in each hand, and instantly opened fire on the heavily armed crowd. In a flash he killed three and wounded several more before any of them could pull a trigger, and the rest broke and ran for it. By the next day the shamed "choppers" buried their dead, hushed the story, and behaved themselves.

Later McIntyre arrived in Pioche when that infamous camp of bad men trembled at the approach of the great Morgan Courtney, deadliest "chief" of them all. Courtney soon met young McIntyre in the street, and having heard of him, told him "Pioche wasn't big enough for the two of them." McIntyre cooly replied that he liked Pioche but Courtney was at liberty to leave! This was the first time a man had crossed the great bully and lived, and the "chief" blustered to no avail. But the men separated peacefully.

That afternoon the entire town managed to keep away from the main street where bullets would soon be flying. Finally Courtney strolled down the walk, keeping an alert eye in all directions, and his hand near his gun. But McIntyre had planned it for a sure thing and ambushed his man. Courtney never had a chance, and died with six bullets in his body and his revolver still in the holster.

McIntyre was promptly arrested, but almost immediately was turned free and the whole camp of Pioche breathed easier for the first time since Morgan Courtney had come to eastern Nevada. First of a murderous influx of professional gunmen who came to be hired by the mines and mills, and remained to bully and intimidate the camp, Courtney was mourned by no one in the entire Pioche area. McIntyre was quiet and peaceful. He dropped out of Nevada history as inconspicuously as he had entered, a young man who minded his own business.

Pioneer Church Financing

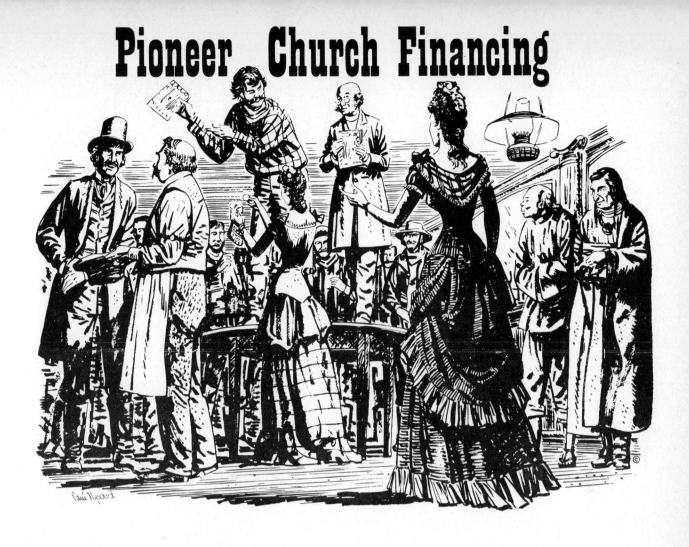

ARLY DAY CHURCH workers in Nevada faced many privations and hardships so courageously, they commanded the respect and admiration of all sorts of people of all faiths. And as a result they often enjoyed unorthodox methods in their fund raising efforts.

Rev. Jesse L. Bennett, a Methodist, preached the first sermon on the Comstock, (on C street), and was amazed to find a hat passed and filled with gold coins. When a "Washoe Zephyr" tore the roof from a new Methodist church in Virginia City, the preacher sold the bricks from the wreckage and rebuilt the church with the proceeds from "the sale."

In Austin the Methodist congregation received many donations of mining stock, which the canny pastor pooled into the "Methodist Mining Company" and sold in the East for $250,000. With this he built the finest church in Nevada with the probable exception of St. Mary's of the Mountain on the Comstock.

The Presbyterians of Virginia City achieved one of the most amazing financial transactions. Taking cash from the church treasury, they plunged on the mining stock market! The stock rose sensationally, and then acting on an inside tip, or else some of the finest judgment in mining history, they sold out at a tremendous profit just before the market broke and the stock plunged in value. They put the money into a new church building and four lots and buildings which supported the church from revenues!

The railroad gave four lots for a Presbyterian church in Elko, and the great Henry Ward Beecher presented an organ. Roman Catholic and Latter Day Saints' workers achieved many spectacular successes in supporting their drives for funds, many of which have been widely told in recent years. The famous Bishop Whittaker conducted the first Episcopal services in Pioche, in 1870, before 150 miners in a saloon; and in Goldfield a meeting was held in the Montezuma Club which subscribed a large fund for the local society for the Presbyterian church.

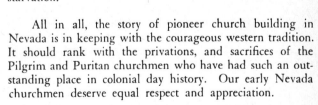

Not all churches found such generous support, however, and in 1873 a kindly and gentle Methodist minister in Gold Hill struggled to keep a large family on a tiny salary. To keep his little flock he often went without himself, and said nothing of his need. And when he died of pneumonia, it was found he had literally died of starvation.

All in all, the story of pioneer church building in Nevada is in keeping with the courageous western tradition. It should rank with the privations, and sacrifices of the Pilgrim and Puritan churchmen who have had such an outstanding place in colonial day history. Our early Nevada churchmen deserve equal respect and appreciation.

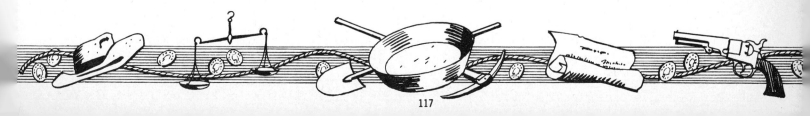

Yellowjacket Fire

Paul Nyrland

FIRE UNDERGROUND! An inexplicable terror known only to those who toil in the dark caverns far beneath the earth's surface . . . and to their families who wait with white, tear stained faces at the hoist . . . the single escapeway from the inferno. Acrid black smoke boils upward from the flaming underground beehive to cloud the sun and cast a funereal hush over the straining crowd, bringing with it the sudden realization of awful calamity.

This was the scene that jarred the Comstock on the morning of April 7, 1869 when fire raged out of control 800 feet beneath Gold Hill in the drifts, chutes and winzes of the Yellowjacket disaster that threatened the lives of a thousand miners, killed 45 of them, raged two months through a subterranean labyrinth of timber and then continued to smoulder for three years in sealed-off tombs.

The relay shift had knocked off at 4:00 o'clock that morning, but one of the miners probably left his candle sticking in a timber. Three hours later between five hundred and a thousand men, working on the day shift, were lowered to the various levels of the three mines. Almost immediately flames were discovered and there was a mad scramble back to the shaft. Cages started humming again to bring men to the surface, but smoke was already so bad that some fell on their way. At Crown Point many of them were overcome by the fumes as they ascended in the cage. Falling against the timbers,

they were crushed as the overcrowded hoist toiled perilously toward daylight.

Grief stricken wives and frightened children crowded the shaft mouth where the dead or horribly burned men were being taken from the cages, where firemen, with meager equipment, bravely descended into the boiling depths to aid the miners. Clergymen sought to comfort stunned mothers or quiet crying children. And down below the flames gained headway.

Firemen and miners fought side by side . . . those trapped in the farthest drifts were warned that gas made escape suicidal, but they knew also that a shift in the draft meant being cooked alive. Water inches deep boiled in puddles where it fell from the red-hot tunnel walls as rescuers sought to quench the flames, but it was no use! By 9:00 that night fire had gained the seven hundred foot level and was burning furiously.

On the third day shafts of the Yellowjacket were covered and steam forced into the deep levels. Four days later the steam was shut off and rescuers again went into the depths to retrieve more bodies. On May 24, nearly two months after the outbreak, workers succeeded in cornering the worst flames and sealing them off where they smouldered for three years to keep the Comstock aware of its worst mine tragedy.

The FABULOUS V&T

FROCK COATED William Sharon was a man who didn't mince words. He visioned control of the Comstock and he needed a railroad to do it. Calling I. E. James to his office, he greeted the surveyor with a blunt question, "Can you build a railroad from Virginia City to the Carson River?" Equally as brief was James' reply, "Yes," and within a month the survey was completed and work commenced on the Virginia and Truckee Railroad, destined to become the most fabulous of all short lines.

Sharon represented the Bank of California, which in turn controlled a number of mills on the Carson River. Using bank credit as his trump card, Sharon was assured of ore for the mills since reduced freight rates would attract shipment of lean ore and even dump material. Timber for the Comstock deep mines was a constant commodity for the return haul.

Chinese coolies, who learned construction on the Central Pacific Railroad, were imported to build the grade and lay the tracks for the V. & T. Fearing cheap labor might invade the mining field, the miners' union drove the coolies from their camps and Sharon fumed for a week before he promised the union that the Chinese would never work the Comstock mines. Work was resumed. Other uneasy moments occurred when the "Big Four" threatened to run a narrow gauge over Geiger grade connecting Virginia City with Reno, but Sharon was tenacious and the steel rails rapidly forged their way from Eagle Valley to the base of Sun Peak. In November of '69 they reached Gold Hill, two months later the first train

rolled into Virginia City and the Comstock took a new lease on life.

Failing to compete with steam power, teamsters went out of business and the V. & T. hauled ore for two dollars a ton to the bank-controlled Union Mining and Milling Company mills on the Carson River. In '73 Mackay, Fair, Flood, and O'Brien hit their "Big Bonanza" and the booming business necessitated an average of thirty trains a day over the twenty-one mile route between Carson and Virginia City. The peak haul was fifty-two trains a day. Railroaders worked a straight eighteen hours out of twenty-four, making four round trips daily. Sharon and his associates, Darius O. Mills and William C. Ralston split a hundred thousand dollars a month in dividends. The Comstock flourished, Julia Bullette was its reigning queen, fortunes were pyramiding and the V. & T. was the lifeline of commerce. Naturally it was a tempting morsel for holdups.

The railroad finally obtained permission to shut down in 1950 as a losing proposition, its rolling stock was sold, its rails torn up for scrap. Much of its ancient rolling stock easily made one of the west's colorful tourist attractions. Brass bound V. & T. engines appeared regularly in motion pictures and were subjects of many coast to coast radio network shows. The Idol of railway societies its yellow Kimball coaches were reminiscent of the day when President Grant rode to the base of Sun Peak to inspect the mines which financed his Civil War campaigns.

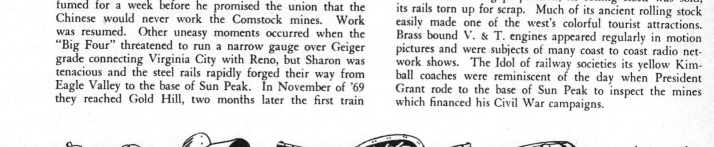

Steptoe Sedans

STAGE COACH TRIPS across Nevada in the early days were always fairly hectic experiences. In addition to the always present threat of an Indian attack, or a hold up by road agents, the pioneer travelers faced the discomforts of clouds of alkali dust, bumpy roads, bitter cold in winter and stifling desert heat in summer. Stage coach drivers, known as the "lords of the road" in their linen dusters, fancy gloves, and deft touch on the reins, were often more interested in setting new speed records instead of the comfort of the bedraggled passengers below.

At certain times of the year there were other discomforts. Early records tell that in 1869 a sea of mud formed a swamp three miles wide at Steptoe Slough, in eastern Nevada. This bog consisted of a soft, sticky, tough clay, covered by six inches of murky water.

Overland passengers were compelled to hire Indians to pack their baggage across the three miles, and to wade or be carried. Ladies usually preferred to be carried across, and a system of sedan chairs was perfected by the Indians to make the crossing. Records tell that four Indians carried a frame, usually made of cottonwood poles, with upholstery fashioned from gunny sacks. The natives would wait until the apprehensive lady passenger was seated in the rough framework, then swing it, tilting precariously, to their shoulders and start off through the muck. Splashing, floundering, and stumbling, they usually ended the trip in a state of exhaustion, and with the fair passenger in a state of nervous collapse. The trip cost forty dollars without any guarantee against a muddy ducking every instant.

Steptoe Slough also presented difficulties for the heavier freight. In 1869 the Central Pacific Railroad and the Union Pacific were rapidly racing to a meeting. It was common knowledge that the completion of the railroad would mean the end of stage coaching. This so lowered the morale of the dashing stage coach organizations that their final operations often became a sorry affair. A traveler arrived on the Comstock Lode during this period with the report that he had seen four hundred bags of mail at the Schell Creek station, on the east side of Steptoe Slough, awaiting transportation across the swamp. The weight of this mail was estimated at twenty-one tons, and there seemed little probability that it could be moved in less than twelve weeks.

A few months later the iron rails were linked at Promontory Point, and the romantic era of stage coach travel to the Pacific Coast came to an end. Stage transportation then shifted to short hauls, side trips, and local travel, and gradually diminished until, generations later, it was entirely replaced by the automobile.

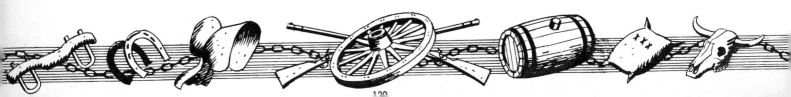

Pony Express Shopping Service

THE ISOLATION of small communities in central Nevada was something to give pause in 1869, and the simplest forms of communication called for a daily performance of feats of courage and endurance which today would be regarded as verging on heroism. The mail rider for the Mammoth district left Austin three days each week, traveling a route through Ione, and into the mining camp of Ellsworth, just over the line in Nye County. The distance was an even 70 miles.

In 1869 the pony rider serving this district was a small and kindly man with the name of Barnes. His regular route in all kinds of weather, called for the full 70 miles each day, and Barnes was known widely as a man who never missed his schedule. He had little, if any, trouble of record with the Indians; but he rode Monday, Wednesday, and Fridays, from Austin to Ellsworth and made the return trips Tuesday, Thursday, and Saturdays. Six days a week he spent in the saddle, covering 70 miles each day.

It is ironic that Barnes' chief claim to fame in Nevada history is not through his endurance, or his faithfulness in performing his duty in time of blizzards, blistering heat, or heavy storm, but rather for his consideration and kindliness for the people living in the scattered little communities along his route. Austin was the "big city" of 1869 to the folks living in Ione, Ellsworth, and a half dozen unnamed or forgotten camps out in the sagebrush.

It was the shopping center, fountainhead of culture, education, and supplies for an area the size of many an eastern State. And on April 15, 1869, the Austin Reese River Reveille mentioned the pony rider serving Ellsworth and Ione as follows:

"The rider is named Barnes . . . a small sinewy fellow, as tough as a hickory sapling. He is so hardy and free that he disdains a coat and rides in his shirt sleeves, heedless of frost or gales. Besides the mail he is 'common carrier' for the people along the route. Three times a week he distributes from ten to twenty parcels of nameless little, but imperative 'wants,' to the men and women in the valley.

He receives the order on his homeward trip (to Austin), fills them in that city and distributes them on his outward trip. He carries the mail, buys tobacco for "the old man's pipe;" medicine for his rheumatiz; picks up all sorts of notions for the "old woman;" Lubin and hoopskirts for the girls; gimcracks for the boys; and soothing syrup and rubber dolls for the baby . . . everything from sole leather to hair pins.

'Barnes performed his shopping service, covering the desert on ordinary cow ponies. In fact, the poor quality of his horses was subject for comment in print at least once. Yet he travelled at a rate of 1,820 miles a month, or 21,840 miles a year, and was hailed by the newspapers of his day as the modest, model mail rider."

In an age of rapid transportation, it is sometimes hard for modern readers to understand the importance of the tri-weekly mail pony and the tie it represented with the rest of the world. For the folks in the little settlements, mines, and scattered ranches south of Austin in the '60's there was no telephone, no daily mail, no paved roads, and the nearest telegraph line was an uncertain strand of wire fastened to cottonwood poles and tree limbs that passed through Austin, from east to west. Barnes was their sole link with the rest of the world.

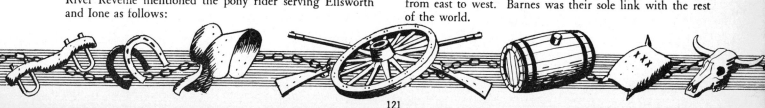

121

Knights of the Road

AT ONE O'CLOCK on the afternoon of September 6, 1867, the Wells Fargo & Company stage drew up at Desert Wells Station, and three men, completely masked and armed with sawed-off shotguns stepped from the doorway.

Taking their places without hurry, the robbers covered the passengers expertly, and ordered them to "get down." There were eight passengers and a driver, all of whom stepped down to the ground with elaborate care, avoiding any appearance of reaching for arms.

Each passenger, upon alighting, was told to keep his hands raised, to face the wall and then lower his wrists behind his back, where they were quickly and efficiently tied. They were also rapidly searched for weapons, but all were unarmed. It was soon evident from the conversation that the bandits had seized the stage station two hours earlier, and had bound the hostler and the cook in the rear of the building.

By now the robbers were enthusiastically searching for money. They went over each passenger carefully, but refused to take any watches, remarking that they were telltale trinkets. They also took great care to preserve and protect the private papers of the passengers, and in general conducted themselves like gentlemen. They did find about $600 in cash, which they kept.

Passengers and driver were then escorted to the rear of the building under guard, while the other two robbers took down the treasure box from the stage, and broke it open.

Then they thought of the team, untied the hostler and stood guard over him while he took care of the animals.

The robbers had prepared and eaten their dinner while awaiting the stage, and they now fed some of the passengers who were hungry, and brought water to all of them. The bandits made every effort to show care and consideration for their victims, and managed to confide to some of the passengers that "unless the quality of passengers on the stage improved, they could not afford to leave the country."

About five thirty they untied the driver and stood guard over him while he released his passengers, and helped them get back up into the stage coach. They kept three of the stage horses, but allowed the driver to depart with the balance of his team, watered, fed, and refreshed.

As the stage drew about a mile down the narrow road, the passengers looked back and saw the robbers lead out their stolen horses, put on blankets and surcingles and ride off toward the Humboldt. So well had they been masked that agents of the company who had been among those robbed, (Dow Huntsman of Cottonwood Station, Charles Share of Westgate, and Butterfield of Butterfield's Station) were unable to describe them other than "medium height, stooped shouldered, and bow-legged." But all members of the party, including Wells Fargo & Company's own men were unanimously enthusiastic over the kind treatment they had received at the hands of the Knights of the Road.

Chinese Labor Trouble

THE YEAR 1868 saw Nevada labor threatened by an influx of thousands of Chinese coolies, imported from the Orient by the shipload, and eager to work for wages that meant starvation to a white man. Much of the labor on the great construction job of the Central Pacific Railway, winding up over the high Sierras and down through Reno, was supplied by great gangs of coolies.

Sharon's crews of coolies would soon lay rail for the V & T Railway down Carson River canyon. Alarmed at the possibility of all these Chinese coolies turned loose and looking for work after completion of the V & T, the Miners Unions of Gold Hill and Virginia City sent a "call to arms" to all labor groups in Nevada. The crisis was only visible in "Washoe," however, and little support was forthcoming from the rest of the State.

A year later found vast hordes of Chinese laying rails on the very slopes of Mt. Davidson! Every day brought the gangs closer and closer to Virginia City, as the V & T neared completion. And with completion would come the end of railway work for the Chinese. Something akin to panic seized the Irishmen and Cornishmen who labored beneath the Comstock Lode in scalding hot water for a wage already low and insecure. The miners resolved on direct action in a series of meetings filled with excitement and determination.

On September 29, 1869, a column of men from the Miners Unions of Gold Hill and Virginia City about 350 strong, marched down from the Divide to the camps of the Chinese labor gangs, where the Overman Mine shaft is now located. The sheriff of Storey County was a man of courage and he dashed in front of the column. It halted, and he read a proclamation to disperse. The men refused, and then the sheriff read the Riot Act.

Good naturedly the miners allowed him to finish, then they gave three cheers for the United States, their drummer beat a quickstep, their fife player skirled defiantly, and the miners dashed on to the Chinese camp. As they approached the Orientals threw down their picks and shovels, seized belongings and deserted the place. Hundreds fled to the hills and others raced for the Carson Canyon or Dayton. Having routed "the enemy" without bloodshed, the miners returned home with flying colors for the appropriate celebrations.

The Unions negotiated for hours with Sharon, and after eight days the Chinese were allowed to return as a "privilege, not a right" with the agreement they would not be hired in the area after completion of the V & T. After the completion of the V & T, the Chinese scattered. For years they were a part of every community in western Nevada.

Sutro's Coyote Hole

ADOLPH SUTRO made his first appearance on the Comstock Lode as an inconspicuous cigar store clerk, but he lived to become one of its best known citizens despite the fact that it took thirteen years to live down the jibes about his "coyote hole."

Underneath the surface, this mild mannered cigar clerk was a born showman and an extremely capable engineer who foresaw construction of a tunnel to drain the deep mines of the Lode. High water in the mines was a consistent hurdle to production and pumping was an overhead to be reckoned with.

In 1865 the legislature of the newly created State of Nevada passed a bill incorporating the tunnel company, and the following year Congress chartered the corporation. Sutro meanwhile contracted with nineteen mining companies for the payment of a two dollar per ton royalty on all ore that would be removed from the Lode through the tunnel, promising at the same time to keep the mines free of water without additional charge. His plan met the solid opposition of William Sharon and the interests he represented with the result that most of the companies repudiated their contracts before work commenced on the tunnel.

Disheartened, but far from ready to quit, Sutro petitioned Congress for a subsidy and tried to interest eastern capital. Failing in America he went to Europe and received a promise of aid from France, but that too was nullified by the threat of war. Then came an unexpected break: in 1869 a fire in the Yellow Jacket Mine took a terrible toll of lives, and Sutro, the master showman, saw his chance. With posters and stump speeches he called on the miners for support of his project which would lessen the danger of disaster. The miners rose in frenzy and on October 19, 1869, Sutro himself broke ground above the Carson River for the tunnel entrance. His project called for millions, and now he met solid opposition from the Comstock Kings, Mackay, Fair, Flood and O'Brien. They

referred to his venture as "Sutro's Coyote Hole." Almost beaten again, Sutro was amazed at the sudden loan of two and a half million dollars from McClamonts Bank of London. His difficulties were not over, but finally in 1878, thirteen years after the beginning of his project he fired the final blast that opened into the first mining shaft, nearly four miles from the tunnel mouth. It had cost five millions and the Comstock had passed its peak, but even so "Sutro's Coyote Hole" paid off in royalties and in one single year drained two billion gallons of water from the deep mines.

Louse Town Track

SARATOGA had the thoroughbreds, but Louse Town had the color! Seven miles down the winding road from Virginia City toward Glendale on the Truckee River, Louse Town enjoyed a bonanza every Sunday during the late Sixties, when miners, muckers and practically the entire citizenry of the sprawling Comstock camps gathered to place their week's earnings on "the ponies."

Here in the dusty half mile oval Washoe's best horses thundered around the sage flat track to the delight of spectators who thoroughly enjoyed an afternoon at the races even though boxes and bleachers were an unthought of luxury. The crowd itself formed the outside track barrier, usually aligning itself with the helter-skelter row of shanty betting booths. But, on the day Ed Kennedy rode the dark-skinned bay that ran away, spectators probably gave thought to the need of some fencing.

Ed was a man of slight build who represented himself as "something of a jockey," and he made the representation to the owner of a horse called Ecliptic. Naturally Ed was in the saddle when the race began. For some reason, still unexplained, Ecliptic decided that the little Louse Town track didn't offer enough room for his flying hooves. Instead of rounding the first turn, Ecliptic took off on a tangent right through the crowd, sending spectators and betting booths flying. Up over the hill he

went, toward Virginia City with Ed clinging tightly to his neck. It was a seven-mile gallop to the Comstock, but if Ed was "something of a jockey," Ecliptic was "something more than a half miler." The big bay breezed right up C street and over the Divide. By the time they reached Gold Hill, Ed figured he had had enough. He managed to dismount rather unceremoniously, but Ecliptic kept right on. A few miners down the canyon who had been unable to go to the Louse Town track that day, got a free show of a real racer. They said the big bay kept right on going until he reached Dayton.

Ed didn't win the race, but his ride made Louse Town famous, and it gained Ed a nickname too. For many years he was "Ecliptic Kennedy" or "Around the Heavens Ed."

The Louse Town track was only one of many activities in a region close to Reno, yet seldom visited these days except by saddle horse or jeep. Louse Town Creek, and environs included an area of active mining, small settlements, woodcutters' cabins, and a stage coach road which wound through some hair-raising country until it finally emerged from Lagomarsino Canyon on the Truckee River and formed a junction with the Central Pacific. Today finds the area visited by prospectors with some formal mining activity from time to time; and a healthy amount of sheep raising in progress.

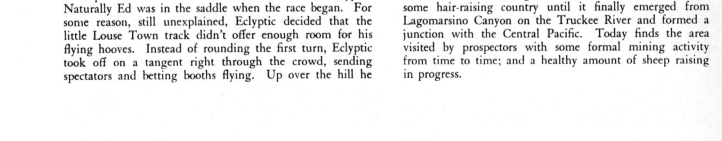

Spaulding's Salt

FORMIDABLE mountain ranges thrusting their high peaks well above ten thousand feet were barriers in the way of early exploration in central Nevada. Towering peaks like Arc Dome, Mahogany Mountain and Bunker Hill along the Toiyabe Range, and the equally forbidding Wildcat Peak and White Rock Mountain in the tumbling Toquimas served to shelter the narrow, sixty mile length of Smoky Valley.

From the '60's to '80's, white men, in their quest for mineral wealth, usurped the wild game salt-licks and churned Smoky Valley's floor to a powdery dust under the iron-rimmed wheels of desert freight wagons . . . Salt from Spaulding's marsh was suddenly in great demand. Quartz mills in Austin and all along the new mining campsites in the Toiyabe and Toquima ranges needed the pure, natural salt for the roasting process by which ore was reduced to metallic silver.

For twenty years the roads from central Nevada camps to Spaulding's Marsh near the head of Smoky Valley, were busy freighting thoroughfares. Ready access to the mills provided a natural market for nearly two thousand tons of salt each year.

Despite demand, harvesting of the salt crop retained a primitive form. Cheap Indian labor was used to cultivate and harvest ten crops each year. There was no surface water on the one hundred acre marsh, but at a depth of about four feet saline water existed. As the sun's rays pulled this moisture upward, a crystal scale would form on the surface. When the scale reached sufficient thickness, it was harvested and a new crop would then develop through the same process.

To harvest this brittle salt layer, Indian laborers, many of them wearing cast-off clothes of their employers, rolled the marsh with a weighted wooden roller, the surface of which was waffled to break the crust. Raking crews followed in the wake of the roller, bunching the salt into piles which in turn were transferred to wheelbarrows. The barrow men transferred the salt across the marsh to the waiting freight wagons and loaded them for their journey to the mills.

In the Seventies, during the peak of milling operations, a new method, designed to speed production was introduced. Operators sought to pump the saline solution through pipes to a nearby area where clay soil would enhance the evaporation. The scheme failed, however, and the owners of Spaulding's Marsh were forced to let nature take her own time in producing the salt crop, a process that had provided a wild game salt-lick long before men mined for silver.

Shotgun Judge

Paul Nyland

THE JUSTICE of the Peace at Tybo, in 1870 was a remarkable character named Dr. J. W. Gally. The good doctor owned half interest in the highly profitable Two Gee mine, operated a lovely ranch, and was so admired locally that his neighbors insisted he serve as Justice of the Peace.

A local mining man and obnoxious bully had been trying to dominate everybody in the valley. And when he pulled a six gun on rancher Alex McKey, his victim swore out a warrant for an arrest. The case was set for the next day by Doctor (now Judge) Gally, and the men brought their wives as witnesses.

Both men exchanged hot words, and soon a nasty quarrel broke out. Finally Newton, the mining man, made a fast move for his holster, and McKey snatched at the satchel held by his wife. But the Justice of the Peace shouted "Order, Gentlemen!" in such a bellowing and commanding tone, that both men froze in their tracks. They turned to find the mild, humorous doctor gazing at them over the twin barrels of his loaded shotgun, and he had both barrels cocked! Moreover, he looked fully prepared to pull the triggers. Promptly the two men were disarmed and a hidden gun in Mrs. Key's satchel confiscated.

The Justice found that Newton should be held on the charge and set bail at $1,000. But Newton growled, "When you want me, you can come and get me in Belmont." The Justice was just putting away his shotgun, but on hearing the remark, he produced it again, cocked, and announced he would hold Newton unless he produced the $1,000 "here and now." Newton wilted visibly, sent for

the money from his friends, and from that time on gave no more trouble in the Tybo District.

Soon after this incident, Judge Gally decided his children were reaching an age when they would require more education than provided in the schools of the Tybo District. So he planned to drive his wife and children to the coast and move to California. He sold his ranch and mining interests, loaded their remaining possessions into a light throughbrace wagon with a four horse team, and drove off for the wagon road over the Sierras.

The nearest route lay to the north, and the Truckee River Canyon. But on passing through Wadsworth on the Big Bend of the Truckee River, they found that deep snows had closed all the passes over the Sierras. So Doctor Gally promptly loaded his team, his wagon, his baggage and his family all on board a Central Pacific train, and they rode over the Sierras and through the snowsheds in short order and finally reached the Bay area by rail.

With both hands full of reins, the Doctor drove his four hysterical broncos up Market Street to the Bank of California where he obtained sufficient cash to complete his journey. With him on the wagon, sat his wife and children, sun-bronzed from the desert winds, filled with wonderment at San Francisco, and a wagon loaded with baggage and heavily armed. The California papers were all agog over the "sun-bronzed people from the desert of Nevada with their wild horse teams." Doctor Gally soon settled in the Watsonville area, resumed the practice of medicine and became an outstanding citizen of California.

The High Heeled Boot

THE CENTRAL PACIFIC Railroad was scarcely a year old when the entire Pacific Coast was startled by news of the west's first train robbery near Lawton Springs on the night of November 5, 1870. Perfectly timed and highly organized the rail piracy netted $41,000 from Wells Fargo's strong box for the daring masked men who politely thanked the express car messenger for giving them a minimum of trouble.

Smug in their belief of eventual success they cached the gold and set out on separate paths intending to let the affair blow over, but they had failed to reckon with the dogged determination of James H. Kinkead, Washoe County's deputy sheriff, whose smart detective work brought seven to justice from the trail of a high heeled boot.

Shortly after eleven o'clock on the night of November 4, as the eastbound Overland Express pulled out of Verdi station carrying a Comstock mine payroll, the engineer and fireman found themselves looking down the muzzles of pistols held by five masked men. They were commanded to "whistle down" the brakes and when the train drew to a halt one of the bandits slipped the coupling pin between the express car and the remainder of the train. Then the engineer was ordered to make full speed ahead. Near Lawton Springs the speeding engine and express car were halted at a barricade thrown across the tracks, and the masked men rifled the express car strong box, waved a laughing goodbye to the trainmen and disappeared in the darkness along the Truckee River. Meanwhile the conductor had eased the remaining cars downgrade, but when he reached the engine at the barricade, the bandits had vanished with $41,000 in gold coin. The train was quickly assembled and pushed on to Reno where a robbery alarm was spread.

Sheriff Charley Pegg and his deputy Kinkead received the word in Washoe at eight o'clock the following morning together with the information that the robbers were headed south, but a full day's search of the Truckee-Carson trail failed to reveal any traces of recent travel. Undaunted by the first day's fruitless search, Kinkead set out for the scene of the robbery and early in the morning of November 7, he found a clue in the light snow that covered the ground. It was the print of a high heeled boot . . . a tiny pointed heel . . . a dandy's boot. Without rest Kinkead set out alone on the trail which led to Sardine Valley in California. There he ascertained that three strangers had stopped on the previous night. One wore high heeled boots. Two had left early in the morning, headed for Sierra Valley. The third had been taken into custody by a hunting party from Truckee.

Despite heavily falling snow Kinkead pushed on to Loyalton and there surprised his quarry asleep in a lodging house, arrested him and confiscated the boots for evidence. The same morning he succeeded in nabbing another suspect on a ranch near Sierraville. Knowing he had made arrests out of his jurisdiction, Kinkead took both men to Truckee to await extradition. A confession "sweated" from one of them implicated a total of seven well-known Nevada men. The information together with court evidence substantiated by the high heeled boots convicted Nevada's first train robbers and recovered the major portion of the $41,000 loot.

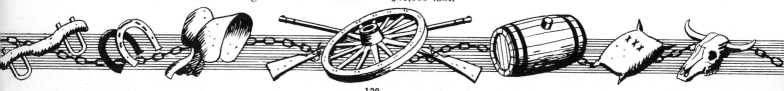

The Molly Maguires

BELMONT, from the moment of the original rush to its lead-silver deposits in 1865, was an orderly mining camp in comparison with some of the other rip-roaring Nevada discoveries.

As the governmental seat of Nye County the community was proud of its square court house as well as the political and social advantages that normally accrued to the county seat. But before the court house was built in 1876, another structure served during many stirring events. Belmont had its moments of apprehension about law and order! Once in particular fear of real trouble spread through the camp when two Pennsylvania coal miners, posing as Molly Maguires, threatened the peace of the community.

Arrested because of their loose talk and threats about "burning down the town," the two were placed in the flimsy jail. Either through cooperation of sympathetic friends or by their own efforts, the Molly Maguires managed to escape and took up hiding in an abandoned mine tunnel.

Barricading themselves in the mine they taunted county law enforcement officials and threw out even more vehement threats concerning their plans for destroying the town. Through some mysterious underground they were supplied with food for a number of days and it appeared that they had no intention of leaving the vicinity of Belmont. Many of the citizens became increasingly apprehensive, and finally the sheriff, braving possible gunfire, entered the abandoned mine. Within a few moments he emerged with the two cowed men whose bluffs proved empty when faced by the determined sheriff.

A group of prominent citizens escorted the Molly Maguires to the low ceilinged basement of the temporary court house. Aided by the light of flares the group drilled two auger holes through the ceiling, threaded the ropes through and knotted them securely to the court house floor. With no more ado they proceeded to hang the two men whose threats had kept the town at nervous tension for weeks.

On the following Sunday, churchgoers who assembled in the court room of the temporary Belmont County court house for regular services, noted two auger holes in the floor, grim evidence of the way Belmont dealt with agitators.

To this day, there are many authorities who claim the Molly Maguires were merely excitable young men who meant no real harm and were victims of an aroused and intimidated community. Opinion was divided in Belmont at the time of the hanging and feelings were strong for a long time. An indication of the bitterness against the men is shown by their burial outside the community cemetery, and the graves are kept outside the fence to this day.

Melodrama at Palisade

TRAIN crews on wood-burning Central Pacific passenger trains enjoyed a well kept secret in the early '70's, and participated in a hilarious conspiracy with the townspeople of Palisade, Nevada. For this rough and ready little town, where the narrow gauge Eureka and Palisade Railway and the ox teams met the "CP," had a tough reputation to live up to.

The crack Overland Limited rolled daily into Palisade, crammed with Easterners who stepped off to stretch their legs. They usually found station and yards filled with tough-looking characters, all heavily armed, and all scowling at each other. Without warning a fight would break out, and in a matter of moments the bandits and gunmen would be shooting at each other and falling in all directions. Most of them seemed to land in large-sized pools of blood!

Half fainting with terror, the railway passengers would creep back to the train under a whistling hail of bullets. Almost by a miracle no passenger or railway employee ever seemed to be hit. Keen observers might have noticed that "dead and dying victims" were usually carried over to the Junction Saloon for treatment, and that at times some of them even returned to the battle.

About the time the Limited "whistled in her brakeman" a band of painted savages usually joined the fray, scalping and stabbing their victims with barbaric abandon. And as the Overland pulled out for the "Far West" and chugged on down the Humboldt, many a white-lipped passenger gave

thanks for having survived such a scene of carnage. They hastened to write letters to friends and newspapers about the dreadful battle and their "narrow escape."

This little pageant of melodrama at Palisade provided a two-fold purpose. Probably its first achievement was to provide the somewhat sparse recreational facilities of Palisade with a game that was hugely enjoyed by all townfolks and all railway men along the division. It filled dull days with excitement and everybody, including the neighboring friendly Shoshones, enjoyed taking part. There was enough of the ham actor in everyone to corn up the production until it stretched credence. A few who insisted on realism usually brought down a few buckets of blood from the slaughterhouse a little while before train time. And when the Overland came down the track almost every able-bodied man, woman, and child in town would be on hand to take part in the "community production."

There was another result of the little game which probably was far-reaching in its results. No chamber of commerce propaganda ever enjoyed more circulation by word of mouth, than the stories of Palisade. Passengers who "had lived through the gun battles of Palisade," soon told and retold the tale, embellishing and enlarging it with imaginary details. A tabulation would have indicated that hundreds of thousands of people must have died violent deaths in the "perpetual warfare at Palisade." No cemetery could have held all the victims. But luckily no statistically-minded soul ever ventured to question the casualty lists, and Palisade kept her reputation for many side-splitting years.

Barleycorn Battle

It WAS 1871, and the tough mining camp of Pioche was attracting miners and desperadoes from all over the west. Every stagecoach brought in a load of heavily armed men, and every sunrise revealed the bodies of many who had met violent death. Men laughed at the sheriff, who reputedly took $40,000 in graft annually. Juries were guarded, not from violence, but from bribery and the guards were hired, not by the law, but by the parties in court. Men and firms with property soon had to provide their own protection, and the town swarmed with paid gunmen.

The mining firm of Raymond & Ely finally imported the great "Chief" and killer, Morgan Courtney, who boasted tailor-made clothes, white linen, clean fingernails, and an absolute dead-eye, coupled with a fast draw. Courtney bossed the Raymond & Ely gunmen.

About this time the Newlands Brothers discovered that a supposedly worthless Raymond & Ely mine was in reality a bonanza of rich ore. They brought in a gang of gunmen from White Pine (later Ely) and jumped the Raymond & Ely mine. Their gunmen were installed as guards, and the shaft area heavily fortified with barricades. Thus installed, they began to take out tons of precious ore. The legitimate owners were furious.

An appeal to the sheriff brought only the advice "to let well enough alone." So Raymond & Ely turned to their new chief gunman for help. Courtney took one look at the heavily fortified mine and realized a direct attack would be costly if not impossible. The mine shaft commanded every approach.

Finally, after careful study, Courtney decided on some strategy. Using a neutral party, he arranged to have a large shipment of very fine whiskey delivered to the fortified mine, as if by mistake. His planning was rewarded when a short time later he heard snatches of song coming down the breeze from behind the big barricades. Later his scouts began to report "glimpses of staggering figures around the head frame of the shaft."

Moving under cover, and keeping his men out of sight, Courtney got his gunmen as close to the barricades as he dared. Then, picking what he estimated to be the right moment, he led them in a swift charge, up and over the barricades in a wild and deadly rush. Only one defender was sober enough to resist, and he was instantly shot and killed. The rest were too drunk to lift their guns, and were easily led down the streets and released.

Raymond & Ely were highly elated at the success of the move, and rewarded Courtney and his desperadoes by allowing them to work the mine for thirty days, keeping the ore for themselves. Records reveal in the thirty days, Courtney and his men realized $15,000 each from the deal, selling the ore back to Raymond & Ely.

But the example of jumping a big mine had set many desperate men to thinking and emulation. In the next few years, many mines were seized and fought over. Gunfire boomed at all hours of the day and night in Pioche, and the cost in lives was heavy. Gunmen were still important, and as "Chief" of Pioche, Courtney was involved many times. His gun was covered with notches, and his name a household word throughout the far west, as he gradually turned more and more into a "bully-gunman." Most people came to fear him and detested his bravado and blustering manner. Finally he met a young man from Elko, with two guns tied low in worn holsters, but the youngster refused to scare other than to take the precaution of setting up a careful ambush.

Tax Collector

JIM KINKEAD was the kind of a deputy sheriff who couldn't be bullied. There wasn't a man in all the time Jim held office in Washoe City who could bluff him, and many were the times he set out alone to bring back two brigands single-handed.

But Jim's duties weren't limited to stopping brawls and capturing gunmen. As deputy sheriff of Washoe County, he was also responsible for collecting taxes, and the problems connected with that office sometimes called for ingenuity.

Early in the seventies, shortly after the Central Pacific Railroad was completed assessment was levied by Washoe County. The railroad, one of the most powerful corporations of its time, immediately protested and a court battle followed. Despite howls of the rail tycoons, Washoe County won the suit and an attachment was issued. It was up to Jim Kinkead to collect the taxes, and quite a problem it was for there weren't many men who cared to buck such a powerful combination as the nation's leading railroad.

Jim thought the matter over and came up with his own solution. Waiting at the Reno station until the first train pulled in, Jim promptly secured the locomotive driver to one rail with a logging chain. Padlocking the chain and affixing his seal, he calmly leaned against the engine and waited. The depot was in an uproar with the telegraph key buzzing the news to San Francisco and back to eastern headquarters. The dispatcher was frantic, but Jim waited, calmly whittling on a willow stick. When the next train pulled in Kinkead promptly chained it down and resumed his waiting position. Telegrams flew faster than ever, and though lots of advice was directed to the dispatcher by the big men of Central Pacific, none of it was worth the telegraph sheets upon which it was written. Jim Kinkead, it seemed, wanted only one answer, that being the tax money which the Central Pacific owed Washoe County.

When the third train pulled in and found itself trussed to the tracks in the same manner as the first two, Central Pacific's directors knew they had been beaten. The Bank of California wired that the tax money had been deposited. Jim Kinkead stopped his whittling, got out his keys, and in a few moments traffic had resumed its flow along the rails of Central Pacific.

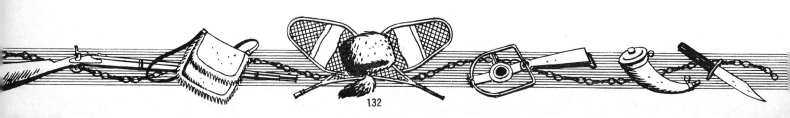

Bandit Jack Harris

PIOCHE in the seventies was considered one of the toughest camps in the west, and not without reason! Hired gunmen were imported at the rate of about twenty a day during boom times to fight mining claim encroachments. It wasn't a healthy spot for a man who couldn't use a gun! As if to lay claim to the sobriquet of "toughest town," early day residents used to point with pride to Boot Row where seventy-five men were buried before anyone in the roaring mining town died a natural death.

But, like any western camp, there was a lighter side to Pioche history, probably best revealed in the exploits of Bandit Jack Harris: Jack, it seems, had a penchant for robbing Wells Fargo Company stages. The rumbling express wagons normally carried a good deal of coin to meet the mine payrolls, and Harris found it a fairly simple matter to waylay the stages on their way to Pioche and relieve them of sizeable amounts of cash. Jack Harris had a way of appearing so unexpectedly that gun play was seldom necessary.

Stage drivers who travelled the Pioche run and the Wells Fargo agent in that town were mighty positive that Jack Harris was the bandit who was causing all the difficulty but they were never able to actually pin any of the incidents on him.

The station agent hit upon a plan: it would be much less expensive for Wells Fargo to pay Jack Harris a stipulated weekly sum provided he would be waiting on the express company's porch when each stage arrived. In that way the frequent robberies would be eliminated, and since Wells Fargo was doing a bang-up business, it could easily afford the payments to Harris. When approached with the proposition, Harris immediately agreed. He didn't want anyone to doubt his respectability, so day after day he arrived at the express company station a few moments in advance of the stage. When the vehicle drew up to the porch Harris would be waiting there with the agent, a thin smile playing about his lips.

Despite this tidy arrangement, the station agent was baffled to discover that the robberies continued at frequent intervals, yet Bandit Jack was always waiting on the porch when the harried Wells Fargo driver drew up to report a robbery.

Jack Harris was keeping his bargain insofar as reporting daily in advance of the stage's arrival, but the station agent didn't know that Bandit Jack still plied his trade. Some few miles before the express wagon reached Pioche, Jack would waylay it, relieve the driver of the valuables and then race back to Pioche by a shortcut in time to be waiting on the porch when the stage arrived.

It was some time before the agent discovered he had made a bad bargain, since nothing in the agreement mentioned the primary purpose which was to put a stop to stage robberies. And then, with its customary vigor, Wells Fargo Company took precautions again against robbery.

Rustler's Rendezvous

Paul Nyeland

HEMMED IN by the stark Hiko range on the east and the equally forbidding Sheep Mountains on the west, Pahranagat Valley threads its slender green way for forty miles between Crystal and Coyote Springs in southern Nevada. Its lush grass and fertile soil form a marked contrast to the brown desert barriers on either side.

Here in the seventies horse thieves found a haven for fattening stolen stock before driving them on to nearby Utah, California and Arizona markets.

The valley was an ideal hideout. Sparsely settled and far removed from any major town, it provided the maximum of protection for rustler bands.

So widespread were activities of the horse thieves that at one time settlers counted as many as 350 brands on the grazing stock. While the horses fattened themselves on the valley grasses, rustlers had a gay time, defying and even encouraging growing hatred of the settlers.

The ranchers didn't take it lying down! Small groups rode together in heavily armed posses, well mounted, and determined to run down and provide necktie parties for some of the unwary thieves, but never in the early years did their action seem sufficient to cope with the entire problem and rustlers continued to use the valley as headquarters.

One one occasion a posse of Utah ranchers caught up the trail of a murderer who had driven their stock into Pahranagat. Arriving in the valley they informed local ranchers of their intentions to lynch the thief and drive their stock back home. Pleased by reinforcements, the ready settlers joined the posse and sought out the particular cavvy of stolen horses. Riding down the rustler at nightfall, they bound him and escorted him to a nearby ranch for an impromptu hanging in the barn.

By lamplight, posse members tightened the noose around the rustler's neck. Just as the leader was about to signal "hoist" a razor sharp voice commanded "halt!" Posse men found themselves peering squarely into the double muzzles of a shotgun protruding through the door. Heaving a sigh, the doomed man loosened the knot. With a flourish and mock courtesy he bid goodbye to his captors. Laughs echoed against the hills as the rustler and his henchman rode off to Crystal for a celebration.

Their insolence so enraged the settlers that a 601 organization was formed and within a few years the valley was peaceful again.

Panamint Bullion

PROBABLY NOWHERE in the west outside the walls of a penitentiary were so many desperadoes congregated as in the Panamint area during the seventies.

Near enough to Death Valley to afford numerous hide-outs, yet far enough from larger cities where law enforcement was becoming increasingly necessary, Panamint offered the excitement of a prosperous mining camp coupled with a certain sense of security for those whose reputations were somewhat shady.

Early locators, almost to a man, were rather tough characters, and the town's cemetery, Sour Dough canyon, was well filled with the gravestones of those who weren't quick enough on the draw! Some of the early investors, who purchased claims from the "shady" element found themselves owning more than they had bargained for. In one instance a group of investors, upon purchasing some Panamint property, found themselves confronted with a claim from Wells Fargo Company because of the original owner's former depredations, and the syndicate paid off an additional twelve thousand dollars to Wells Fargo to obtain clear title.

Largest investors in Panamint properties were Senators John P. Jones and William Stewart who formed the Panamint Mining Company with capital stock of two million dollars. They paid approximately a quarter of a million dollars for some of the more prominent claims to get the company into production.

The two senators along with their mining operators soon realized that they had purchased something of a "pig in a poke." The town continued to be a hangout for desperadoes, and many of the original owners, who had sold

their claims, remained in the vicinity noting the mining milling developments with avid interest. It was apparent that the major problems would not be limited to the production of ore, but would encompass the peril of safely transporting the bullion to market.

After due deliberation, following a request for service from Senator Stewart, Wells Fargo Company "guessed not" on Panamint. Company officials evidently felt the district was too tough, and that the hazards of transporting the bullion through a country where so many bandits waited, wasn't worth the risk of service. Disheartened by the Wells Fargo turndown, Senator Stewart did not give up hope.

Since there was only one road out of Panamint, Stewart realized that bandits intent on robbery of the bullion in transportation would necessarily have to carry the stuff by mule back to evade being caught. Hence he developed a scheme which worked. He ordered several large molds, and when milling commenced, the bullion was poured into the molds, emerging in huge round balls, weighing 750 pounds each. Such was the weight and shape of the valuable bullion that bandits were unable to load it onto mules, and after one attempt at robbery, they gave up in disgust. In fact, they called upon Stewart and other mine owners and roundly cursed them for the scheme which so thoroughly put an end to their own well laid robbery plans.

Laughingly, the teamsters employed by mine owners, moved each wagon load through the town and to safe destination, without even so much as a guard. Panamint was tough, but the tough element lacked the brains to cope with mine operators.

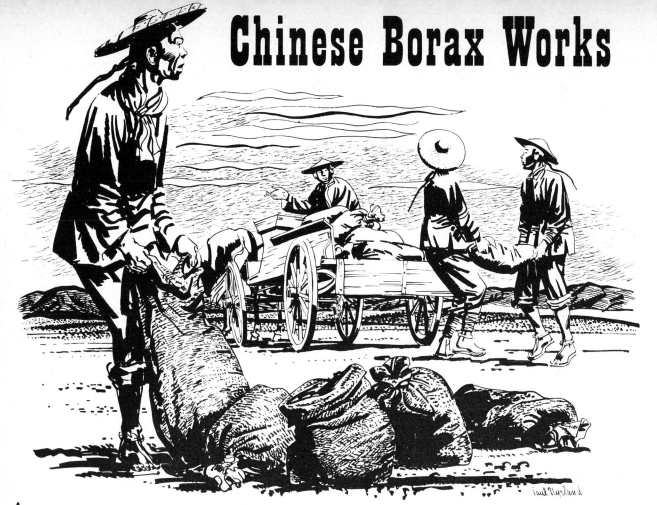

Chinese Borax Works

AS YOU DRIVE along the highway, some 25 miles south of Mina, you pass the old Columbia Marsh, an area which was extremely active and colorful in the '60's and '70's. Here in 1865 started the town of Columbus, providing salt and water for the mills working the silver, and later those from booming Candelaria.

Activity at the salt marshes had started in 1864, and during the Candelaria boom the rich silver ore was freighted down to the mills on the backs of Mexican pack trains. In 1871 a former Comstock miner arrived on the scene. He believed the marsh contained borax and succeeded in refining some in a wash boiler. A year later William T. Coleman entered the borax business but soon sold out to Borax Smith of Twenty Mule Team fame, who continued there through the '70's.

Columbus was as wild and woolly as most pioneer Nevada boom towns. A man was lynched at the old slaughter-house a mile west of town and there were numerous shootings. But Columbus got most of its color from the Chinese laborers who were brought in to work the borax.

At one time there were more than a thousand coolies working on the marsh. The heat had proved too great for white laborers, and the work was almost entirely done by Chinese. They spread out over the vast marshes in little groups, wearing wide straw coolie hats, long "pig-tails," shirts outside their pants, trousers rolled up out of the mud, and light sandals. They worked seven main boilers, scattered out in the brush. The boilers were fired by sage-brush, and Chinese gangs stripped the desert for this fuel as far south as the old Dyer Ranch in Fish Lake Valley. The marsh water containing soda, was boiled in these crude vats, the Chinese stirring it with long handled shovels until it was syphoned off into galvanized tanks and crystalized.

Transportation on the soft marsh was limited to very light wagons, drawn by two horses, and handled by Chinese drivers and swampers. The finished product was freighted to Wadsworth and loaded on the Central Pacific during the '70's and later in the '80's it was hauled to Candelaria instead, usually in 100-pound sacks.

Old-timers told how the Chinese and their wagons crawled up the steep grade into Candelaria, emptied their load, and returned to Columbus by an even more precipitious shortcut. There were no brakes on the little wagons, and as they bounced down the grade, the wagons crowded the teams, the teams would begin to bolt, and the Chinese drivers would get panicky. They always entered Columbus'

main street at a terrifc speed, hanging on for dear life and shouting and screaming at the horses at the top of their lungs in Chinese. The coolies never learned to return to town in any different manner, and it became a daily feature of life at Columbus.

The thousand Chinese lived in adobe huts for the most part. Many had cellars for opium dens underneath but these were ignored by the white employers whose main policy was to "keep John Chinaman at work."

Columbus produced borax until about 1890, but the main interest withdrew in 1875, marking the start of the downgrade which sooner or later comes to every mining camp.

Bullwhacking Sleepers

Freighting BY OX-TEAM was a big industry in eastern Nevada in the 1870's, and "Bullwhackers" drove thousands of teams between Pioche and Toano and Ward. If an animal appeared exhausted it was un-yoked and left to graze at any convenient spring. On the return trip the outfit would pick up the rested oxen. Such animals were called "sleepers," and it became common to "pick up sleepers," leaving oxen of your own for other future teams.

Often owners would ride out and round up "sleepers" when the number turned loose became large, and some mining districts in Nevada were discovered by men riding out "to gather up sleepers." A code became established by which freighter outfits returned animals as often as practical and kept an eye out for each others property.

The big bulls were branded with burned initials on their horns, and ownership was carefully observed by the reputable big outfits. But one Bullwhacker named Humpy Baker had a reputation for picking up too many "sleepers" on slightest provocation.

One day Charlie Coats rode up to Sacramento Pass in a region of lush rich range grass among the junipers where he had left a number of oxen to graze on a recent trip to Eureka, and to his surprise met Humpy bound for

Ward with two wagon loads of lumber and two of Coats' own oxen in his string! Infuriated, the mild mannered Coats yanked out his six gun and shoved it into Humpy's face. He yelled at him to "un-yoke those sleepers damned quick."

Humpy Baker had no idea who Coats was, and for a minute he hesitated. A flourish with the gun decided him, however, and with a resigned shrug, he stepped to the head of his big team and un-yoked a span of oxen. Then he un-yoked the next span, and soon, his trembling fingers had released every big bull in his whole outfit! It was composed entirely of sleepers! Humpy had no bulls of his own in his entire string, and it was obvious to Coats that Humpy's freighter business was being conducted through the unintentional courtesy of all other ox freighting outfits in eastern Nevada.

The tender-hearted Coats for all his bluster, realized the predicament in which this placed Humpy. Brandishing the gun he yelled at the terrified Bullwhacker, demanding if he had a file in his tool box. When Humpy produced it, Coats told him to "file the C. C. Brand (Charlie Coats' own brand) off the horns of those two bulls and keep them, but if I ever catch you west of the White Pine Mountains again, I will kill you on the spot."

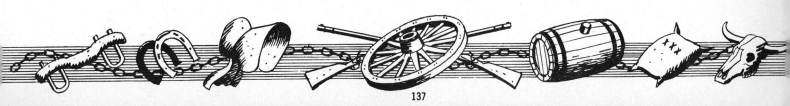

Snowshoe's Lost Mine

THREE MEN, Pony Bob Haslem, Hank Monk, and Snowshoe Thompson, were well known to the pioneers of western Nevada in the '60's, because each in his own way was an outstanding example of the best traditions of the service he represented. Pony Bob's name was synonymous with the Pony Express; Hank Monk's was linked firmly with the Pioneer Stages which rumbled between Genoa and old Hangtown . . . and, of course, Snowshoe Thompson, hero of them all, braved the Sierras' passes to carry mail in the dead of winter when snow isolated the frontier and brought a halt to all other means of transportation.

Though his prodigious feats on skis will remain one of the outstanding examples of pioneer spirit, John A. Thompson was remembered by many persons for another virtue, that being his strict adherence to the truth. Little wonder then that Snowshoe's Lost Mine created more consternation in the '70's and '80's than the Breyfogle, the Gunsight, and the Peg Leg all put together.

Snowshoe Thompson knew every foot of ground between his home at the eastern base of the Sierras, up over that tumbled mass of mountains to Placerville. He had reason to know it because he carried the mail for years through howling blizzards, sometimes at night with only his own intimate knowledge of the country to bring him safely to his destination.

Many were the times during the years before his death when he brought tremendously rich specimen rock to his Diamond Valley home after a trip through the mountains. The chunks of quartz were heavily flecked with gold, and Snowshoe often remarked to his wife that he would work the mine when his other work was over, but death overtook him before his daily duties came to an end.

On his deathbed Snowshoe said he could see the outcroppings of his mine from his bedroom window. Samples of the ore were in his home to prove that his story was more than a myth, and for years after his death the entire countryside was combed without success.

Every square foot of ground between Horseshoe canyon and Hawkins Peak was thoroughly covered by prospectors and friends eager to find Snowshoe's Lost Mine, but today the fabulous find remains one of those secrets that have caused hundreds to risk limb and fortune in the hopes of locating untold wealth. Along with Breyfogle and Gunsight, Snowshoe's Lost Mine is still undiscovered, still somewhere in the Sierras waiting to make some lucky prospector wealthy and independent.

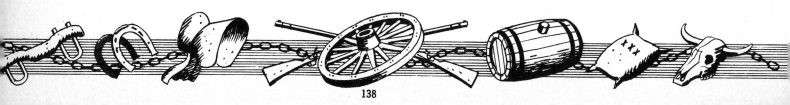

The Bride Stayed 3 Minutes

PIOCHE WAS SETTLED in 1864 and within the space of six brief years became the roughest, toughest, wildest camp in the entire West. Guns were the only law and Pioche made Bodie, Tombstone and other better known towns pale in comparison. Some 75 men were killed in gun fights before the first citizen died peacefully in Pioche!

In 1871 a young Illinois attorney arrived with his bride. For days they had been jolting over dusty desert roads, roasting in the daytime, and freezing during the hours of darkness. Wayside stage coach stations had little in the way of decent accommodations, often jamming all travelers into crowded quarters. The food was indifferent at best, the danger of renegade Indians always an unpleasant possibility, and the chance of stage coach holdups an equally nasty consideration. Since leaving Salt Lake City the stage had moved in the midst of a perpetual cloud of white alkali dust which filled the inside of the vehicle like a fog. It penetrated the lungs, eyes, clothes, bags, trunks, and possessions of every passenger. So when they dismounted finally in the center of the raw little camp at Pioche, it was with alkali reddened eyes, shortened tempers, and upset feelings which provided an emotional setting for the scene which then followed.

While the bridegroom handed down his wife from the stage to the board walk, a deputy sheriff standing nearby on the street corner espied three desperadoes standing on the other corners of the intersection. In the space of the few seconds required by the bride to walk across the board walk from the stage to the hotel door, the deputy drew his pistols, aimed, and killed each of the three desperadoes across the street!

The bride entered the building in an acrid cloud of blue gun smoke, accompanied by the echoes of the fusillade, the screams of the dying victims, and the shouts of the excited throng on the street!

Within three minutes the bride was back on the stage headed for home. Pioche was too much for her!

Old-timers used to wager on who would survive the day's shootings. The area was fantastically rich and produced more than $40,000,000 in ore. Excitement was always forthcoming. . . . In 1871 a fire burned part of the town and touched off 300 barrels of gunpowder which flattened the rest of the community and most of the population with it.

Pioche is still active, but is now law-abiding, friendly, and quietly progressive. Low cost power from Boulder Dam is expected to bring much growth to this colorful and picturesque area and many travel-experts feel a tourist industry could be built on the exciting relics of early day Pioche. Pioche rose to a population of 6,000 at one time and while it is now smaller, has enjoyed a steadier production from its mines than most camps and in many ways has brighter prospects for a prosperous future. Old-timers claim the camp "has only started."

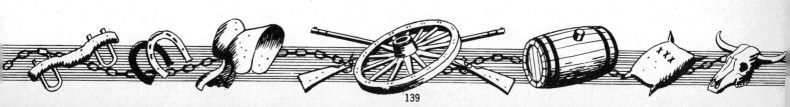

Embattled Mr. Lake

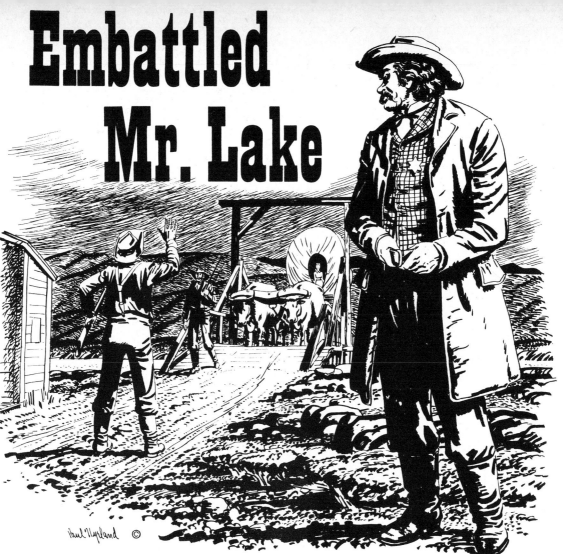

Paul Hyland ©

MR. LAKE stood in the middle of a pasture that, 70 years later, would be the heart of downtown Reno, and cursed the district court, the Washoe County sheriff's office, and fate in general. The county was trying to take away from him the great grand-daddy of the Virginia Street bridge, and it had been a beautiful paying proposition. Every time a husky miner or a Bonanza King in booming Virginia City wanted steak, it came from a critter which had to be driven from ranches in the north down across Mr. Lake's toll bridge, and up the road to the Comstock. And Mr. Lake collected from a dollar to a dollar and a half per head for every animal that crossed his bridge.

It had all started in 1859 when W. C. Fuller of Susanville put up some small buildings where the Riverside Hotel now stands, and operated a makeshift ferry boat across the Truckee. A few months later a rickety low wooden bridge replaced the boat, and the place was known as "Fuller's Crossing." It was a losing struggle, however, and Fuller, forced to sell his clothes for seed corn, spent his first winter wearing a blanket tied around his waist with a rope. In 1862 the bridge washed out, and discouraged Mr. Fuller sold out to M. C. Lake of Honey Lake Valley.

The newcomer was enthusiastic and energetic. He promptly rebuilt the bridge, and also opened a small store and tavern where trade became very brisk. He also charged toll when people or livestock used the bridge. The huge herds of cattle driven from the ranches of the north to feed Virginia City's growing thousands provided Mr. Lake with a little bonanza all his own. The place was now known as "Lake's Crossing." Mr. Lake's new bridge was washed out

in 1863, the same year he had built it. Undaunted he put up a better structure, and it lasted until high water took it out in 1867. Again he rebuilt. And then, on New Year's Day, 1870, he opened the first hotel in the Truckee Meadows, known as the Lake House.

Mr. Lake's troubles really came a year later. In 1871 his charter for the toll bridge ran out, and Washoe County was to take over ownership of the bridge and let the public use it without charge.

Mr. Lake couldn't bear to lose his beautiful bridge and his growing volume of toll charges. On one technicality after another he delayed the legal action of the county. Finally he dug a trench around the bridge, armed a guard over the place, and continued to take toll. Evidently this worked, at least briefly, for finally, in desperation, the county was forced to take the matter to court and filed suit against Mr. Lake.

The law upheld the county and Mr. Lake's bridge became public property. A year later (1872) the county replaced it with an ultramodern iron bridge which had quite a history of its own. This iron bridge stood at the Virginia Street crossing for 33 years. Then, as the present bridge was built in 1905, the old iron bridge was moved down to Rock Street. There it connected Mill Street with East Second Street until its downfall in the flood of 1950.

Little did Mr. Lake in his fight with the sheriff, or Mr. Fuller darting about in his blanketed kilts, dream the eventual fame of the crossing would be a legendary spot, celebrated in stories, books, plays, and motion pictures, where giddy divorcees were said to throw away their rings.

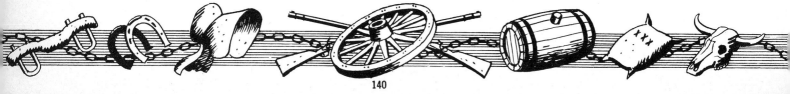

The 601

Paul Nyland

LAWLESSNESS HAD reached a peak in Virginia City during 1871! Cold blooded killings became the rule rather than the exception. Knives and guns were commonly used to settle the smallest disputes, and the Comstock was rapidly gaining a tough reputation! Seemingly from nowhere there sprang into being a secret organization known as the Six Hundred and One, a masked group of vigilantes, whose rapid dispensation of fatal justice was accomplished in the dead of night without benefit of court and jury trial.

Decent citizens had nothing to fear from the 601, but the seamy side of Virginia City soon learned respect for the organization which methodically terrorized desperadoes and killers. No one knew exactly who belonged to the 601, but it was presumed that the organization's membership was composed of the mining town's leading citizens.

Near midnight on March 24, 1871, at least a few Comstock citizens witnessed the 601 in action. To their knowledge, it was the first concerted effort of the secret group, and it served to notify the entire mining community that lawlessness would no longer go unheeded.

Late stragglers, homeward bound from Virginia City's night spots, were surprised as they approached the jail to see that building surrounded by a large group of armed, masked men. The stragglers who sought to approach picket lines were warned to "go back!" With the exception of that curt warning, not another word was spoken by the masked men who fingered their rifles as if they meant business. Mean-

while, well inside the picket lines, a group of some thirty 601 members had entered the jail, aroused the sheriff and jailer, taken possession of their weapons and proceeded on to the cell occupied by Arthur Perkins Heffernan, who a few days before had shot and killed another man in cold blood. Opening the cell door by the light of torches, the vigilantes told Heffernan, "Come out, we want you!" With no more ceremony than that, and with one boot missing, Heffernan was escorted out the back way to a shaft near the Ophir works. The noose suspended from a hoist frame cross-bar, was placed about his neck, and he was made to stand upon an old timber placed over the gaping shaft. When the signal was given the plank was yanked from under his feet, but Heffernan had anticipated the action, and just as the word was given he leaped high into the air in order that the force of his fall would bring quick death.

In the morning the coroner who went to the Ophir works to cut down Heffernan's body, found a note attached to the dead man's shirt. It was a small card upon which were scrawled the numerals "601."

This first example of swift justice was enough to prove that the vigilantes were serious, and the necessity for such fatal action steadily declined. Undesirables were presented with "tickets of leave" which meant that they were to stay away from the Comstock region. One man, served with such a notice, decided to return after a short absence. It was pure folly. The morning following his arrival his body was found dangling from the end of a noose which was swung from a mine flume. Pinned to his shirt was the 601 card.

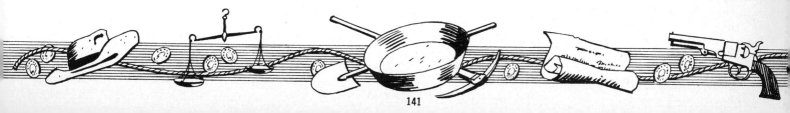

The Big Break

OVERPOWERING a handful of guards, twenty-nine men, including some of the most desperate criminals in the west, broke out of the Nevada State Penitentiary on September 17, 1871. For thirteen days part of Nevada and bordering California counties were gripped with terror as one of the frontier's largest manhunts developed.

Among the convicts who staged the big break were members of a gang which had been sent up for stage robbery near Aurora. Their conviction had been due in part to the testimony of an Aurora resident, Horace Poor. When the twenty-nine men scattered in smaller groups to make good their escape, some of the stage robbers headed southeast intent upon seeking revenge for their conviction.

They waylaid and killed sixteen-year-old Billy Poor, a mail rider and brother of Horace. Switching clothes with the dead youth, they left his body along the roadway dressed in prison garb, and then fled toward the Mono Lake country in California.

The killing of one man during the prison break, plus the wounding of others and the murder of Billy Poor, shocked the country. Hastily a posse was organized in Aurora and the convicts' trail was picked up south of Mono Lake. Meanwhile the town of Benton had been alerted, and the deputy sheriff with a ten man posse followed the gang's trail into Long Valley and up Mount Diablo Creek to the sheer granite walls of Convict Lake where a pitched battle took place. During the melee a Benton merchant and an Indian guide were shot. Armed with powerful Henry rifles, the escaped prisoners easily held off the posse.

Major Egbert of Fort Independence, some one hundred miles south of the battle scene, armed five soldiers and set out to join the other pursuers. Fearing capture because of the ever growing strength of the posses, the prisoners split up, seeking to slip away singly, but the watchful pursuers nabbed three of them by the name of Black, Morton, and a youth, Roberts. The latter received a serious head wound during the gunplay.

Realizing futility of resistance, the three were placed in a wagon, and Morton, upon his own request, drove the team to his own hanging. The posse members, soldiers and their prisoners drew up at an abandoned cabin and for two hours the convicts were questioned concerning the whereabouts of the other escapees. At length a vote was taken on each man. All present were in agreement that Morton and Black should be hanged, but the vote tied on Roberts and his life was spared.

By moonlight on the night of October 1, thirteen days after the big break, Morton and Black swung from a hastily erected gallows. The posse action had its effect. Within two months eighteen of the original twenty-nine escapees were either captured or killed. Not one of the other incidents, however, was packed with the battle drama or the impromptu necktie party at which the convict Morton, shook hands with his executioners before the hanging. Since that day, eighty years ago, the little lake at the base of the towering Sierra in Long Valley has been known as Convict Lake.

Chinese Jackpot at TUSCARORA

THOUSANDS OF Chinese coolies had been engaged by the management of the Central Pacific Railroad during the construction of the roadbed and the laying of steel rails across Nevada desert. When the project was completed the Oriental laborers had to look elsewhere for employment. It wasn't strange that some two thousand of them, stranded in Elko county, journeyed to the eastern slope of Mount Blitzen where Tuscarora was booming.

The district is said to have produced between twenty-five and forty million dollars in silver and gold ore. Chinese coolies, used to the hard work of labor gangs, are accredited with a major proportion of the Tuscarora output, since they gleaned metal from claims which had been abandoned, as the white miners moved on to more fertile fields.

During the fourteen years of Tuscarora's peak operation, the surrounding hills were completely denuded of scrube pine and sagebrush. Collection of the wood and tough brush required the services of almost as many men as did operation of the mines since the fuel was needed to maintain pumping and milling operations. Even today the hills for miles around the old camp are completely barren.

Tuscarora was considered a particularly rough camp and, to illustrate a fondness for the personal setting of troubles even after law enforcement agencies had been established, pioneers still tell the tale of a grudge fight:

A man named Rockafellow had been in the habit of using violent and profane language in public against a Major John Dennis. So widespread had Rockafellow's

abuse of his fellow citizen become that the zealous sheriff arrested the offender. Major Dennis immediately went to the justice of the peace and bailed Rockafellow out for the "pleasure of beating the tar out of him." Despite his pains and the desire for personal revenge in the form of fisticuffs, however, Major Dennis received a sound flogging!

The Crime of '73

VIRGINIA CITY'S barren hills fairly gushed silver in the sixties. So fabulous were shipments that the Comstock region gave aspects of becoming an unending source of white metal. Its profits built railroads and pipelines, established banks and governed commerce, paid a major portion of Civil War debts, established the stock exchange in San Francisco and constructed mansions on Nob Hill. This impact of wealth was apparent not only on a regional plane, actually development of the great ore bodies had farreaching international significance that resulted in foreign pressure from France and England to demonetize silver and bring about the "Crime of '73."

While mining tycoons were driving deeper shafts, unravelling engineering problems and arranging better transportation, France and England viewed this immense production of silver with apprehension. They commanded top position in world monetary circles . . . a position which depended entirely upon the gold standard. According to the theory of England's Sir Thomas Gresham, financiers must make money scarcer. Gold production was on the decline, while silver production was increasing rapidly. If silver could be demonetized then the U. S. Civil War bonds, blocks of which were held by France and England, would be worth more.

Emperor Louis Napoleon sent a special emissary to study the Comstock mines and his report furthered the anxiety of France. In 1867 the United States sent John Sherman, representative from Ohio, to the world monetary conference in Paris. En route to the French capital, Sherman visited English bankers and financiers. As a result he introduced a resolution at the conference which pledged representatives to establish the gold standard in their respective countries.

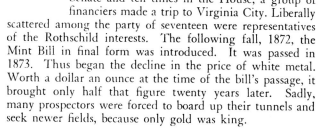

Outgrowth of this resolution was the so-called "Mint Bill," introduced in Congress in April, 1870. Its aim was to revise the mint and coinage laws of the nation. Whether by mistake, design or "expert routine" the silver dollar was omitted from the bill, and thus began the controversy which is still a western issue.

During the time the bill was on the floor of Congress, it was introduced nine times in the Senate and ten times in the House, a group of financiers made a trip to Virginia City. Liberally scattered among the party of seventeen were representatives of the Rothschild interests. The following fall, 1872, the Mint Bill in final form was introduced. It was passed in 1873. Thus began the decline in the price of white metal. Worth a dollar an ounce at the time of the bill's passage, it brought only half that figure twenty years later. Sadly, many prospectors were forced to board up their tunnels and seek newer fields, because only gold was king.

Joke at Columbus

Paul Nyeland

I T WAS New Year's Eve, 1873, at Columbus and women for the big dance were scarce. One American girl had come in from Fish Lake Valley, and a Chilean woman was playing a guitar as part of the orchestra. Except for the one girl, the floor was filled with men, half of whom were designated as "ladies" by the handkerchiefs tied around their arms.

When the fun was at its height, a Mexican named Victor Monega objected loudly to the Chilean woman playing for the dance. He snatched her guitar, smashed it to bits, and slipped out the door. A respected restaurant keeper quietly remonstrated with the Mexican over his conduct, and in a flash the latter slipped a long knife into his heart! Sobered by the sudden tragedy, the dance broke up, and the town hunted for Monega. In a few minutes they had him in the town jail.

Soon a delegation of leading citizens called on the two Columbus police officers, detaining them in a friendly fashion, with plenty of drinks all around. The officers were not harmed, but soon found they could not leave a room in which a party was rapidly developing in place of the ruined New Year's Ball. Columbus was bound to have some form of fun "to see in" the New 1874. Meanwhile, another committee quickly removed Monega from the jail and strung him up on a huge butcher's windlass normally used to hoist the carcasses of beef. It was a

cold, white, moonlit night, almost as bright as day. Out on the silvery marshes the coyotes howled. If Monega made any sound, it was drowned out by the hearty guffaws of the "committee," the creak of the huge wheel, and the sudden deadly tightening of the noose at his throat. The "committee" then joined the party with the officers and had a few drinks.

Two of the lynchers were sent out to cut the body down but soon came back. Although the corpse was visible in the bright moonlight from any point on the main street, the men claimed they had been unable to find Monega, and a few more rounds were enjoyed. Another "committee" went out "to search for Monega" and had just started to lower the body when it gave a convulsive kick, so they stopped and returned for another drink, reporting they could not find Monega.

It turned into quite a hilarious party, everyone enjoying the good joke on Monega. In the morning the corpse was tossed into a hole and covered. But it seemed Monega had the last laugh on the committee. A few days later a deputy sheriff from San Bernardino county arrived and advised them Monega was wanted for the brutal murder of a California family. A reward of a thousand dollars had slipped through the hands of the impulsive committee, a little too anxious to play a joke on Monega.

Belleville Hits Water

MANY A NEVADA town was built on a dusty, dry site, and only a desert dweller can appreciate the true value of water. Belleville in 1873 had no water and teaming it to town made it more rare and precious than gold.

Plans were made for running a pipe line for miles across the arid desert for the new eight stamp mill. Meanwhile, it was almost cheaper to drink whiskey. The whole town dreamed of a well, and hotel keeper Johnny Nicholson hired a crew and sank a shaft in the hope of getting water. The entire town was agog, and watched each shovelful of dirt for moisture. But it was a sad and discouraging piece of business.

One blistering day, when the perspiring well diggers were eating lunch in the hotel, enjoying a brief respite from the hot sandstorms and the white alkali glare, a few practical jokesters dumped a whole barrel or two of precious water down the well shaft. The well diggers soon returned to the job, and gave the first man down the shaft the usual brisk ride on the windlass bucket.

They were thunderstruck to hear a loud splash from below, and frantic screams for help from drowning! Men came tumbling from nearby doors. The loafing windlass crew sprang guiltily and excitedly from the cool shade. Unbelievingly, but hastily, they hauled up the windlass lifting to view a man soaked to the skin and shaking with panic. Instantly, as reason dawned, pandemonium broke loose. The town had water!

Men beat on tin pans. Work stopped at the new mill. Chinamen fired crackers. Proudly the owner of the new well opened his bar stock to the whole town! Liquor flowed in all directions. It rapidly turned into the biggest town drunk in many a year, all under a white hot desert sun.

Men lined up at the bar. Barrels were rolled outside in the dust and broached as there was no longer room indoors. It was the granddaddy of all gigantic parties.

And like so many good parties it was followed by a king-size hangover. Tottering up to the shaft the next morning, nursing throbbing heads and queasy stomachs, the well digging crew had the additional shock of discovering that all the water had seeped away! Realization of the hoax led to an outraged search for the identity of the jokesters but history fails to record their discovery.

Belleville finally got pipe line water from the mountains, but lost the milling business to Candelaria. When the Carson and Colorado Railroad was under construction the town enjoyed a temporary recovery and boom as a work camp and terminus. It had a few ups and downs but eventually gained the ghost town status of so many little mine and mill towns, which it keeps today.

Claim jumping at
EL DORADO

CLAIM JUMPING in a mining country is comparable to cattle rustling on the range land—a pretty dirty business! One of the best known examples of its far-reaching effects is the tale of the Queen City incident at Nelson, originally called El Dorado in southern Clark County.

In the middle seventies an organizer of doubtful scruples decided to jump the rich Queen City claim in El Dorado Canyon. To aid his plan he employed three desperados, promising each of them five thousand dollars for their participation. Secretly he arranged with one of them to kill the other two and even more secretly, he planned to murder the remaining one of the trio to cover up the entire transaction when the Queen City became his property.

One of the trio, who bore an English name, counted three killings to his record; the second, a Frenchman, was a known murderer and the third was a half-breed Indian lured into the scheme by the promise of dollars. Shortly after the three employees had succeeded in running off the Queen City's assessment workers, the Frenchman launched the second part of the scheme. One early morning as the half-breed was washing his face in front of their shack, the Frenchman put a bullet hole through his back. The half-breed grabbed a powder keg and knocked his assailant down, then fled to the cabin, grabbed a rifle and shot the pursuing Frenchman. Fearing repercussions the half-breed

made for the hills leaving a trail of blood.

Word got around in El Dorado that the Indian had attacked the Frenchman and the entire camp joined a posse search for the half-breed, following a blood trail which led them to a scooped out glory hole on a steep hillside. From this vantage point the half-breed held off his pursuers for two days and nights before the blazing sun and unbearable thirst caused him to give the sign of surrender. The first man of the posse to reach the glory hole put a bullet hole

through the half-breed's head and the rest of the citizens buried the body where it lay.

Acquisition of the Queen City by the man who planned the affair was a hollow victory for he was afraid to venture near the property after dark, and during daylight he swore that the ghost of the half-breed lurked there. Part of his fear is attributed to the fact that the Frenchman did not die from his wound and another of the trio also lived to plague the owner with the ever present possibility of revealing the entire story.

Hot Water Plugs

Paul Nyyland

AROUND 1875 the miners who dug in the Comstock Lode were "picked men," strong, young, vigorous, and paid the highest underground wages in the world. Working in the depths, they stripped to the skin in the terrible heat, swinging picks, shoveling, tramming ore, carrying timbers and risking their lives. Miners' skins were lily white from underground work in blinding steam. Heat radiated from the very rocks. Metalwork on cages blistered the skin on touch, and buckets of ice water and cold air were pumped through pipes to bring some relief to the men. These miners and all Virginia City residents since, have been proudly known to the world as "Hot Water Plugs." And they still glory in the title.

A typical experience indicates the courage of the men who worked under such conditions. A young miner was running a Burleigh drill in the face of a crosscut about two feet from the bottom, on the 2,000 foot level. Suddenly, without warning, the drill penetrated through the rock into a terrific stream of scalding hot water, producing 24 "miner's inches of flow." Instantly it spouted steam and hot water across the drift, spreading as it flew.

Soon the entire open space was filled by this huge jet of scalding water. It even blocked the crosscut where the man who had been running the machine stood. He was held close prisoner and dared not move. Hemmed in between the hot rocks of the tunnel wall and the great gushing waterfall of steam and hot water, he was in immediate danger of suffocation. But, thinking fast, he quickly opened the exhaust valve of his drill and a welcome blast of cold compressed air roared out, cooling and protecting his head and allowing him to breathe.

Meanwhile his fellow workers heard the commotion and rushed to the rescue. Bringing hip boots and gum coats, and hats, they outfitted their largest man. Protected by these garments from the hellish stream, he dashed through it, carrying an extra coat, boots, and hat. The trapped miner made a quick but cautious change, and the pair, taking a deep breath, made a joint dash for freedom.

They made it without other harm than superficial burns and badly scalded legs. And, according to newspaper reports published several days later "the torrent of scalding water was still roaring from the drill hole in the rock face." So much water and such high temperatures did much to make the cost of mining exhorbitant.

Lady Fence Builder

IN 1870 the grounds around Nevada's new capitol were a notorious eyesore. Several ladies' groups in Carson City had been complaining bitterly, and they now began to heckle the legislature with an organized drive for a beautification program. They were so persistent that in 1875 the legislators finally surrendered and authorized an iron fence and gates, set in a stone foundation. They also placed advertisements seeking bids in certain California newspapers.

The lowest, and successful bidder was one H. K. Clapp, and only after all the papers were signed, was it learned that the "H" stood for Hannah, and that the new capitol fence would be built by a A WOMAN!

Miss Clapp had carefully figured the cost of the fence when computing her bid. The iron-work cost her $5,500 and was fabricated by Robert Wood & Company of Philadelphia. It cost her $950 in freight alone before the sections of the fence could be unstacked from the little wooden cars of the V & T. But, by the first of August, in 1875, the first of the fence sections began to arrive and the lady fence-builder put her crew to work.

The actual assembling of the fence was done by Z. B. Ravenelle, a contractor, with the help of a single laborer. The foundation of the fence was made of sandstone blocks, quarried at the nearby State prison. Ravenelle smoothed and shaped them, and his man put them in place. In their enthusiasm to get on with the job, the helper laid a section

of foundation one day when Ravenelle was away, and the entire job had to be done over again but nobody seemed to mind. Holes were drilled by hand in the sandstone, the iron fence posts set in the holes, and then flaming brimstone or sulphur poured in to set them fast. On September 1, 1875, the fence was all in place and painted brown.

Hannah Clapp was easily an outstanding woman in pioneer Nevada. She came west with a covered wagon train in the late '50's and so interested a chief of friendly plains Indians, that he offered a valuable band of ponies to the wagon train leader in exchange for her!

On arrival in Carson City, she associated with Miss Ella Babcock and operated a co-educational school, a most unusual and radical idea in those days. The school operated successfully for about 25 years until the infant University of Nevada moved from Elko to Reno. At that time she was made a member of the faculty, and in fact, she and President LeRoy Brown were the entire staff of the university and taught all subjects.

In her later years, the name Hannah Clapp appears many times as a suffrage leader in Reno. She was an outspoken leader for women's rights and it was believed she contracted for the capitol fence just to show that a woman could be a successful contractor as well as a man. The infant frontier State of Nevada produced a surprising number of talented leaders in the struggle for women's rights.

Bullion Bullets

BROADHORNS BRADLEY was a worried man during the first week of September, 1875. Rumors had been filtering across the executive desk for a number of days telling of trouble with the Goshute Indians in Spring Valley. Now the situation appeared beyond the rumor stage. Governor Bradley was sincerely worried as he glanced at a letter before him demanding troops to quell an uprising at the Cleveland ranch.

Since his office was over three hundred miles from the scene of the incident, Governor Bradley couldn't possibly know that reports from eastern Nevada had been highly exaggerated. He did know that the pressing demand for troops and arms indicated near panic in the White Pine area, and his decision resulted in orders to Eureka and Pioche that Volunteers were to seize horses and supplies and march immediately to the relief of the besieged Cleveland ranch.

Preparations were under way for the "military" almost as soon as Bradley's orders arrived in Eureka. Ex-soldiers from the Civil War, Federal and Confederate alike were eager to answer the call. Guns and supplies were short, but ammunition for such a campaign was almost totally lacking. Eureka was a lead center and leaders of the expedition quickly applied to the operating companies for enough of the heavy metal to manufacture their own bullets. With a sly wink the mining men informed their visitors that it was impossible to dispose of company metal except through regular channels, but they reckoned as how it would be a pretty difficult matter to trace the stuff "if some of the stock piled bullion should disappear." The military took the hint. That night little fires glowed all over town as volunteers heated and molded their bullion bullets.

At daylight a marching column set off for Spring Valley, Not astride a conventional charger, but rather in the comparative comfort of a parasolled buggy, rode Major John H. Dennis, commander of the expedition. The tattered blue and grey uniforms of his volunteers strung out loosely behind his vehicle across the dusty sagebrush country, but as the sun caught their ammunition belts there was a distinct glint from the shiny silver bullets.

Upon reaching Spring Valley, Dennis and his volunteers came upon a goodly number of Goshutes, all apparently engaged in the peaceful occupation of pine nut picking.

The sight of marching men with ready rifles duly impressed the Indian band, and if any hostilities had ever been intended, they were dissipated right then. It was the last serious threat of Indian uprising in Nevada, and though it wasn't necessary to fire a single shot, Eureka's bullion bullets had served the cause of peace.

The Great Fire

Paul Myrland

A THIN BLACK SMOKE spiral, barely distinguishable in the half light that engulfed Virginia City at dawn October 26, 1875, rose haltingly toward a patch of sun on the high tip of Mount Davidson. Halfway to its goal a playful Washoe zephyr sweeping down the hillside, caught the column in its funnel and dispersed it eastward over Sugar Loaf.

A keen-eyed watchman could scarcely have determined its origin . . . and at six o'clock in the morning such an individual would have been hard to find. It was an hour before shifts changed in the teeming mines, the one period during Virginia City's hectic 'round the clock activity when the streets were deserted, a brief respite in which the camp prepared for another day. Yet the base of the column hovered above "Crazy Kate's" rickety wooden boarding house on A street, a shanty that clung to the steep slope of Sun Mountain, directly in the west wind's path.

Inside rivulets of fuel from an upset coal-oil lantern fed the flickering flames as they ate into tinder dry floor boards and gulped with increasing appetite upon tasting cotton batting in the chinked partitions and the smooth muslin base of curling wall paper.

Moments later sleepy residents, coughing smoke from their lungs, plunged from doorways. Fire bells clanged! Flames had attacked three other buildings with a terrible spurt of energy. Before volunteers could man the pumps a section of the city was already doomed by a sheet of white hot flame. The playful zephyrs turned to demons! Sucked into the vortex, they emerged in great puffs to scatter flaming debris over an even wider section. Hoistmen tied their whistles down and Virginia City awoke to screaming noise, confusion, and smoke. Snatching small possessions here and there, residents fled up the mountain slope for protection or joined volunteers to combat the fire. Within the space of six hours flames were to consume a half mile square area of the town with damages running well over ten million dollars.

Piper's Opera House, the International Hotel, the court house, all went up in puffs of smoke as the scorching flames raced through the city. Dynamiting crews commenced blasting to save valuable property. Detonations shattered windows and spewed forth even more fire.

At the sound of blasting, a throng gathered in front of the newly erected Catholic Church. The brick edifice was squarely in the path of the devastating flames. As dynamiting crews approached, the throng fought them back, reluctant to sacrifice their church. Suddenly, in front of the flames, appeared the giant figure of Bishop Patrick Manogue, famous priest of the Comstock, who had labored long to build the edifice for his people. He talked earnestly with a pleading mine superintendent, and then with sudden determination, ordered the throng to clear a way for the dynamiting crew.

Seconds later with a great roar the majestic church crumpled in a pile of rubble. Tears stained the smoke-blackened faces of Father Manogue and his people as they hastened past their house of worship, but as if by miracle the long tongue of flame that first reached the twisted wreckage, sputtered, and died. With new heart fire-fighters checked the flames saving the remainder of the town and all the producing mines.

Less than two years later, the new St. Mary's of the Mountains, a stately gothic structure that stands today, rose from the ashes where the Great Fire was halted.

The Field of Honor

BOOT HILL, better known in polite parlance as a cemetery, remains today the single thing of permanence to remind us of the violence that was once a part of the hard-bitten mining camps in which it flourished.

Hasty words, imagined insults, cheating at cards, and even more often, the jumping of claims, resulted in rather fatal consequences for those who were "slow on the draw." The first twenty-six graves which formed the nucleus for Virginia City's sizable cemetery resulted from this quick form of "lead poisoning."

But there were instances in which such disputes were settled by the more gentlemanly form . . . a carry over, no doubt, from the strong southern influence which was present in practically every boom mining region of Nevada. In fact, duelling became such a fad in the sixties that it was outlawed by statute and every public office holder was required to assert in his sworn oath that he had never actively participated in a duel, either as a principal or a second. Apparently legal aspects failed to curb the appetite for this manner of settling differences and many were the instances in which opponents met on a hillside or in a secluded ravine in the grey morning hours to uphold their beliefs on the field of honor.

Usually a slug in the leg, the thigh or the arm was deemed sufficient reprisal, but it was not always so. As late as 1876 when Jefferson Canyon in Nye county was at its mining peak this gentlemanly form of homicide took place in the true sense of the word.

An argument arose between two citizens of Jefferson and it was agreed that the matter should be settled with pistols. As per arrangement they met in the early morning at the place designated by seconds and were informed that each was to walk 25 steps in the opposite direction and then commence firing. Evidently the strain was too much, or else he miscounted; at any rate one of the adversaries turned on completion of the seventeenth step, took aim and fired. His pistol jammed and he found himself facing the deliberate aim of his opponent a split second before the fatal bullet struck him.

In the eyes of a grand jury that was summoned to investigate, the law is all right when it applies . . . the members failed to bring an indictment against the victor.

Comstock Soup Kitchen

WHEN THE Consolidated Virginia, greatest of the Comstock mines failed to pay its regular monthly dividend of $1,080,000 in January 1877, the market crashed, and thousands of prosperous citizens of Virginia City were reduced to begging in the streets.

Virginia City jails were soon jammed with vagrants, and hundreds of starving, desperate men roamed the town. Robberies became common and the threat of mob violence haunted the entire Comstock Lode.

Mrs. Mary Mathews, who ran a lodging house, and her close friend, Mrs. Beck, discovered good food was being wasted in restaurant garbage barrels, and these two women resolved to salvage enough for a soup kitchen. In a day or so they had converted an old carpenter shop into a kitchen, using borrowed stove and cracked china. They obtained clean left over food from restaurants, broken food packages from grocers, wilted vegetables, good meat scraps from butchers, day-old bread from bakeries. A dairy donated milk.

They obtained some cash donations, which enabled them, with the offer of food and lodgings in their own homes, to hire an old man as a dishwasher and a girl as waitress. Soon these two courageous women were feeding 500 people a day!

The surplus was given to the starving Paiutes and Chinese who were in need, and the whole town pitched in to give them help. The two women rose long before daylight, and often worked late into the night. They were helped by the hungry folks themselves, who scrubbed down the floors, chopped wood, hauled water, and performed much of the manual labor.

The "kitchen" kept entire families alive, and many of its patrons were women and children. At times men who were drunk were made to walk up and down in front, until cold sober, and then were made welcome with free food. For breakfast they served coffee, bread, butter, cold meats, hot potatoes, and hash. Dinner featured soup, vegetables, cold meat, bread, baked beans, pork and coffee. Supper was the same, except small bits of pastry were often included as dessert.

As time came for the soup kitchen to close, the two women put up hundreds of lunches for the men to carry as they hiked to other towns seeking work. Those who remained in Virginia City found the various churches and charitable organizations then organized to carry the load, and the soup kitchen project came to an end.

An almost identical incident took place in Las Vegas in 1932 when two newspapermen organized a similar soup line at the Busy Bee Cafe, until the Red Cross could take over. They gathered old bread, vegetables and groceries around town and fed hundreds of men for several days.

153

Pancake Peak

ONE OF Pioneer Nevada's most dashing bandits was A. J. "Big Jack" Davis, and even today the number of robberies he planned and carried out remains a mystery. So charming, pleasant, and personable was Big Jack that folks could hardly believe he was a criminal . . . until he was one of the band who held up the Central Pacific's Overland Limited in 1870, captured, found guilty, and served a sentence. Big Jack's personality even charmed the authorities and when he showed them where some of the loot was cached he got off with a very light sentence.

Before that he had led a stage coach robbery on Geiger Grade at midnight. A pretty young lady was aboard, so Big Jack provided her with carriage cushions and blankets and soothed her while his band blew open the express box. Then he opened a case of champagne and passengers joined bandits in a few polite toasts before Big Jack rode off in the night.

Big Jack and his men had a method using signal fires from mountain peaks at night to indicate the number of guards riding the stages. On this particular evening the southbound stage from Eureka to Tybo carried shot-gun messenger Eugene Blair and with him an extra messenger, Johnny Brown. Blair had never lost a gun fight with a bandit, and enjoyed a widespread reputation as a steady, crack shot with iron nerves.

As the big stage rumbled and creaked along the dirt road, a few miles north of Willows Station, Johnny Brown noticed a beautiful red star shining through the twilight near the mountainous horizon of the Pancake Peak. He mentioned it to Blair, adding that "it looked sort of double."

But down in the shadows of Willows Station, Big Jack and two of his men also decided it was a single light. The two signal fires placed so close they looked single was a blunder that would have tragic consequences. Big Jack had surprised the station hostler and a visiting rancher and tied them up inside. Now the signal fires incorrectly told him that only one shot-gun messenger rode the stage. They could already hear the horses coming up the road.

As the stage pulled up the bandits called out, "Eugene Blair, surrender!" For a moment the messengers thought it was a practical joke on the part of the hostler but when a second order demanded, "Get down and surrender" they knew. Blair jumped to the ground and ran around toward the open barn door. Two shots blazed but Blair had ducked. They passed over him, hitting Johnny in the leg.

Blair rolled over on the ground and Big Jack jammed a shot-gun into his chest but Blair brushed it away with his left hand and the two men scuffled. Finally they parted enough in the dark for Johnny, up on the stage to make out the two forms and he promptly shot Big Jack, wounding him so that he died in an hour or so.

The other bandits immediately ran for their horses and escaped in the darkness but were later captured with Tom Laurie, who had built the signal fires too close together.

Ward's Quick Justice

THE MINING CAMP of Ward in White Pine County leaped into existence in the spring of 1876 and soon became a bustling town since it offered a central location for commerce with the entire Ward district. Though lawlessness was prevalent in most new camps, Ward's citizenry managed to curb most of the troubles that had plagued similar mushrooming mining villages. Perhaps it was because the citizenry had a way of silent yet fatal treatment which soon indicated that the town was not going to wink its eyes at crime.

In the fall of the first year the town's even tenor received a sudden jolt when one of the leading citizens was murdered. A rough, who followed the new camps, had evidently put the squeeze on this respected businessman for some cash, and upon being refused lay in wait for his victim. When the latter passed down the street he was felled by a bullet.

The killing naturally caused a flurry of excitement, but unlike other camps where talk of lynching always followed such an affair, there was not even a hint of mob action, yet the following morning the rough's body swung from the limb of a tree on the outskirts of town. Various questionable characters soon quietly moved away after this demonstration. The local citizenry had handled the matter with dispatch and it wasn't until nearly a year later that the next hint of crime was dealt with almost as effectively.

The roads between Ward, Eureka, and Wells were teeming freight routes and the stages, operating along the same roadways, were doing a large business. In the fall of '77 as one of the stages approached town, the driver and messenger were brought up suddenly as bullets whistled over their heads and two bandits suddenly appeared in the roadway. Calmly the messenger directed two well aimed shots in the direction of the masked men. One of the latter dropped in his tracks while the other took off across the brush in an evident hurry despite leaving a trail of blood which impeded his progress.

Quick action of the stage messenger put a stop to any more robbery attempts. The second gunman was caught and imprisoned. Ward had a way of nipping crime before it got started, and old-timers feel that it was the experience of the town's citizenry, many of whom had seen a lot of raw western life in other camps and were determined to keep Ward free from such troubles.

The Christmas Dance

TWENTY-THREE people made up the little town of Bunkerville in 1877, as the first year of settlement ended at Christmastime. It had been a struggling year, with no time for fun or recreation in the face of a serious effort for sheer survival. But crops had been good. It was decided to celebrate with a Christmas Dance.

Bunkerville consisted of a community dining hall, built with rough planks, and six adobe walled houses, roofed with mud and tule leaves. A dance pavilion was built for "the Party," adjoining the community dining hall, with a floor of rough planks and two walls of canvas. The rear wall was actually one side of the dining hall, and the remaining wall was left open, with a huge bonfire lit nearby for light and heat.

A few rude kerosene lamps gave some illumination, and music was supplied by Ithaner Sprague with his accordion. Settlers came from near and far, by wagon, saddle horse, or on foot. Since there was no cash available, admission was paid in potatoes, pumpkin, squash, or other produce. This was piled near the musicians stand.

And since there were no baby sitters, every family deposited its infants in a long box behind the accordionist. Big tables groaned under stacks of refreshments for the dancers, who tromped and stamped with huge work shoes on the rough planking. The Mormon people have always loved to dance and this was their very first opportunity in more than a year.

They danced with such enthusiasm that every few minutes the floor was cleared so the rough pine splinters could be swept away. The dancing continued until daybreak, when weary couples sorted out their own slumbering children from the heap back of the musician, and made their way again by wagon, saddle horse, or foot, to their homes out in the sagebrush. It was the first dance and it had been a tremendous success.

Records tell this community experimented with joint ownership of all property, labor, and profits in a mild and friendly sort of "pioneer communism" from 1877 until the early 1880's when the experiment was abandoned and private ownership customs were adopted and of course continue to this day. Other primitive socialistic experiments also faded away, but the enjoyment in dancing of the pioneer years still continues as a community-wide form of popular recreation.

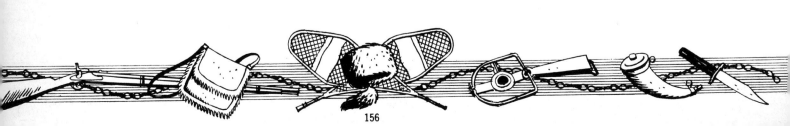

Still Unexplored

NEARLY SEVENTY YEARS ago, Absolom Lehman, pioneer eastern Nevada rancher, was hauling timber from the Snake Range to his valley home, when the off horse of his logging team stumbled and sank shoulder deep in the apparently firm hillside surface. Seeking a clear path down the mountain, Lehman had unknowingly driven his team over a crusty portion of earth where a series of underground caves rose within inches of the surface. Thin overburden gave way to the unexpected weight of the horse and Absolom Lehman became the first human to glimpse an underground art which nature had been carving and etching since days preceding the ice age.

The discovery aroused local interest. Lehman and others in the valley made preliminary explorations, but it was not until years later that the full importance of this subterranean wonderland was fully realized. It is now a national monument administered by the Park Service. Lights were installed to guide tourists through the twisting half mile length of beautiful stalactite and stalagmite formations to view the glistening fairyland that burrows two hundred feet below the surface. Even now some of the smaller chambers are not accessible to visitors since reaching them is a matter of arduous exploration. Various state agencies, and chambers of commerce in eastern Nevada have been interested in developing the caves as a tourist attraction of wide appeal.

Scientists say at least twenty-three thousand years have passed since the first water percolated through limestone and commenced carving Lehman Caves. The minute drippings may add only an inch each one thousand years to the size of the rare underground formations, yet some of the columns in the vaulted caverns reach a height of sixty feet.

In more recent years other caves have been discovered in the same area, principal among which is Whipples Caves, to date only partially explored. Many explanations for the caves exist, and most of them harken back to Lake Bonneville which once in the dim past inundated most of eastern Nevada and western Utah. Slightly off the beaten path, Lehman Caves nonetheless draw numerous interested sightseers, and with the eventual completion of transcontinental highway U. S. No. 6 the fame of these underground caverns is expected to vie with Kentucky's Wind Caves and New Mexico's Carlsbad.

LIGHT and H'IST!

AT THE WESTERN base of the Desatoya mountains, directly astride transcontinental U. S. No. 50 lies Eastgate, one of the best known early day stage stations, where travel-weary fortune seekers welcomed a night's rest, and cow-hands and trail riders would alight to "hoist" some liquid refreshment. A tufa block house erected in 1879 is still scarred with hundreds of names of those who partook of Eastgate's refreshment and hospitality.

The stage station had its fun with tenderfoot travelers, leaving many of them wide eyed in amazement at the apparent swiftness of western justice. A favorite stunt was the staging of a fictitious shooting. The victim, apparently "murdered" was carried out of sight and immediately the "killer" was seized and charged, not with murder, but with cattle rustling. Vaqueros of the nearby ranges thus succeeded in duly impressing greenhorns that the killing of a man was a trifling offense compared with cattle rustling.

While visitors gazed in horror the killer-rustler would be strung up before their eyes. Though the rope appeared to be stretching his neck, it had actually been cleverly con-

cealed around his shoulders. As the body dangled in the breeze, the avengers pretended to riddle it with bullets. Many were the travelers who set off again in the morning on their westbound journey, firmly convinced that they had seen an actual murder and lynching party. To say that they were duly impressed with the fact that cattle rustling was a heinous crime, is putting the statement mildly.

For many years, even after the turn of the century, Indians of the entire region used to gather at Eastgate in the narrow canyon mouth for their fandangos and pow-wows. The best reason for selection of the conference place seems to spring from the fact that George B. Williams, owner of the Eastgate ranch, used to provide beef for the barbecue which always concluded the gatherings.

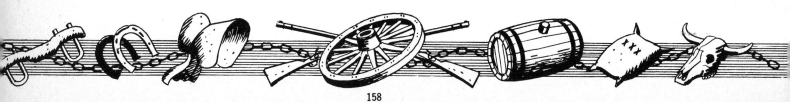

The Fish Creek War

DWARF CEDAR and nut pine, burned in kilns to produce charcoal, was the principal fuel for Eureka smelters during the boom days when tons of lead and bullion moved to market from the rugged little mining camp. Because of the undiminishing appetite of the furnaces, charcoal became a major business with Eureka.

In the late summer of 1879 all the scrub timberland adjacent to Eureka had been depleted and it was becoming increasingly necessary for the Carbonari (name applied to the Italian immigrants who manufactured the charcoal in their stone kilns) to move farther and farther away from the town to sources of timber supply. The greater hauling distance, in addition to the added expense of setting up new charcoal camps, clearly indicated to the Carbonari that their charcoal should bring greater returns at the Eureka smelters.

The mine managers and smelter operators failed to agree with the Carbonari viewpoint, however, and flatly refused to pay the thirty cents a bushel price which the charcoal burners requested. Standing firm, the mine managers stated that they would pay 27½ cents a bushel and no more.

Maddened by resistance to their request, the Carbonari marched upon Eureka, gathering sympathetic members of their trade along the way. On August 11, they took possession of Eureka in a-by-no-means peaceful manner. The Charcoal Burners' Union, which numbered several thousand men in its membership, prevented any deliveries of charcoal to the smelters. The rioters defied police authority and refused to allow the arrest of any of their numbers. In addition they completely controlled the charcoal pits thus making it impossible for mine owners to transport charcoal to the slowly dying furnaces.

The governor was urged to call out the militia to quell the "insurrection." Major Butler in San Francisco took the required action, but a lull ensued during which the Carbonari awaited expected action and prepared to enforce their stand.

On the sixth day after Eureka was taken over, a sheriff's posse of nine men attacked the charcoal ranch at Fish Creek about thirty miles from Eureka and opened fire on approximately one hundred Carbonari stationed there. Great excitement followed the clash. It was claimed that the Carbonari were well armed, but it was also noted that five of them were killed, six wounded, and that the sheriff's posse suffered not a scratch. A coroner's jury cleared the posse of blame, and the Fish Creek war brought a sudden end to the rioting as Carbonari returned to the kilns and once again charcoal was shipped to the smelters.

The Common Council Saves the Day!

IGNORING AUSTIN'S contention that its location on the Overland Trail plus the immensity of its mining wealth, made that thriving central Nevada city a "natural" rail center, the Central Pacific Railroad nonetheless laid transcontinental tracks ninety-two miles north of the Lander county seat. With the completion of the railroad the heavy freight which had once flowed through Austin, was diverted from the mining capital.

Isolated more than ever by a complacency which had failed to foresee this turn of events, the citizenry began to raise a cry for rail connection with the outer world. Such transportation, it soon became apparent, was the only guarantee to Austin's future. Freight from Battle Mountain was at the rate of $1.25 per hundred pounds, more if the roads were muddy. It was a sad blow to Austin's bright future, especially when commonplace ore was running seven hundred dollars a ton, and high-grade up to five thousand, a fabulous sum, even in comparison with the Comstock.

It remained for M. J. Farrell to revive the railroad fever in 1874 with plans for a narrow gauge from Austin to Battle Mountain. Lander county answered his impassioned pleas with the promise of a $200,000 subsidy provided the road could be completed in five years. Nevada's governor "Broadhorns" Bradley was opposed to railroads, but despite his violent veto of a legislative measure approving the project, Farrell succeeded in having the veto overridden. Real heartbreaks were still to come. Four years passed without action, capital simply couldn't be interested and the dream of a narrow gauge became "Farrell's Folly."

Pulses quickened when the Central Pacific evidenced interest in 1878, but again there was a lack of action, until suddenly on August 30, 1879, Austin was electrified by the news that the powerful Phelps-Stokes syndicate had taken over the project and would commence work at once.

It was a race with time, only five months remained to claim the $200,000 subsidy.

General Ledlie, the contractor, was a man equal to the task. Within less than a week, grading and track laying were underway. The new year passed and the race quickened. With seventeen days to go "end of the track" was still twenty-five miles from Austin. General Ledlie increased his crews. The thunder of spike mauls split the bitter cold desert nights as hundreds of laborers graded frozen ground and laid steel rails by the light of torches and bonfires in a frantic race with time. Their efforts were cheered by Austinites who drove out to the scene to urge them on.

On the fatal ninth of February two miles separated Austin's city limits and the toiling crews. It seemed a dismal situation until Austin's Common Council met behind locked doors in an extraordinary session. To claim the subsidy the tracks must be within the town limits by midnight. "Why not," said the councilmen, "extend the city limits to prepare for a town growth which the railroad assured." A unanimous "aye" was the aldermen's answer. Ten minutes remained before midnight when General Ledlie's crew crossed the new city boundary, the last half mile of track being laid on a bed of solid snow and ice, but what matter? The subsidy was claimed, and Austin had a railroad!

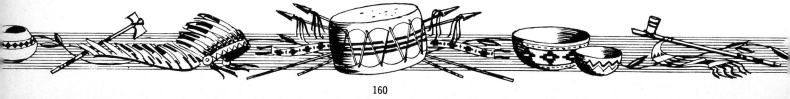

Logging by the V Flume

FANTASTIC WEALTH spewing forth in a continuous stream of silver from the Comstock Lode created many industries that were to thrive long after the deep mines were boarded up; others lived a short, full life, riding the white metal crest, and then disappearing almost as suddenly as they sprang to life.

Most fabulous of these was lumbering! The hydra-headed Comstock had an insatiable appetite for timber; a craving which consumed nearly seventy-three million feet of lumber each year, while necessary adjuncts to the business of mining gulped up another quarter million cords of wood annually.

It was a hunger that could not be denied! As men burrowed into the steaming depths of Sun Mountain, they were closely followed by sturdy timber sets to form a giant maze of underpinning for the thin earth crust above. Men's greed for silver was surpassed only by the mines' propensity for lumber. From Virginia City down through Gold Canyon and clear to the Carson River was another sprawling "above ground empire" of mills and hoists craving cord-wood to fire its boilers and treat the cold blue ore. Such was the demand that the eastern Sierra slope soon became denuded of stately pine, and even the roots were torn up and used for charcoal to feed the furnaces.

To J. W. Haines of Genoa goes credit for the develop-ment of an engineering marvel, designed to supply timber quickly and efficiently. His invention was the V-Flume, a sectional wooden trough, manufactured from two-inch planking with each section so carefully fitted that there were no apparent breaks in the entire length. The flumes followed natural grades, crossing canyons on overhead trestles, winding in gradual curves from the summits to valleys below. Through these flumes flowed a turbulent stream of water capable of carrying sixteen inch square timbers up to thirty feet in length at speeds from fifteen to sixty miles an hour.

At flume's end, Washoe and Eagle valleys, the timbers were shunted into stacking yards to await rail transportation over the V and T to Virginia City. Ten flume companies—operating in 1880—maintained eighty miles of flume.

The entire Lake Tahoe region became a logging camp almost as far as the eye could see. French Canadians, Italians and Chinese were employed as wood choppers in the forests. The rough timber was snaked to the lake or hauled by oxen-powered wagons. Here it was rafted to such mill points as Glenbrook where it was sawed into planks, scantlings, boards and square timbers, then trans-ported to the summit and dumped in the V-Flume trough for a swift, white spray ride to the valleys below, eventually to be buried in the caverns, stopes and drifts of Sun Mountain that men might mine more silver.

"She Burns Green, Rosie!"

SKIRTING the eastern rim of Death Valley, the Funeral range is as forbidding as its name, and the fact that these peaks look across a sullen desert toward Specter mountain and the Skull range further east, does little to encourage the spirit of adventure in timid souls.

But Aaron Winters and his frail, Spanish-American wife, Rosie, ventured into this ghostly country in the late seventies and settled in Ash Meadows. A hillside dugout near a tiny trickling spring was their homesite and they eked out a bare living from the unyielding desert. Often their fare consisted of mesquite beans and chuckwalla meat, primitive food of the Indians. Despite the rigorous life, Rosie maintained a link with civilization. An old starch box, used for a dressing table, supported a cherished collection of bottles that had once contained such feminine niceties as Magnolia balm and Florida water.

Despite the knowledge that his wife longed to leave the desert, Aaron Winters couldn't bring himself to quit his prospecting and settle down to city life. Deep in his mind was the thought that somewhere in this barren country untold riches were waiting just beyond his grasp.

One night in 1880 a lone prospector wandered upon the Winters' Ash Meadows abode. As customary on the desert, the Winters asked the prospector to share their meager evening meal, and after supper the wanderer began telling of the Borax discoveries further north around Columbus.

Listening intently, Winters asked numerous questions concerning the tests that would prove the presence of borax deposits. In detail, the visitor enumerated the ingredients, which, when mixed with borax and fired with alcohol, would produce a green flame.

No sooner had the prospector departed than Aaron Winters took off on a long trek to San Bernardino to obtain the chemicals. Upon his return, he and Rosie travelled by foot over the Funeral range into Death Valley where Aaron suspected the existence of borax. Making camp late in the evening at Furnace Creek, they scooped out a borax sample and mixed the powdered chemicals.

In the eerie desert darkness, streaked only by the pale light of the moon, Aaron fired the sample. Breathlessly they waited. Then he shouted, "She burns green, Rosie, we're rich!"

The test was accurate. Within a short time the properties he located were sold to William T. Coleman and Company for twenty thousand dollars, and Coleman started the Harmony Borax Works on the floor of Death Valley. It was this property, the result of Aaron Winter's green flame, that later obtained prominence through twenty mule team transportation.

The Slim Princess

RAILROADS WERE a booming business in Nevada during the eighties. Short lines such as the Virginia and Truckee, made fabulous fortunes for their owners. The great Central Pacific was doing a thriving transcontinental business, and little feeder lines which hauled Nevada ores and bullion to the main line railroad, were repaying owners' investments at an amazing rate. It was a crazy decade of speculation in railroad building when investors could visualize fortunes through the medium of transportation.

A child of this great desire for expansion was the Carson, Colorado Railroad, fondly called the Slim Princess. Organization of the company was completed in 1880 with Henry Yerington as the builder and Darius O. Mills as the financial "angel" who supplied the money from his New York office. By late spring of 1881 a hundred miles of trackage had been completed through the desert regions from Mound House, just east of Carson City, to Hawthorne on Walker Lake. The road was pointed for the Colorado river to tap the great potential mineral resources of half the State of Nevada, but for some reason revenues on this first one hundred miles failed to meet expectations. Instead of pursuing the original course the roadbed took off toward the mining country surrounding Candelaria. It wound up and over the White Mountains, finally coming to a halt at Keeler, California, on the shores of Owens Lake, three hundred miles from its starting point.

Wiseacres insisted Yerington had lost his compass and that the Carson, Colorado should change its name to the C and O since the letter O symbolized its destination—nothing.

Upon its completion, D. O. Mills came out from New York to ride his Bonanza line. After traversing the entire route Mills told Yerington "either this line was built three hundred miles too long or three hundred years too soon!"

And so it proved to be, at least financially. A few sporadic shipments of ore from Esmeralda county, bolstered now and then by rich rock of the Darwin area, kept the railroad running. When Tonopah was discovered and Sodaville became a freighting center, the Carson, Colorado was quite busy, but as mining dwindled and highway transportation took over most of the traffic, the Slim Princess became more of a sentimental connection with the mauve decade than an actual transportation arterial.

Many are the Nevadan's who remember riding the route to Keeler when the fireman would get out to put ashes on the icy track so the little engine could gain traction over Montgomery summit, and just as vivid are the memories of times when passengers and crew would ride in the open door box car taking pot-shots at jackrabbits along the right-of-way; when the engineer would stop the train if someone's hat blew off, or pause for an hour or two while the conductor, later a governor of Nevada, drove by buggy to his sweetheart's ranch for dinner.

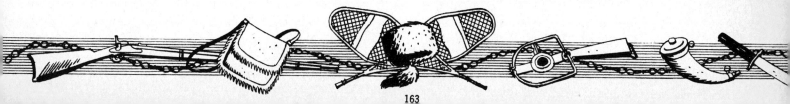

Milton Sharp

Gentleman Bandit

Paul Nyland

FAMED FOR his charming manners, his good looks, and his cultured habits of speech, Milton Sharp made a specialty of single-handed robberies of the stages along the Smith Valley Road from Carson to Bodie and Aurora. In June 1880, he robbed a stage near Wellington and while being hunted for that holdup, broke his rule of working alone for the first time, and had a helper.

A detective tracked him by moonlight to his hideout, and Sharp's man opened fire. The detective returned the fire, killing the man, but Sharp then ambushed the officer, wounding him in the arm. In the resulting melee, Sharp caught a nearby stage driver off guard and made away with the big express box of bullion bound for Carson!

Stories vary, but either laundry marks on the slain man's clothing, or his carpet bag led detectives eventually to a San Francisco rooming house where Sharp usually took his loot following each robbery, for living in the greatest luxury available on the coast! Here Sharp was arrested, taken to Aurora and jailed.

His keepers let him have a pen knife with which he carved toys for the jailer's children, 'til one dark night he used it to dig through the mortar, lifted the bricks out, and squeezing quietly and breathlessly through the wall, escaped. But again he was caught, and returned.

This time he was shackled with heavy leg irons, but again he made a desperate escape on a cold November night, and dragged the heavy shackle across the bleak, freezing desert, to Candelaria. Cautiously he threw sand on the window of a friend, hoping to get help before he froze to death, but the sheriff arrived at just the wrong moment. And now he went to the penitentiary at Carson!

Again he escaped, and dropped completely out of sight. He had succeeded in reaching New Orleans, started an honest business, married, and had two children. Respected and well liked for years, he relaxed and enjoyed life until during a Mardi Gras he saw, and was seen, by a man from Nevada!

He informed his family he was "called away for an indefinite period," went to a nearby county and gave himself up. He was quietly returned to the Nevada prison where he appears to have been a model prisoner with no more escapes until, a few years later, Governor Colcord pardoned him.

He then returned to his family, became a respectable citizen, and records indicate he lived out his life as a popular and honest man.

164

Blue Dick's Funeral

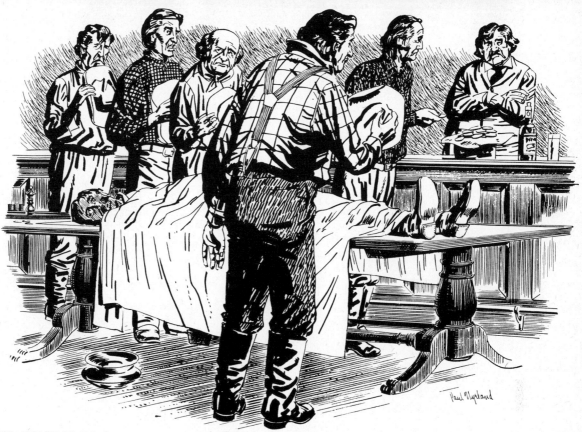

ENTERTAINMENT IN the raw, new mining camp of Candelaria was scarce, so the residents went to extreme lengths at times to provide original forms of diversion. One of the most widely told tales, and later related by Wells Drury, was one concerning Richard (Blue Dick) Hartman, who had been in a mine blast accident which peppered his face with gun powder, resulting in a vivid blue complexion.

Blue Dick came to Candelaria with the reputation of a fearless gun fighter on the Comstock. He was envied, hated, and feared by a man named Joe who was a great bully and hanger-on at the Northern Belle Mine, and the Roaring Gimlet Saloon.

One morning, the story went around the camp that an unknown gunman had killed Blue Dick, and the body had been laid out in McKissick's Saloon. Most of the miners rushed down to see, and the barroom soon filled to capacity. Sure enough, over in one corner reposed Blue Dick, laid out in state on a gaming table. A sheet covered the body except for his big brogans, showing he had died with "his boots on."

The crowd began to eulogize the departed and it was decided he should have a "genuine first class funeral." The barkeep put up the first twenty dollars for the house, and once the ball started rolling, the crowd began to toss contributions into Dick's stetson which lay on the table beside him. When the pile of money overflowed out of the hat, onto the table, and finally on the floor, one of the boys asked to see the man who had been the pride and fear of Candelaria.

The sheet was pulled back, and there lay the hero, steel gray eyes fixed on the ceiling. Just as one spectator thought he saw an eye quiver, the right eye of Blue Dick solemnly winked! A shout went up, and Dick rose to a sitting position. He got up, swaggered to the bar, and as

the barkeep walked over with the heavy hat of money, he roared, "Set 'em up." The cheering crowd then proceeded to drink up the entire proceeds of Blue Dick's funeral fund.

By now it was time for the second shift to come off work at the mines. Blue Dick hastily returned to the table and the sheet was spread over him again. As the boys came down the street they were told the sad news, so they hastened down to see the body and to contribute to the funeral fund. It was just about this time that Bully Boy Joe appeared. Looking for the barkeeper, he saw the crowd milling around the body on the table. One miner spoke up, "Joe, our old friend Blue Dick is no more." But unlike the others, Joe had no praise for his rival.

"It's lucky somebody plugged him," he announced, "or I might have had to do it myself, for the good of the camp."

At these words, Blue Dick sprang up from the table, enraged. Draped and entangled in the sheet, he made a dash for Joe. The latter, thinking he had seen a ghost, turned ashen, and finally finding strength in his legs, bolted through the open door and headed across the desert for Columbus. Dick was right behind him, cursing, shouting, and shooting but fear lent such wings to Joe's legs that he outraced the danger. Dick gave up the chase and returned to drink with his friends who had so openhandedly contributed for his funeral.

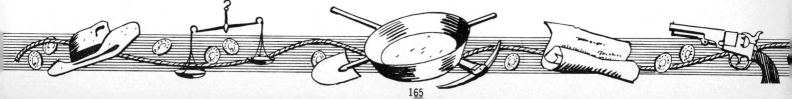

Cherry Creek's Match Race

CHERRY CREEK, like most mining towns of the '80's, was plentiful with cash money when anyone made a proposition that sounded like a good bet. The miners from Star Hill, usually flush on pay-day, were ready to risk their earnings on most any type of sporting event. Favorite by far was a good horse race!

Such was the interest in racing that Star Hill miners had acquired a little saddle horse which had never been beaten in a match race and they were willing to back the pony's speed with their pay checks. Aware of this desire for competition, Keough, a rancher who resided near Cherry Creek, quietly arranged with a friend in Hamilton to import a speedy horse named "Muggins," which he knew could outrun the Star Hill pony.

In due time Muggins put in an appearance in Cherry Creek disguised as a pack animal, and, within a few days Pat Keough had arranged a match race with the Star Hill saddle horse for a small bet, expecting to clean up the following day with heavy side bets.

Noting that Muggins was a newcomer to Cherry Creek, the Star Hill miners were just a bit leary about betting

heavily on their own pony until they had some sort of an idea concerning Muggins' speed. So, at midnight on the day prior to the race, a few of the Star Hill miners stealthily took Muggins out of the stable for a pre-race match with their own entry.

Pat Keough had been wise enough to figure on just such skulduggery and he had taken precautions earlier in the evening by nailing a four-pound shoe on one of Muggins' back feet and removing a front shoe. Then Keough had concealed himself in the sagebrush to watch the trial heat.

Of course the Star Hill entry won in a walk and the miners were overjoyed. The next day they appeared in town, pockets heavy with "betting money." Before the race got underway seven thousand dollars was riding on the outcome.

Muggins loped home to an easy victory just as Keough had known he would, and the puzzled Star Hill miners watched their money change hands. They hadn't reckoned with the fact that two could play the same game, and in the dark of the prior midnight they had neglected to notice that Muggins was running under a severe handicap.

Pickhandle Gulch

FROM '64 until the early eighties nearly twenty million dollars worth of silver and gold ore lay sweltering under a yellow-white alkali blanket at Candelaria awaiting development.

In the closing year of the Civil War a Mexican prospector discovered unmistakable signs of silver deposits seven miles from Rhodes Marsh in Esmeralda county, and a year later laid claim to the most promising portion of the prospect. But, for some strange reason, no steps were taken toward development and the property was forgotten until some five years later when it was re-discovered.

Like any new strike Candelaria flourished since gold as well as silver ore proved a valuable part of the deposit. Before long the Northern Belle became one of the state's leading producers.

Problems of providing for the ever increasing influx of miners and their families were multiple. As soon as the Northern Belle proved its worth telegraph lines were strung across the dry hot desert to Candelaria. The townsite was so barren of vegetation or water that the telegrapher had to seek out the 1700 foot level of the Mount Diablo shaft before he discovered a spot damp enough to attach his ground wire.

Nine miles away a tiny spring became almost as valuable as the mineral properties. Water hauled to Candelaria sold for a dollar a gallon, and even at that price was in great demand. Realizing the potential of the camp, the White Mountain Water Company set about running a pipe line to Pickhandle Gulch, just below Candelaria. At the same time the Carson-Colorado railroad commenced a feverish race with the water people to bring train and freight service to the new camp.

By 1882 Candelaria was the largest town in Esmeralda county and the race between railroad and water company to bring their services to the flourishing camp reached a frantic pitch.

On February 25 a trickle of water began flowing into the reservoir at Pickhandle Gulch and the price of this precious commodity immediately tumbled from one dollar to five cents a gallon. A week later the first train of the C and C rolled into the station and Candelaria was able to shed its role of outpost town.

One of the immediate effects in the transformation to city status was the sign Barber Leo Eberle put in his window. It announced "baths at a reasonable rate . . . Hot water $1.25 . . . cold water 75c."

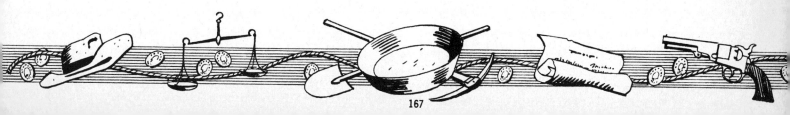

Chieftain's Death

SOME PEOPLE believe when old Chief Winnemucca, the Great Poito of Pyramid Lake Battles, lay dying, he really wanted his young squaw and his baby to be with him in the hereafter. Others have maintained the old chief really thought his young wife had bewitched him. At any rate he accused her.

We know that the time was October 1882; at the south end of Surprise Valley, over the line in California. And the young squaw, realizing her fate tried suicide, but was cut down from her attempt at hanging. Promptly she was taken to a spring, given a ceremonial bath, sprinkled with fine ashes. Then she walked, barefoot and naked, to a low hill covered with sagebrush. Here a cleared space of 100 feet in diameter was ringed with sagebrush fires. And here she was tied in the center of the circle, one ankle secured by a buckskin thong to a low stump, a few inches high. Eyewitnesses report she held her two-year-old baby in her arms, a bright eyed papoose.

A neat pile of stones, a little larger than baseballs, lay near the clearing. The Indians joined hands and began to swing around the circle of fires, chanting as they danced. Soon one Indian stepped into the circle and gave a long ceremonial speech. He stopped, approached the terrified squaw, seized the baby by the heels, whirled it around his head, and dashed its head against a rock, crushing it to death. Then he silently stepped back into line.

Again the Indians chanted and danced around the circle, until the same Indian came opposite the pile of stones. Stepping forward, he picked up one and threw it, striking the squaw heavily in the side. He took his place again and the next Indian threw. Again and again this was repeated until the squaw was lying unconscious on the ground. Then one Indian raised a huge boulder on high and crushed her head. The two bodies were then covered with piles of sagebrush, and a fire lighted which was kept roaring high all night.

Back in the brush teepee, old Winnemucca lay wrapped in rabbit skin robes, with his feet covered with warm ashes. He visited briefly with his grown children while they fanned him with brushes made of sagebrush twigs in the smoke-blackened wickiup. The place was packed with people. He was anxious to learn of the ceremony and fell silent after receiving a full report. Presently he turned his face to the wall, and in a day or so, he too died. His burial place is presently unknown.

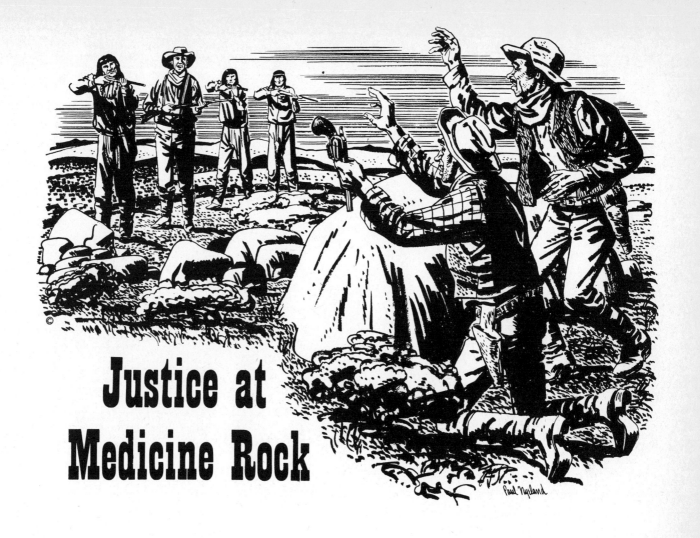

Justice at Medicine Rock

W HEN TWO Nevada bad men named "Rockwell" and "Tex" started out to make a stake in 1882, they didn't care how they made it. Whether it was for horses, or guns, or just for sheer "sport" nobody knows, but they began by slaughtering an Indian family in the Armagosa Valley. One little boy, left for dead with a pick buried in his side, eventually crawled to help, gave word and finally recovered.

Meanwhile Rockwell and Tex cached extra rifles and horses at Lida's Little Mill, and rode up to Silver Peak. They were in the act of staging a holdup at Chiatovich's store when a levelheaded Mexican named Antone Bacock opened fire on them, and killed one of their horses. The bandits rode double and tried to reach their cache.

Evidently they were cut off from their extra horses by Bob Stewart who was operating Little Mill. At any rate the bandits fled south on foot, armed only with revolvers. Word instantly flashed out on the Indian "grapevine" the same vicious white men who had so brutally massacred the little Indian family were the same group of men now described as escaping bandits.

So Indians, Shakespeare, Black Montezuma Dick, and Butcher Jake left Lida in hot pursuit. They soon got within range but the bandits were clever at using big boulders for cover, and were excellent marksmen with their revolvers.

The hunt soon turned into a chase, with life or death hanging in the balance. Relentlessly Stewart and his three Indian companions followed the bandits, firing every time the desperate men exposed themselves. They in turn invoked every trick possible, as they retreated through the desert. Although firing was heavy, progress was fairly rapid, until finally the bandits' ammunition gave out in the vicinity of a huge Medicine Rock held sacred by the Indians for ceremonial purposes.

Here the bandits were cornered and helpless to defend themselves. The four grim hunters came closer and closer, and despite pleas of mercy, relentlessly shot them down. Rocks were piled on their bodies, and in recent years passersby claim to have seen their bones, still mingled with the boulders not far from the sacred Medicine Rock.

Disaster
at Genoa

A LONG WINTER was almost ended in the little town of Genoa, when on the night of March 16, 1882, an amazingly heavy snowstorm struck and continued falling all night long. About 4:00 A. M. it piled so deep that the steep slopes above the town could no longer hold it, and with a shattering roar, an avalanche broke loose high and to the left of Water Canyon.

The deep rumble of the plunging mass of snow, ice, rocks, trees, and brush had barely awakened the pioneer families below, when it struck, and as it swept over rows of homes, it left death and destruction behind. First in its path was a cabin in which an Indian family of six were sleeping. They never awakened and later were found dead, all in bed. The next house was sheared off so cleanly that Mr. and Mrs. Minrod Bowers were killed as they lay in bed, but two men guests who slept on the floor escaped, one with a broken shoulder, the other uninjured. The wreckage of this house was deposited down in the main street of Genoa.

Far below, Mr. and Mrs. Borline heard the roar and raced to safety with one child, but another youngster was smothered in the snow. The Gray family next door were alarmed and escaped, too, but their barn was demolished and their home smashed badly. At daybreak they found their horse, standing bewildered, nervous, but unscratched, on the top of their house, some 14 feet above the street level, and it took them three hours to get him down.

Other homes were smashed, other people injured, but the freak slide was no sooner over than the little town started digging out. Lawrence Frey, the town milkman, drove his herd of cows to and fro, packing down the snow to allow men to work. Only the tips of the cow horns could be seen above the snow. Searchers ran iron rods down through the snow, their dogs sniffed for the scent of dead or injured in the resulting holes, and then crews of men went to work with shovels. It was several days before all bodies were found and many weeks before the wreckage of the shattered homes was removed from the main street and rebuilt, back high on the slopes above. Genoa recovered however and soon took its place again as an important Nevada city.

Comstock Traffic

I T WAS NOVEMBER 14, 1885, and the good people of Virginia City were all excited about the reckless driving and dangerous traffic on the Comstock. There was even talk of a safety program! And then came a traffic accident which set the whole territory on its ears.

Virginia City is built on a steep hill, and streets running down it are virtual cliffs. Fill these narrow thoroughfares with excited teams and anything could happen. Down from C street ran D street, where deliveries were made to the rear doors of many important C street hotels, restaurants, and stores, and to the front doors of more dubious forms of enterprise along D street.

The morning of November 14th a swill cart, piled high with barrels of garbage rattled down D street. Something frightened the nervous horse and he bolted, bit in teeth. Two boys were driving the swill cart, and one of them, young Martin, instantly leaped to safety. But Pat Hanifan stuck to the seat. Between Sutton and Union streets the swill cart reached a terrific speed, and at that moment, plunged broadside into an overloaded vegetable wagon, creaking behind a laboring four-horse team.

The splintering crash could be heard clear up on the Divide! Tons of garbage and fresh vegetables were littered for scores of yards in all directions.

Young Hanifan was catapulted from the swill cart, landing on his head and suffering a long scalp wound and bruises about the legs. The swill cart rebounded several feet in the air, hurling additional garbage into the doors and windows of several buildings. The blow killed one of the wheel horses on the vegetable wagon and dashed the two riders, Luigi Picietti and Natale Menante, to the ground. Picietti's leg was fractured and Menante dislocated an ankle and suffered bruises on the face. Both men were immediately given first aid by Dr. Zangerle, who announced they would soon be up and about.

Meanwhile, the remaining horses of the vegetable wagon team went completely hysterical and began to plunge violently, dragging the shattered wagon and dying wheeler across Sutton avenue. There spectators seized them and quieted them, until they were soon unhitched and led away quietly.

The vegetable wagon and team belonged to "Black John," an Italian rancher "on the Carson River below Cooneys." The swill cart was the predecessor of the garbage collector of today, but instead of paying to have garbage removed, it was deemed a favor to the person who gathered it, to "give him your swill" for his hogs. Regular collectors of swill were always on hand and actually competed for the privilege of hauling away garbage.

Emma Nevada

PIONEER NEVADA produced one truly great opera star, and she never forgot her childhood friends and companions. When, after triumphs all over the world, she returned to Austin on December 4, 1885, a special train bearing leading citizens travelled with her. She was met at the station by a gaily decked carriage, drawn by all the young blades in town. The Lander Guard Band struck up "Home Sweet Home," and she swept in triumph up the main street. The whole town heard her concert that night in the old Methodist Church, loaded her with massive floral tributes, and rocked the building with applause.

Earlier she appeared in Virginia City under similarly enthusiastic conditions, where 2,000 Comstockers cheered. In Reno the whole town lined the station platform just to see her private car pass by. Her trip to Nevada was made at her insistence, as part of a triumphant tour of America after the Queen of England had given her a diamond necklace worth $100,000.00.

Emma Nevada was born Emma Wixom at Alpha Diggins, California, February 7, 1859. Her father was Dr. Wixom, originally of Michigan, and her mother was a dealer in a pioneer gambling hall. In 1864 the family moved to Austin, Nevada, and the little girl, who had been singing to the birds and to the music of the camp blacksmith forge, now found herself singing "John Brown's Body" at the parade of the famous Gridley sack of flour. Her father was one of the Gridley auctioneers, and very prominent in Austin.

Little Emma sang at the dedication of the Methodist Church and attended the old brick school. Her mother died when she was 13, and a few years later she entered Mills Seminary (now college) and there continued her study of music.

Her early life in Austin had been very happy, and she also thoroughly enjoyed Mills, where she remained to do postgraduate work in languages.

In 1877 she went with a group to Europe, but remained to study music under Mme Marchesi in Vienna where her voice was described as "wonderful." Her father soon joined her, and later managed her concert career in Europe, and some of her tours in America. She was an instant success and tremendously well liked everywhere. She was married in Paris, sang at the coronation of King George, and became a very great and gracious lady of tremendous popularity on both sides of the Atlantic.

But no matter where she travelled, or to what heights she reached, she never forgot her childhood in Nevada, her pony rides among the desert wildflowers, and her many friends in the sagebrush State. She often described pioneer Nevada to her European friends and for years was an informal "ambassador of good will for the entire State of Nevada." She died in Liverpool at the age of 81, on June 26, 1940, a gracious old lady, loved by all her friends and remembered by oldtimers in many mining camps.

Taxpayer's Journey

TAX PAYING has always been a serious business, but in 1886 in the rugged desert State of Nevada it often had melodramatic overtones. When Aaron Winters reached old age, he quit his mining and borax activities in the area around Death Valley and "retired" to the comparative ease and quiet of running a ranch in Pahrump Valley. But once a year the old man had to drive from Pahrump, in the extreme southern end of Nye County, to Belmont in the northern tip, to pay his taxes.

It was a grim trip of three to four days each way, through some of the roughest, most arid desert on the continent. He drove his team by way of natural watering places, and his route included stops at Silver Peak and the old San Antone Station (northwest of Tonopah in the San Antone Desert). This station and a mill had been built in 1865 and camels were used to haul salt there from the marshes at Rhodes and Columbus. It was a busy and colorful spot when old man Winters spent the night there in 1886 to feed and water, and rest his team on his way to Belmont to pay his annual taxes.

Winters was a tough old rooster and had already killed a man or two before his famous borax discovery in Death Valley. This morning at San Antone he rose early, took his tax money bag of golden eagles from his pillow, stuck his revolver in the holster, and went outside to his team. He threw the money sack in the jockey box of the buckboard wagon, where he could drive and keep an eye on it at all times, left his team a few moments to get a bite of breakfast and to pay the station keeper. Naturally light on his feet, he stepped noiselessly to the door and found a large, red haired tough going through the jockey box and in the act of lifting out the sack of gold! Winters beat him to the draw, firing once and killing the bandit instantly. The body lay covered with a blanket on the board walk for another day until the coroner arrived from Belmont and ruled the killing "self defense." A so-called "Black Bart," who had been an accomplice of the dead thief was jailed in connection with the attempted robbery, but escaped and left the country.

The inquest over, Winters again hitched up his team and drove on across the desert to Belmont, where he turned his golden eagles over to the treasurer without incident, and started again on his return journey back to Pahrump. To him, it was all in the course of a trip to pay his taxes.

Later the incident was retold, and in the telling it became embellished until several versions are in circulation. The most widely told account (but not supported by sufficient facts), has it that Winters expected to be robbed and he resorted to strategem. He was said to have strapped a worthless gun in holster to the dashboard of his wagon, and hidden a very fine Navy revolver under the seat cushion. Near Belmont he was held up by two robbers who made him hand over his cash and dismount. Putting on a show of fear, Winters made his captors jeer and laugh. One of them seized the worthless gun and turned to show it to his partner. In that instant the old man snatched up the good revolver and killed the nearest robber. The other begged for mercy, and walked in front of the wagon into Belmont. He was said to have worked on Winter's ranch later in Pahrump. Few known facts support this latter version.

Pot Shots at Pahrump

AMONG THE FAMOUS dead-shot gunmen of the early west, there is a special niche reserved for one of the quickest on the draw, one of the most deadly of them all. For Gordon Ellis not only dared his victims to draw first, and then moved almost faster than the eye could follow; he not only **never** failed to hit where he aimed; but he had an aversion for murder . He always crippled his men by shooting them in the leg!

Ellis had sold a borax claim near Death Valley, and then dropped over into lush Pahrump Valley for a visit at Bennett's Ranch. Here were big orchards, fresh green vegetables, and much green whiskey. It was a real oasis to the prospectors and miners from the parched and blistering deserts. Here, as usual, was a large crowd of men getting a brief refreshment from the arid country. And here Ellis ran into trouble.

The first day he had an argument with a Mexican, and, according to his custom, promptly shot him in the leg. Legend has it that there were many of Ellis' victims in that area in those days, easily identified by a limp or by crutches. On the second day Ellis had another argument with an Irishman by the name of Pat Shea. Again Ellis made his famous lightning draw, and again he drilled his victim in the leg. But Pat Shea refused to quit. From the floor he described Ellis in magnificent if unprintable language until the gunman, literally dancing with rage, shot him in the other leg and strode out the door.

But too many Pahrump men had an "Ellis-Limp" and this latest shooting was one too many for public opinion. The men blocked Ellis' path and compelled him to return.

Pat Shea was not appreciative and he turned his flow of adjectives on a by-stander. This man dared Pat to stand up on his shattered legs and fight, throwing his six gun on the floor. Shea actually dragged himself to his feet and tottered a few steps until he got near the gun. He picked up the weapon and cocked it. It so unnerved Ellis to see his victim walking with a loaded gun that he dashed for his horse, hitched at the doorstep. Shea called on Ellis to come out from behind the horse, as he did not wish to injure the animal, but Ellis in a sudden panic, tried to hide behind the terrified and plunging mare.

Thoroughly unset by now, Ellis tried a fast pot shot from behind the horse and hit Shea in the groin. But the bleeding Shea refused to fall. Propping himself, he calmly fired two times in rapid succession, the first doing little damage, but the second drove Ellis to the alkali ground in his death throes. Then Shea slowly slumped to the door sill, but again pushed himself up in a sitting position. Weak from loss of blood, he took both hands to lift the heavy six gun to aim again. The barrel wobbled, and the crowd of excited men were surging to and fro across his line of fire. Impatiently he called to them to get out of his way so he could get another shot at Ellis.

But Ellis, dying at the feet of his horse, heard him, and called out, "Don't let him shoot. I've got enough." And almost immediately he died. Shea recovered, but there was no arrest, and no trial. The men found $100 on Ellis' body, which, the records say, was "just enough to pay for a proper burial." And since that day the "Ellis-Limp" has disappeared from Pahrump Valley.

Wovoka, Indian Messiah

A STRANGELY potent medicine began brewing along the shores of the West Walker in the waning years of the Eighties. Like early morning pogonip, that mantles bare limbs of trees and bushes, it clung to the Redmen, blanketing the Paiute tribes first, then spreading east of the Rockies into Sioux territory.

It was a doctrine that spread like magic because it sprang from the vision of Wovoka, prophet of the Paiutes, messiah of the Redmen. In a brief eighteen months the weird Ghost Dance of Wovoka's teaching spread an alarm through the west for it heralded a possible uprising of the Redmen. In the Sioux territory, Sitting Bull, he who massacred Custer's band at the Little Big Horn, died as the direct result of Wovoka's vision.

To the Paiutes the teachings of their young medicine man had long been recognized. To the whites, this kindly Indian was plain Jack Wilson, who worked on a Smith Valley ranch. He had studied the Bible and seemed deeply interested in the ways of the white men . . . even taking his employer's name as his own.

In the closing months of '88 Jack Wilson became seriously ill with a dangerous fever. During his illness an eclipse spread fear and wonder among his Paiute brothers, and such was the excitement that Jack Wilson became delirious. He saw himself transported to the Spirit World where he received a revelation. Upon recovering from the fever he called in the tribal leaders to listen to the meaning of his vision. All the Indians, he said, would soon be restored to their rightful inheritance and be reunited with their departed friends. By inference Wovoka's vision meant that the Whites would disappear. All the tribes, he said, must prepare for this day by practicing the songs and dances he would teach them. Principal among these was the weird and rhythmic Ghost Dance in which men and women of the tribes joined hands and shuffled slowly in a circle, keeping time to a chant.

Like all doctrines that foresee the culmination of a people's most ardent desire, Wovoka's wonderful vision spread rapidly through the western tribes, the Paiutes, Crows, Cheyennes, and Arapahos and then flashed across the Rockies into the land of the Sioux. Everywhere the doctrine was accompanied by a studied practice of the Ghost Dance. This sudden activity on the part of all tribes, who for more than two decades, had listlessly accepted the westward movement of the White Men, sent a trembling fear through cities along the Pacific slope.

In the Sioux territory the Ghost Dance brought on an impatience for the promised disappearance of the Whites, and aggravated by local conditions, the Sioux went on the warpath. Sitting Bull was killed during December of 1890 and ten days later the massacre of Wounded Knee occurred. Those were the major outbreaks brought on by the teachings of Jack Wilson, the Paiute's Wovoka, whose vision came as he lay ill on the banks of the Walker in Nevada.

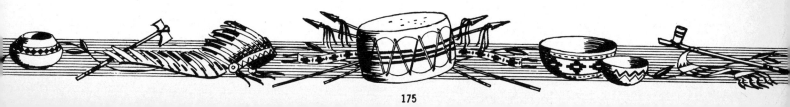

Milk Maid Bonanza

Paul Nyeland

As THE HUGE power shovels load the vast, complicated conveyor machinery these days in the big mine at Round Mountain, it's interesting to reflect how a cow had a direct bearing on the first discovery of gold in this placer area; even as another famous cow had a bearing on the history of Chicago.

In 1888 the Stebbins family lived at a stage stop in the mouth of the Jefferson Canyon, and one day the family milch cow, "old Dolly," was missing. Laura, the young daughter was sent out to find her, riding side saddle and dressed in a gingham apron and calico sunbonnet. "Dolly" was found, in due course, and on the way home, the young lady noticed some peculiar rocks. Now all pioneer Nevada children grew up on the lore of prospecting and Laura was no exception. She stopped, filled her apron with the rocks, and made a note of the location.

After supper Laura broke up the rock and panned it just for fun. To the amazement of the family it showed "color" in abundance. Laura made several trips for more rock and soon had a little vial well filled with gold dust. The family showed it to friends who immedi-

ately started panning the area. Meanwhile Laura's gold was sent to the Mint in Carson and earned $500.00, which was a considerable sum in those days. But the professional miners did not seem to "have the touch" of the young girl and they failed to produce the rich showings she had found. Soon they were discouraged and quit.

The district was more or less dormant until Louis Gordon made some important discoveries at Round Mountain in 1906, and in 1907 "Dry Wash" Wilson found placer where the present workings are in progress. The Stebbins family profited in the development of the area, however, in contrast to many similar instances, and were among the early locators in the Round Mountain District. In fact, prospecting was so ingrained in this family that Mrs. Jack Stebbins was said to have carried her small baby on her back while prospecting in this district.

It was also said during the Tonopah strike, many people prospected the Round Mountain area, some leaving "pay ore" unrecognized on the dump to ride away disgusted. It was a tricky, deceptional sort of country with unfamiliar looking rock.

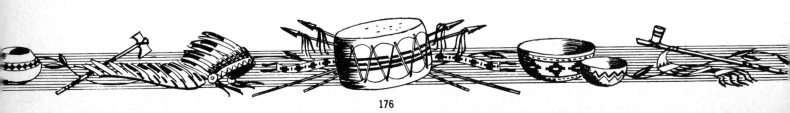

Mob Justice at Eureka

Paul Nysland

THE WINTER OF 1888 found the mining town of Eureka seething with excitement! For ten months the camp had been seeking to identify a man guilty of an alleged rape, but evidence of any kind had been skimpy. Phil Paroni, a local merchant, had been singled out and subjected to two trials and a Grand Jury investigation, and some folks refused to accept the decisions of innocence.

A masked mob seized Paroni at his home one night, marched him to the lime kiln west of town, stripped him to the waist and poured hot tar and shreds of paper over him. For a time the mob debated firing the tar and burning him to death, but finally tied his hands behind him and sent him on his way to the railroad tracks and out of town on pain of death. He later freed his hands but saw so much activity and excitement in town it seemed possible they might really kill him, so he made his way up the tracks.

He had only one shoe, his bare foot was badly cut and swollen, and the night was far below freezing. A bitter wind swept across the desert, and out in the blackness howled a circle of coyotes. He tried to find the smooth ties in the dark for his cut foot, but the starlight was too dim to see anything but the reflection on the rails.

Staggering along, he soon realized he no longer felt the bite of the cold wind and so must be freezing himself. So he ran, until exhausted, to keep warm. Alternately walking, stumbling and running, he covered twelve miles before he made out the warm yellow windows of the little section houses at Diamond Station, heard the barking of the dogs and saw the door swing open. Barney McCook, section boss, stood with lantern in hand for a moment, trying to make out the nature of the strange creature standing half frozen in the tracks in the dead of night. Then he took him in, bathed him, scraped off the tar, fed him and put him to bed. After a day's rest, Paroni borrowed some clothes from McCook and returned to Eureka to face his accusers since his conscience was clear, and he felt that to run away would be to admit a guilt which did not exist.

Back in Eureka he felt he recognized some of his tormentors but was unable to prove anything. The incident served to clear him completely, however, in the minds of his fellow townspeople. It was deemed a blotch on the reputation of Eureka, and it was evident the members of the mob were heartily ashamed of the parts they had played. Paroni continued to live there, became an honored citizen and finally served as County Commissioner.

The Terrible Winter of '89

SNOWFALL WAS early and heavy in December 1889, and Nevada stockmen were jubilant at the end of a "dry spell." But the snow continued, and by mid-January train service at all Nevada points was at a standstill. From Wyoming west, the country was in the grip of a disastrous winter. Sheep and cattle starved and froze. Trains were stalled. The Sierras were blocked, as fires in the snow-sheds had left the tracks exposed.

A herd of wild horses, huddled and were frozen in their tracks near Virginia City. Cattle losses were 50 per cent. A band of 400 sheep froze in one night in Reese River. Everywhere mail was carried by sleigh and finally on snow shoes. Antelope bands starved at Wells and in Reno it was 42 below zero. One family drove 500 cattle to Elko by sleigh, but lost all the cattle and barely escaped with their lives.

All mines at Virginia City were closed as snow blocked the ore tracks, and food supplies ran so low the town was in danger of starvation. Finally, ranchers near Dayton ran sleigh loads of potatoes to the mouth of Sutro Tunnel. The potatoes were loaded into ore cars and underground trains hauled them to the C & C shaft. Tons of the "spuds" were lifted to the surface in Virginia City, amid the cheers of the populace.

In Reno the harassed Southern Pacific was caring for 600 unwilling passengers who were stranded, and the yards were jammed with snowbound trains waiting to get over the Sierras. For weeks the V & T, Carson and Colorado, and Eureka and Palisade railways had been snowbound. The roof of Piper's Opera House fell in under six feet of snow. The 600 "guests" of the Southern Pacific at Reno petitioned for free rides back to Ogden and a detour through the Southwest to the Coast. The railroad stalled, until finally, on January 30, the tracks over the Sierras were clear and twelve locomotives began blasting on their whistles, calling passengers from hotels, saloons, and other points of local interest. Soon mobs of passengers jammed the Reno platform and filled the street as they hauled out baggage and loaded up. The townspeople cheered the passengers and the passengers cheered the trains, and at 1:30 in the afternoon the first of a long series of trains chugged out. It was a scene of great excitement, equalled only by the great Reno fire, and still later by the great Reno flood.

Meanwhile the rest of the State dug itself out. Many cattle and sheep outfits were broke, bodies of animals littered the range for miles and commercial life was almost at a standstill. But the thaw continued and most stockmen were saved. Another week or so would have ruined the entire state. It had no real parallel in Nevada history until the dramatic winter of the Hay Lift, years later.

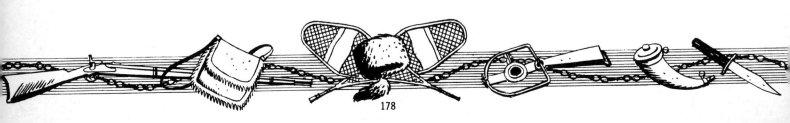

Maker of Widows

SILICOSIS WAS a foreign word to the vocabularies of young farmers who were lured across the Nevada line from St. George, Utah, to the thriving camp of Delamar in the mid-nineties. Even veteran Cornish miners who forsook the Mother Lode of California to pursue high wages of the new camp would have questioned the meaning of the word. But they all learned about the Delamar Dust!!

Three dollars a day was a fabulous wage for the young Mormon men of Southwest Utah who had been raised on backbreaking farm labor to earn a bare living. Delamar offered hard cash for their pockets, the chance to make a stake, enough money to marry and settle down. Besides the work wasn't too hard even though it took the laborer underground or into a dusty mill.

For the "Cousin Jacks" it was a new strike which challenged their knowledge of mining and offered good pay to boot. They were intrigued by the fact that the man behind actual development was none other than Captain Joseph Rafael Delamar, a fabulous native of Holland, who seemed to possess the magic touch.

Hard quartzite of the mines produced an abundance of dust both underground and in the mills. So thick it was that many of the new workers, especially the young men from St. George, many of whom had brought brides to the mining camp, began to suffer coughing spells. It wasn't long before their bright dreams of fortune faded into the realization that they had contracted the "dust." Within a year many of them, some just out of their teens, had succumbed to miner's consumption. Yet, as in any thriving mining camp, work progressed at an even pace and other young farmers, as well as more Cornish miners appeared at Delamar to take over the waiting jobs.

Death did not diminish. From miners up through the mill, even to the superintendents, Delamar dust continued to claim its toll of the men workers.

Black dresses for women became a style imposed by the necessity of attending funerals. No actual figures have been substantiated, but many who worked the Delamar lode say the town's population at one time numbered between five and six hundred widows of St. George men who had come to Lincoln county to work in the mines.

With the advancement of engineering methods early in the twentieth century and purchase of the Delamar properties by the Bamberger interest, the first major change was to bring in water and abolish dry mining. The new method stamped out death from the dust, but in the short preceding years the cemetery had grown measurably and Delamar had established its reputation, known the world over, wherever miners gather, as the "Maker of Widows."

Ferris' Wheel

Paul Wyland

BILLIE CRADLEBAUGH'S bridge spanning the Carson River on the old Overland Trail, was a landmark to westward bound pioneers. The rickety wooden structure afforded easy crossing of the last water barrier, and from the river bank emigrants peered apprehensively at the towering Sierra summit above Genoa, only remaining obstacle between their wagon trains and the fabulous golden land of California.

But, to one pioneer, Cradlebaugh's meant more than the dream of gold! He was young George Washington Gale Ferris, Jr., who had crossed the plains with his parents when he was five years of age. The Ferris family settled not far from Cradlebaugh's in Carson Valley and whenever George was missing from home, he would, like as not, be found at the bridge contemplating the huge undershot water-wheel as it turned slowly in the river current, hoisting water for travel-weary stock. Observers say young George used to lie on the river bank for  hours idly chewing on a blade of grass, seemingly completely absorbed by the motion of the big wheel, and the way it lifted water to feed the stock troughs.

Two score years elapsed before his youthful dream became a reality, but in 1895, the world was startled by a brand new type of entertainment . . . the Ferris Wheel at the Chicago World's Fair. Rising two hundred fifty feet from the ground, the big steam-driven wheel was capable of carrying sixty persons in each of its thirty-six cages. This ponderous mechanical wonder, weighing over four thousand tons, was an immediate sensation. As many as two thousand persons could ride at one time. For fifty cents each, they were permitted to travel two complete revolutions of the wheel, which took twenty minutes. For most of them it meant the first time they had ever been able to view the surrounding countryside from such a vantage point.

George Washington Ferris planned his wonder well. A thirty-three inch steel forged axle supported the weight of the big wheel, the axle alone accounting for seventy tons of the over all weight. Power was supplied by two huge one thousand horse power steam engines fired with coal. It was a real triumph!

George Ferris had labored long and hard to realize his dream, borrowing money from every conceivable source, and endangering his own health by acting as engineer, promoter, financier and operator of the Ferris Wheel. One season at the World's Fair was enough to prove that he had not dreamed in vain. His backers were financially rewarded by success of the venture, and Ferris, himself, had given posterity one of its most popular sources of fun.

Today's county fair gayways and beach amusement parks still depend upon the looming bulk of the Ferris Wheel, outlined by sparkling lights, to let the world know a fun festival is in progress. Strange it is, that this symbol of the circus and the carnival was born from a dream of a small boy who watched a water-wheel turning on the little Carson River in Nevada.

Solar Plexus Punch

GENTLEMAN JIM Corbett could handle his fists. He had displayed that fact very successfully on September 1, 1892, when he defeated the great John L. Sullivan in New Orleans to become the first Marquis of Queensbury champion. It took twenty-one rounds to conquer John L., but the tricky maneuvering of the master boxer coupled with stinging blows of his big gloves finally told on the rugged ring veteran, who three years before beat Jake Kilrain in a seventy-five round match that marked the last of the bare knuckle bouts.

It was only natural then that the eyes of the sports world turned to little Carson City when the championship bout between Gentleman Jim and Bob Fitzsimmons was set for March 17, 1897. As much as a month before the match Carson's main street looked like a section of San Francisco with banners proclaiming the headquarters of the leading newspapers. Dispatches kept the wires hot, and although the spring weather was extremely raw, the sportsmen didn't seem to mind.

Arrangements were made to stage the championship fight at the Carson race-track, under the direction of Dan Stewart. An English firm is said to have approached the two principals prior to the engagement, promising a total of two hundred thousand dollars for movie rights provided the bout went twenty rounds.

St. Patrick's Day dawned clear and warm, and a gay crowd milled into the outdoor race-track arena. The gate take was only eight thousand dollars and it had already cost Dan Stewart some fifty thousand dollars to get the champion and the challenger into the ring. For the first few rounds the champ and Fitzsimmons felt each other out. Some spectators whispered that the two had an agreement to keep the bout going a full twenty rounds. Whether the whisper was truth or a rumor will never be known.

At any rate Corbett shot a stinging blow at his adversary in the sixth and Fitzsimmons reeled with the punch. Maddened, he came back at Corbett, and if there was ever an agreement to keep the fight going any specified number of rounds, it ended right there as the fists began to fly in earnest.

Gentleman Jim was a conceded master of boxing, but Fitzsimmons was a wary foe who carried a shocking amount of power in his long bony arms. In the fourteenth round Fitz landed his famous solar plexus punch. It sent Gentleman Jim to the canvas, momentarily paralyzing him. And, though he tried vainly to rise, he heard himself counted out and saw freckle-faced Fitzsimmons take the championship belt he had worn for five years.

The English firm refused the movies because the bout didn't go the full twenty rounds and the film was dumped in the lap of Dan Stewart. It was a lucky break for him, for although he went deeply "in the hole" on the fight, he is said to have netted about a million on the movies. And Nevada became increasingly known as a site for great fights.

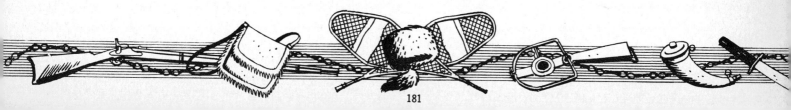

Tonopah's First Funeral

THE GOOD HEARTED and enthusiastic people who swarmed into the raw new camp of Tonopah following the discovery there of valuable ore, went through many trials and tribulations and ordeals which later became part of the history of the State. It was a new experience for most of them, that early fall of 1900, when the first resident died and the people of the new camp were called upon to give him a suitable and decent funeral.

The dead man was a geologist named Weeks, who had succumbed to a heart attack.

Later many others died from what was known as the terrible "Black Death of Tonopah." But at the time of his funeral, Weeks' chief claim to fame lay in being the first corpse at a Tonopah funeral, and the most interesting thing at the time was the funeral itself.

There were no undertaking parlors in the primitive new camp, so Walter Hollis, who had been a carpenter in Belmont and had some experience as a sort of undertaker there, laid out the dead man as best he could without embalming materials. He also made the coffin from pine lumber, and in the funeral procession, Hollis drove the wagon that carried the corpse. Mrs. Charlotte Nay got all the women of the camp, and the men who could sing as a choir. It soon developed there wasn't a hymnal nor a Bible to be had in the entire camp. But they eventually put enough lines together to reconstruct a hymn or two. They found a cook who had a fine voice, and soon the new choir was organized. Thus reinforced the new choir soon got under way and its rehearsals later became a part of Tonopah history. The choir included Tasker Oddie, who later became governor and senator, Bill Marsh, Joe Nay, the cook, and most of the women of Tonopah who could carry a tune.

Meanwhile various committees had gone ahead with the other details of the first funeral. The only buggy in Tonopah was commandeered for use as a mourners' carriage for the widow and her young son. A buckboard wagon was pressed into service as a hearse, with Hollis as driver. Since there was no other place to ride, Mrs. Nay and Miss Hughes rode with Hollis. It was a most unusually hot day and the condition of the corpse was almost too much for the people riding in the buckboard.

Most of the remaining women and children of Tonopah rode in the funeral procession aboard the town water wagon, driven by John Nay.

The population of the new mining camp was predominantly male, and most of the funeral procession consisted of the men who marched behind the water wagon.

The Odd Fellows mustered an informal marching group, wearing sashes fashioned from a fine linen bed sheet. The coffin was swathed in a black silk skirt.

The "first funeral" procession wound down through the town and out to the new graveyard below Tonopah. The whole camp turned out to give John R. Weeks a decent burial and later established the Tonopah Public Library with books which were donated in Weeks' memory by his brother, an Alameda newspaperman. For years it was known as the "Weeks' Library."

The Reno Wheelmen

SPEED BEGAN to make its appearance in the west at the turn of the century. The sprocket and spoke boys who could send their geared up bicycles around an oval track at forty miles or more an hour were the foremost exponents of fast travel that was to become characteristic of the twentieth century.

Recognized from San Francisco to Salt Lake City as a team of speed demons were the famed Reno Wheelmen, who annexed the Pacific Coast championship in Sacramento on July 4, 1900. The ten-man relay team brought Reno's name to the forefront of the sports world, and, as always with champions, the Reno Wheelmen were often called upon to defend their laurels. A scant three months after winning the coast title, the team was challenged by San Francisco's Olympic Club and the Olympians arrived at the old Reno Race Track with ambitions of victory and a plan which they felt would secure their intentions.

Well over two thousand ardent cycling enthusiasts turned out to watch the heated competition, major event of the annual fair, and it soon became evident that the Olympic Club plan for victory had been well mapped. The expertly coached Olympians resorted to a rather unethical practice of "hooking one." Each rider in turn would trail his flying opponent just close enough to be pulled along in the semi-vacuum without undue exertion. Every rider did a stint of five miles and when three relays had been completed without any appreciable gap between riders, it looked as if the Olympians would stick to their Reno opponents like flies to honey until the last five miles when their star sprinter would turn on all his power in the final lap.

But the Olympic Club had failed to reckon with the seasoned experience of King Ryan, Reno trainer. King saw through the plan long before the first fifteen miles of the fifty mile race had been ridden, and he set about concocting an idea of his own which succeeded in out-generaling the Olympics.

Arthur Peckham, fourth rider of the Reno Wheelmen, was a strong cyclist and his wheel was equipped with an extra large gear which could generate tremendous speed. King instructed Peckham to make a poor pick-up and thus lose the Reno lead on the first lap of the fourth relay. So well did Peckham play his part that the stands gasped as his wheel slewed around on the track. In fact, he made it appear that he had lost balance and would fall. It was just what King wanted, the Olympic rider shot well into the lead.

Then it was that Peckham went to work. He got the big gear under control and started pumping with strong legs. He whizzed by the Olympic Club rider at forty miles an hour and though the Olympian tried desperately to "hook on" again, Peckham's speed was too much for him, and at the end of the twenty mile mark a great gap separated the two teams. So jubilant were the remaining Reno riders that they really "poured in on," each wheelman accounting for another large margin of lead. When the last Reno rider finished the fifty mile course, his Olympic opponent still had to ride another mile and five-eights alone to complete the required distance.

July 4th in Nevada

NEVADA MINING CAMPS used to celebrate the Glorious Fourth with an enthusiasm and originality which always more than made up for any possible lack of professional smoothness. A glance back 40 to 80 years ago this week reveals a great deal of fun and a hilarious good time were had by all Independence Day.

July Fourth dawned with every mining camp and cowtown in the State heavily draped in red, white, and blue bunting. Gasoline buggies and earlier carriages and wagons were all smothered with elaborate decorations. Kids paraded variously as "Uncle Sam" or "The Goddess of Liberty" and firecrackers popped in every direction. It was a great day.

Most mining camps, around the turn of the century, staged fights between ornery Jackasses. Many were held in the very center of town, to the tune of heavy betting. Burro races were held for boys and girls of various age groups, with prizes from $10.00 on up. Of course horse races were a fixture from the very earliest days and accompanied by feverish betting.

No July Fourth was complete without muckers contests and competing drill teams. Champion muckers and drillers came from miles around and the competition was terrific. A few of these contests are still held today, but they are found largely in isolated mining camps where a lively local interest in mining skills persists.

Many mining camp celebrations featured a championship baseball game between local mill and mining teams, with special talent smuggled into town for the Big Day. And a high point on most programs for decades in Nevada was the July Fourth Squaw Race! These were usually held down the main street, with a sack of silver dollars waiting at the finish line for the winner. Jim Butler in Tonopah was said to augment this race with showers of silver dollars tossed exclusively to Indian children, (to the great chagrin of their white playmates).

Boxing matches were regular events, and the July Fourth fight card and match-making would dominate mining camp conversation for months before "The Day". And no Independence Day Program was complete without "The Orator of the Day" (usually a prominent attorney) followed by a huge dove or sagehen stew and barbeque. Volunteer Fire Departments usually held races with carts or pumpers, joining the rest of the town that night at the Grand Fourth of July Ball which inevitably climaxed every Independence Day Program. The biggest day of the year in Nevada ever since has continued to be the Glorious Fourth.

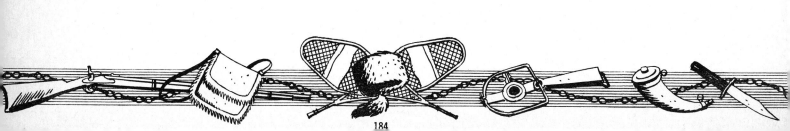

Bony's Bath

ALL THE OLD TIMERS knew the hot springs at Silver Peak Marsh were famous for medicinal qualities, but the proprietor, Bony Aguilar, never patronized his own establishment. In fact, within the memory of the oldest settler, no one had **ever** known Bony to take a bath.

Bony was originally one of the Mexican miners, who with their Indian helpers, burrowed into the hills of that district for silver. They crept on hands and knees into tunnels too low for stooping, dragging out behind them buckskin sacks of ore which they reduced in tiny arrastas, still visible today. But Bony's lot had improved, and for generations, he had rented the tubs of hot water for bathing, and told tall stories about his old wound from an Indian stone arrowhead.

Bony was a friendly little old man, but as he got older near the turn of the century, he was seen less and less often down town. His hot baths were still patronized but his saloon had less and less business. He was well-liked, and as colder weather came on, he added more layers of garments as his age increased. He seldom seemed to get warm in summertime. He complained increasingly about his old wound from the Indian arrow, and told tales of the early Mexican mining days around Silver Peak and the primitive methods they used to burrow like animals into the desert hills.

When Bony died the citizens deemed him worthy of a real funeral like all old-timers. Then they found a problem. The stooped, secretive little man had never bathed! In two generations he had never removed his clothing. As garments wore out he added a layer of new, until at the time of his death he had at least six pairs of overalls, and more shirts . . . each layer firmly cemented with alkali dust and encrusted with grime.

Brooms were used to dust him off on the outside, and then in despair he was slung by ropes over his own hot baths, and soaked therein for the first time. Then, and only then was it found possible to lay him out for the respectable burial which every old-time miner felt was his due. He was the last of a generation of Mexican miners and his funeral was attended by just a few "old-timer" friends.

Queen of the Silver Camps

MODERN NEVADA has its roots in Tonopah. Many of Nevada's leaders got their start in the famous old silver camp and Tonopah traditions, customs, and philosophy are today accepted throughout the entire state. The influence of mining camp honesty and liberality are reflected in Nevada attitudes on almost every subject.

Tonopah is said to have been discovered by Jim Butler's burro. Legend (and probably truth) has it that the prospector picked up a stone to toss at the offending beast and the rock looked like ore. Too broke to pay for an assay, Butler's appeals for an assay on a share basis established fortunes, built Tonopah, put Nevada on its feet, sent a senator to Washington, created a great political organization, later rebuilt San Francisco after the fire, and started a series of great mining camp booms.

In the fall of 1901 eastern capital moved into Tonopah and the real rush started. The railroad was extended south, water was piped in and churches, saloons and an opera house soon followed. By 1913 production reached the peak

of $9,500,000. Tonopah people were willing to rough it but had a taste for the best. Their social life, clubs, dances and banquets had the best money could buy. Oysters, quail, champagne, and flowers graced the tables and formal attire

was the rule. The town was founded and run by prospectors and was the most orderly of mining camps in history.

Today finds Tonopah still active. Mining has dropped off but a huge air base nearby created a wartime boom that seemed like old times. Experts know and agree that huge bodies of silver ore still lie deep beneath the colorful Tonopah hills and every Nevadan is confident that the old camp is anything but dead.

Tonopah Water Wagon

ALTHOUGH THE NAME "Tonopah" means water-brush, and discoverer Jim Butler claimed to have named the famous silver camp for springs known to the Shoshones by this name, it's a fact the town is located on a desert spot where there is no water.

For many years after Tonopah was established as a great strike, water was peddled from wagons at a dollar and a half to two dollars a barrel, or fifteen to twenty-five cents a bucket! Water was hauled in tank wagons from Rye Patch in Ralston Valley; and even after a pipe line brought water to town, most people still bought from the water wagons. Few of the early houses and shacks had water piped to them.

Early residents of Tonopah love to tell of the many ingenious ways they learned to get the most from each precious drop of water. Rinse water was saved to wash laundry, and water from laundry was saved to scrub and mop floors. Baths were few and far between. Lavatories were expensive and outhouses were common even in the "twenties."

Water for livestock presented a serious problem. Most of the stage and teaming outfits maintained their own water wagons, and no teaming outfit was allowed out on the desert without water barrels. Most of the hauling was to the nearest rail point, at Sodaville.

One story, told by many old-timers and since published, tells of the problems faced by miners in obtaining a bath. A leading barbershop is said to have provided bathing accommodations in a highly effective but primitive manner. They dug a hole behind the shop, and sunk a barrel in the ground. Over this was a grating, arranged so it could be teetered back and forth by a man standing on it. A framework supported an old kerosene can overhead, with holes punched in its bottom. A miner standing on the wooden grating could teeter it back and forth, thus working a pump which forced water from the barrel up through pipes to the kerosene can overhead.

It then sprinkled down, making a shower-bath on the man teetering the grating. The water was thus used over and over again, effecting a great economy. Ore sacks were fastened around the frame for privacy.

One version has it that the bather undressed in the tent barbershop, paid his "four bits," and got a bar of soap and a towel. Quickly he ducked out and under the "shower" where, with teeth chattering, he rapidly teetered the wooden grating and was rewarded with an icy trickle from the rusty kerosene can overhead.

Tonopah later was typical of many desert mining camps in its frugal use of water. And the stories of former residents of the many ways found to save the precious fluid will some day make a hilarious book. But a "dry camp" is no laughing matter in the desert as any old-timer will attest.

First in the Nation

GRAND COULEE, Boulder and the mighty Shasta win recognition today as the largest of huge government reclamation projects, but to Lahontan Dam on the Carson River belongs the honor of "First in the Nation." Here in the once arid sagebrush land was realized the first construction project under the newly passed National Reclamation Act.

A scant half-year after Congress approved legislation in the summer of 1902, work commenced on the Truckee-Carson project. Spurred by the action of men like Francis G. Newlands, who had seen Lahontan Valley and all the Carson Sink land suffer from flood and drought, progress was rapid. Within two years an unlimited supply of water nourished thirsty land, and the following season, in 1906, crops flourished as an intricate 608-mile canal system brought an abundant and steady flow of water for irrigation.

Cost of the powerhouse and dam at the head of Lahontan Valley was nearly a million and a half dollars while construction on the canal system, drains and diversions was another six and a half million— a tremendous sum at the turn of the century when public sponsored irrigation projects in desert lands were termed "radical, irresponsible, and visionary."

In return, however, one hundred thousand acres of semi-arid land became potentially productive. Today nearly seventy thousand of those acres are under water right contract and ranchers of the Fernley, Hazen, Fallon district appreciate the foresight of the wise men who pushed their dream to realization, for not only is there water, but power as well.

Fed by the watersheds of the Truckee and Carson rivers with part of the Truckee being diverted at Derby, Lahontan Reservoir now covers ten thousand acres forming an irregular lake five miles long and about half that distance in width. Less than a century ago Pony Express riders traversed what is now the reservoir lake bed as they sped the precious mail along the desolate leg of its journey between Salt Wells and old Fort Churchill, military outpost against the Indians.

In 1919 the Truckee-Carson project was renamed in honor of the man who took the lead in desert reclamation. It became the Newlands Project after the late Senator Francis G. Newlands. Today bountiful crops of the entire valley are testimonial to his belief that desert soil needed only water to give it rich productive ability.

Black Death

ON MANY occasions during Nevada's hectic mining history, the roar of a cannon signified momentous happenings: the hanging of a desperado, raising of the flag, warning of an Indian uprising or the announcement of election returns. But, from among these numerous incidents, the booming voice of a single artillery piece in Tonopah on New Year's morning, 1902, is outstanding!

Not only did this signal welcome the new year, but it called lessees from their feverish labors deep in the rich gold bearing desert mining lode, and scarcely had the echoes ceased to rumble when the scourage of Black Death swept through the flimsy shanties and the mountainside caves to claim a terrible toll.

Jim Butler staked out his claim to the choice Tonopah lode areas in 1900 and soon a makeshift town sprang up around the diggings. Slight attention was given sanitation facilities and the water supply was two miles distant from the mining activity. Butler was easygoing. Within a few months fifty separate leases were operating along his properties. Miners lived in makeshift houses constructed of tin coal-oil cans, combination mud and bottle huts, barrel stave shacks or hillside dugouts.

There was little time to arrange for proper sewage or garbage disposal, consequently the helter-skelter growth was accompanied by increasing swarms of flies, but even then citizens weren't troubled . . . everyone, it seemed, was making money and that was their reason for coming to Tonopah.

On the twenty-eighth of May, 1901, Jim Butler sold the Tonopah Mining Company to a group of Philadelphia financiers, but Jim protected the leasers. Terms of the sale included an agreement forbidding the new owners possession until the following January 1. This entitled the leasers to seven months' productive work, and each one took advantage of the situation to get out as much ore as possible. Digging increased at a feverish pace as the months rolled by, and on the last day miners worked through until midnight.

On the stroke of twelve the cannon roared and workers left the mines to head for the nearest saloon. Celebration was in order. In the small hours of the new year's dawn miners trudged home to their chilly makeshift cabins to rest. Almost as if by signal the Black Death, a form of pneumonia, swept the camp. Not a woman was stricken, but dozens of miners died in a matter of hours after they contracted the fearful plague. Horror accompanied the scourge. Brave wives nursed their husbands who were too ill to move, but others fled wildly from the town.

Though the new owners had taken over, two months elapsed before a sufficient number of miners returned to Tonopah to commence the new operations.

Bully's Luck

"TWO GUN" Mike Kennedy was the toughest man that ever came out of the East. At least that was Mike Kennedy's brag, and he seemed pretty well on the way to making it stick as he bullied the citizens of Sodaville for many weeks before his bluff was called.

Sodaville in 1904 was a pretty tough town to bully because it was just about the most important stop between Reno and Tonopah where all the railroad freight destined for the mushrooming Nye County silver camp was unloaded and transferred to stages for the desert haul. It was also a place that saw lots of boomers and numerous toughies during their brief wait for transportation to Tonopah. But "Two Gun" Mike bluffed out his claim until he ran into a quiet and peaceful miner one night.

James Lund was in from the diggin's for a little fun one Saturday night, the same night that Mike Kennedy was particularly vociferous. Though unarmed, Lund called "Two Gun" Mike's bluff, and Kennedy invited the miner to shoot it out. The two squared off in the center of town as residents took nearby cover. They blazed away and the "toughest man ever to come out of the East" fell with six bullets lodged in his body. Slightly bewildered, but unscratched, James Lund walked back into the saloon for another drink, and the congratulations of bystanders.

Sodaville had its light side, too, for instance, the time that an unthinking storekeeper, deciding to have a little fun, appeared behind his counter one Saturday night in a Hallowe'en mask. It was a sad mistake as the place was filled with Indians.

Suddenly sighting the apparition behind the counter, the redmen bolted for the great outdoors. Not bothering to seek the door, they plunged through the window glass and made for the sagebrush. Not even pleading, could again induce them inside the Sodaville store, for they were convinced that the devil had appeared among them and they weren't aiming to be present for a second visit.

Desert Fire Drill - 1905

IN NEVADA'S pioneer mining camps, water was always scarce, and fire a constant threat. Hardly a camp went through its cycle of boom and bust without at least one epic conflagration and many of them had several. With water selling in early day Tonopah at a dollar a gallon, it was obviously a rare and precious commodity.

Fire protection thus was vital and the volunteer fire companies became the aristocracy of dominantly masculine communities. In Tonopah, in 1905, there were 100 members with five hose companies of ten men each. The volunteer firemen formed what amounted to an athletic club, with a complete gymnasium at the fire-house. They held boxing matches and other events, and guarded the election of new members with jealous caution.

These Tonopah firemen made quite a colorful picture in their strenuous activities. They wore little white caps, red shirts, and white pants for social affairs. On the 'shirts in white lettering appeared "T. V. F. D." for Tonopah Volunteer Fire Department.

Each hose company of ten men stood watch for a day, or day and a night, in a rotation system. So rigidly were they trained that the average hose company on receiving an alarm could get to the fire at any point in Tonopah, with the cart and have water playing on the blaze within three minutes. Fire drills were held in the evening, two or three times a week.

In drawing the hose cart to the fire, the lead man was called the "Spike" while the two nearest the cart were known as the "Wheel Horses." The nozzle man and the plug man rode on the carts and the entire group was trained repeatedly as a team until every motion became automatic.

As the Fourth of July approached each year, the fire drills were held almost every evening. Tonopah always had a gigantic Fourth of July celebration, the climax of which was a championship race between hose companies from every section of Nevada.

These races were usually held from upper Main Street opposite the Elks Building, down to the corner of the Mizpah Hotel. The rules called for each hose company to make a standing start, dash down the steep street to the Mizpah Hotel, and have water streaming through the nozzle. Hose Companies No. 1 and No. 2 of Tonopah were always among the leaders of the State in this event and became the favorites of the people of the silver camp and the heroes of its small fry.

Nevada history makes much of its volunteer firemen, from the aristocratic hose companies of the Comstock to the exclusive Curry and Warren engine companies of Carson City. The larger cities of the State now have paid professional firemen, but the colorful volunteers have by no means disappeared from the scene.

In every small town today in Nevada you'll find one of the most carefully disciplined and socially exclusive groups to be its volunteer fire department. They have made the transitions from hose carts to steamers, from foot carts to horses, and from horses to trucks without so much as changing a by-law or a regulation.

Brawl at Bullfrog

IT WAS AFTER midnight, October 13, 1905, at the Combination Saloon in Bullfrog. The new camp was booming, with tents and shanties built out over the desert in all directions. And the Combination was jammed with men from every corner of the world.

The poker table had been attracting heavy play, and A. J. Jodoin, a young stone mason, was well ahead of the game. Chips were piled in front of him, and his pockets sagged with silver.

He and an onlooker, Bob Arnold, got into in argument over who carried the most money. Hot words flashed, and Arnold, who was a huge man, pulled out a six-shooter and beat Jodoin over the head, gashing his scalp 'til he bled freely.

Jodoin rose to fight, but, being unarmed, thought better of it, and fled up the main street with Arnold in hot pursuit, cursing and shouting at every step, threatening to "shoot him down like a dog."

Next day at noon, Jodoin appeared at the Combination Saloon again, met Arnold, and the quarrel was immediately renewed. Jodoin backed up toward the door, started to remove his coat, and dared Arnold to step outside to fight. But Arnold evidently had no stomach for a free-for-all fist fight in the dust of Bullfrog's main street, and refused to step outside. Jodoin then shouted, "You big cur, you're not man enough!"

At this point Arnold reached for his gun, and poker players, bartenders, customers at the bar, and onlookers all plunged for cover, in a clanging welter of brass spittoons, shattering chair legs, and overturning tables. Jodoin made a hasty snatch for his gun; but before he could pull it out, Arnold fired, and missed.

Jodoin took hasty aim through the smoke and pulled the trigger, hitting Arnold in the abdomen, but the big man still leaned on the table, raised his gun, and emptied it at Jodoin. Miraculously the smaller man was not hit in the hail of lead which struck all around him, splintering the swinging doors. But he was so rattled that his next three shots missed Arnold by a wide margin, and the big man slumped to the floor.

The rising tide of faces from behind tables, bar, and furniture took quick stock of the situation and Arnold was soon laid out on the billiard table where he died 35 minutes later. Jodoin was held before Judge Norris, with Assistant District Attorney Thomas prosecuting. Arnold and Davis, two youthful attorneys who stepped off the stage as the shooting took place, obtained their first case by handling the defense. A coroner's jury, however, brought in a verdict of "self defense" and Jodoin was released.

Difference at Silver Peak

Paul Nyland

TEMPERS WERE short and minor differences were often magnified in the narrow and bitter confines of mining camps; and Silver Peak was no exception during the boom of 1905. One story, still debated by old timers, is that a gunman named Cook started trouble when he kicked a pet dog belonging to popular and gentlemanly McIvor. At any rate the dog incident, or some similar episode, caused bad blood between these two men, and their feelings were soon chafed raw in a community so small they saw each other daily; and where the only recreation included large quantities of dubious quality liquor.

Cook was a rough and rugged professional gunman from Arizona, handy with a nasty tongue and six-shooter alike. McIvor was slender, quiet, well-bred, and a drifter like others in the camp. After days of angry and increasingly bitter relations, the two men met one day on opposite sides of the main street. The hand which first moved toward a gun holster was never seen, but in a flash, both men had swung into the protection of doorways, and instantly their revolvers were blasting across the narrow street, filling the air with heavy smoke, bits of flying wood splinters, and the shattering shock of gunfire echoing in between buildings.

Cook backed into the frame of the entrance to Tom Cartee's Saloon, while McIvor ducked behind the jamb of the door to John Shirley's Bar, across the street and at a protecting angle. Both men fired several shots at relatively close range.

And right through this deadly hail of lead and powder smoke, happily loaded with raw whiskey, waving an empty bottle, and singing a popular Spanish War song, "Goodbye Little Girl, Goodbye . . . " staggered a town character known simply as "The Frenchman." This worthy, dipped, and weaved right through the line of fire, singing all the time! Emerging without a scratch, he continued on down the street, still singing, and still oblivious of the battle in progress.

It soon ended. Cook aimed a heavy slug through the protecting door jamb, and it splintered the plank and penetrated McIvor's abdomen. He slumped to the board walk, and was immediately carried upstairs to his room nearby. A Doctor Harper was summoned to help the wounded man, and promptly found himself embroiled with an indignant landlady who demanded the dying McIvor be hauled out of her place at once because his blood was staining the floor.

Once again the gunman, Al Cook, was tried for murder, and again he was freed under a verdict of self defense.

Ghost Town

Hemmed IN by sullen brown slopes of the Funeral Range dipping westward into the weird abyss of Death Valley and eastward toward the mysterious underground Amargosa River, lie the ghostly ruins of Rhyolite, for three short years most fabulous of Bonanza Road's gold camps.

Two score years ago Rhyolite was a city of eight thousand gold hungry miners who believed in the fable of the lost Breyfogle mine as they wormed three million dollars worth of precious metal from barren hills before the ore pinched out.

Today even the trains which once swept these riches to market, are long since abandoned. It is said they add their low moaning whistles to the ghostly echoes which swirl around the gaunt spectres of steel and masonry, gradually being swallowed by shifting sands and desert heat.

Ruins of the town sit high on a slope commanding a view south for miles across the shimmering Amargosa Desert, from Cararra on one side to the mountain of shifting sand on the other, and all of it borders the blistering depths of Death Valley.

Alone among the wraiths of the past stand two battered structures, the Bottle House (now a museum) built from the excess of materials as muckers slaked their desert bred thirst with iced Rhyolite beer and cast aside the bottles; and the old depot which once sought prominence as the Dearborn Street Station of the West.

Tonopah and Tidewater was Borax Smith's dream of empire as he pushed steel rails northward from the Santa Fe Railroad in a race with J. Ross Clark's Las Vegas and Tonopah Railroad that connected with the Union Pacific. Hardly had either of the steel ribbons begun to tap Rhyolite's riches than desert ghosts started their encroachment on the camp. Rails were ripped up and put to other uses years ago.

And for decades, the old roadbeds made passable but rugged highways for desert travelers, the gaps where bridges had been removed providing an additional hazard for the more sporting drivers of early day automobiles.

But desert rats claim trains still puff through Rhyolite's ghostly silence on dark, windy nights.

First Train Into Ely

OLD-TIMERS IN eastern Nevada still refer to September 29, 1906, as **"The Day,"** marking the arrival of the first train at Ely, and the start of mining operations which would produce $550,000,000 in metal and build some of the state's largest communities.

"The Day" was the climax of several years of engineering, and of much excited planning on the part of White Pine Committees.

It all started when old Isaac Requa poured some of the great wealth he won on the Comstock into the little Eureka and Palisade Railroad. When some 20 years later, the fortunes of the Eureka mines slumped, the railroad slumped with them. Isaac's son, young Mark Requa, was given the job of managing the railroad, and he began to search for new mines in eastern Nevada. Eventually he bought a copper property at Ruth for $150,000 and soon found the entire region was tremendously rich in the red metal. Requa quickly interested eastern capital in the development of the mines and started a new railroad from the north.

Special trains were made up for the "first day," at Salt Lake City, Ogden, and Reno. All Ely was decorated, and the old county courthouse was completely covered with sagebrush wreaths. Rates from Ogden were $10.50 per round trip, $2.50 for Pullman cars, and the trains were to stand on a siding with their own dining cars. Local committees went out to Cherry Creek and rode in with the first train, which was gay with flags, bunting, and sagebrush wreaths.

There were loud cheers, whistles, and salutes by the band as the first train steamed in. Many grown people had never seen a train before, and most of the Indians refused to venture within several hundred yards. When the engineer leaned out of his cab and yelled "Look out folks, I'm going to turn her around" and blew his whistle, it so unnerved the crowd that hundreds broke and ran in all directions!

The first train was from Salt Lake City, and was the signal for the big barbecue to start. Tons of meat and huge kettles of beans had been cooking, and there were scores of washboilers of steeping coffee. A Nevada whirlwind suddenly caught up the paper plates and in a second the air was filled with white plates and napkins soaring into the sky.

At 2:30 the Ogden and Reno trains arrived, Mark Requa drove the last spike, made of pure Ruth copper (now in the University of Nevada mining museum) and a three day celebration was launched. Held's band played in the unfinished Northern Hotel, there was dancing in the streets, baseball games, and miner's double drilling contests. And within a single year Ely's population went from 500 to 3,000; she had over a $1,000,000 spent in new buildings, and the area became one of the most important sections of the entire State in wealth, progressiveness, and enterprise. The future of the area looks better now than it has in years.

Goldfield

LUSTY SON OF Nevada's great silver camp at Tonopah, was Goldfield where miners clamored for the right to work for $3.50 a day and came out of the mines at shift's end worth over a hundred dollars in fine high-grade concealed beneath their fingernails or in the creases of their clothes; where muckers paid more to sleep for an eight hour shift than they could make in wages; where champagne and Pousse Cafes were ordinary thirst quenchers; and where Tex Rickard gained world renown as a promoter by staging the Gans-Nelson Battle of the Century.

Eleven million dollars in jewelry gold came from the mines in a single year—the amount lost through high-grading could never be computed. A claim that lapsed for lack of assessment work, brought a million and a quarter in cold cash. Townsite lots on desert wasteland soared to as high as $45,000 apiece. Nat Goodwin and Ella Goodrich, deans of the comedy theatre, were secured to open the opera house. The Federal government found it necessary to send in U. S. Army troops to preserve order during labor difficulties. And a two hundred room brick hotel was erected to care for the thousands of transients and the elegance of the social life outdistanced anything thus far seen in the west. Tex Rickard of Klondike fame ran the Northern Saloon and it was there that decision was reached to match Joe Gans and Battling Nelson for the world's lightweight championship.

On September 6, 1906, the bulging boom town of twenty thousand practically split its seams as population doubled for the historic struggle. A month before the Goldfield Athletic Club had raised $110,000 in 24 hours to meet Nelson's demand of a thirty thousand dollar purse, largest offered to that time in ring history. The battle is well remembered by many. Negro Joe Gans emerged winner of the lightweight crown after forty-two rounds of titanic battling, and Tex Rickard was on his way up the ladder to fame as a promoter.

Today, Goldfield lives in the firm conviction that such fabulous wealth cannot just disappear, and recent developments there tend to lend credence to the belief.

"Little Joy's" Grave

Paul Nyland

THROUGH the hot desert nights, the weary mother nursed the dying child, bathing her feverish brow with Goldfield's precious water, chinking the cracks of the shanty against blistering hot winds and the clouds of white alkali dust with the smell of sun-dried sagebrush. Miners' wages bought little in medicine, and every day "Little Joy" sank lower and lower.

And now the child lay in a tiny unmarked grave in the desert cemetery, a rag doll still clutched in one small hand. Discouraged, the family was preparing to return east, for this camp of great riches for many, had proven a heart breaker for them.

Unable to bear the thought of leaving "Little Joy" out among the Joshua palms, in an unmarked and forgotten grave, the mother decided to take direct action. Gravestones shipped into Goldfield were fabulous in price, and this family was penniless. But down the street a new school building was under construction! That night the mother waited until the last crowds had left the streets and the camp slept. Then she trudged through the dust, pulling the toy wagon of the golden haired tot who slept out on the hill. Luck was with her, and she reached the new school building site without a sound. There she selected a block among the cut stones, ready for the masons, and praying that it would never be missed and her theft would be forgiven, she struggled, tugged, and wrestled the rock up a plank and into the toy wagon.

Furtively she pulled it down the street, and on out to the cemetery. Again she was not detected, and at last at the fresh grave, she unloaded the stone. With borrowed chisel and maul, she amateurishly hacked out the letters, chipping and cutting the rock, making mistakes in her haste, for it was now getting light in the east.

It was a hurried job, but she was not seen on the way home. And if a building foreman found a stone missing, or a cemetery watchman discovered fresh rock chippings, no one said a word as the little family packed up its goods and left Goldfield forever.

And to this day, visitors to the Goldfield cemetery are shown the tiny grave, the rough stone still standing, with the crude letters "JOY" hacked at midnight by a loving mother's hands. Goldfield has never forgotten, and on every Decoration Day for nearly a half century, the old timers of the famous camp have remembered, and decked "Little Joy's" grave with flowers.

RILEY GRANNAN'S Funeral

"IT DON'T AMOUNT to anything; it's all a joke." Those were the words on the lips of Riley Grannan when that world-famous plunger of the turf died at Rawhide.

His funeral was typical of the raw, new mining camp where an empty chewing tobacco can with an appended ox-tail served as the post office because folks were too busy mucking pocket gold from the steep canyon walls to pay much attention to matters of lesser consequence.

But they all halted their labors for Riley Grannan's funeral! Begrimed miners mingled with satin-clad dance hall girls, saloonmen, promoters and rounders in the cortege that followed Riley's remains to the "preachin'." Gathered around the bier was as sincere a throng of mourners as ever met at the coffin-side of a friend, and before the obsequies were through there was not a dry eye in the crowd. W. H. Knickerbocker, former clergyman, delivered the eulogy.

"He was born in Paris, Kentucky," Knickerbocker said, "he died in Rawhide. He was born in the sunny southland where brooks and rivers run musically through luxuriant soil; where magnolia grandiflora like white stars glow in a firmament of green; where crystal lakes dot the greensward and the softest summer breezes dimple the wave-lips into kisses for lilies on the shore; where the air is resonant with the perfume of many flowers. This was the beginning. He died in Rawhide, where in winter the shoulders of the mountains are wrapped in garments of ice and in the summer the blistering rays of the sun beat down on the skeleton ribs of the desert. Is this the picture of universal life?

"He was a 'dead-game-sport.' I say it not irreverently, but fill the phrase as full of practical human philosophy as it will hold, and I believe that when you say one is a 'dead-game-sport' you have reached the climax of human philosophy.

"And now the time has come to say goodbye. The word 'farewell' is the saddest in our language. And yet there are sentiments that sometimes refuse to be confined in that word. I will say, 'Goodbye, Old Man.' We will try to exemplify the spirit manifested in your life in bearing the grief at our parting. Words fail me here. Let these flowers, Riley, with their petalled lips and perfumed breath, speak in beauty and fragrance the sentiments that are too tender for words. Goodbye."

* The above is only a partial quotation from Mr. Knickerbocker's eulogy which is well worth reading.

The Unsinkable Saloon

OF ALL NEVADA'S brave mining camps, none had more spirit than Rawhide, the town that survived fires, flood, panic, bank failures, robberies, and a setting amid arid, barren, light-yellow hills, swept by winds and blizzards! Rawhide was built in 1907 and backed by Tex Rickard, George Graham Rice, Nat Goodwin, and others.

Lumber was teamed from Schurz, and desert roads crawled with dusty wagons, mule spans, and ancient autos. Adventurers from all over the world crowded into the sun-blistered camp. Water was scarce, and from the first the town dreaded fire. The first one broke out July 20, 1908, and as the volunteers raced to put water on the blaze, hundreds of passersby swiftly lifted, by main strength, the adjoining tents and cabins and **carried** them away, thus isolating the blaze!

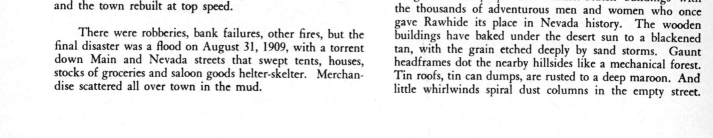

But in September almost the entire camp was destroyed by fire and lay in ashes. Offers of help poured in by wire, but a mass meeting decided "Rawhide would pay for everything and accept no charity." Funds were raised and the town rebuilt at top speed.

There were robberies, bank failures, other fires, but the final disaster was a flood on August 31, 1909, with a torrent down Main and Nevada streets that swept tents, houses, stocks of groceries and saloon goods helter-skelter. Merchandise scattered all over town in the mud.

The Fountain Saloon Building, on Nevada Street, was whirled around, lifted by the flood and carried, plunging, dashing, turning dizzily down the street while the bar-keep yelled for help and the customers hung onto the bar for dear life. The crest of the flood passed, dropping the saloon a block or so down the way and facing on Regent Street. The Press-Times announced that the Fountain Saloon, although sadly twisted and in a new location, was "almost immediately able to dole out the needful."

And needful it was, because Rawhide was done. The spirit was still there. The leasers still worked but output got lower and lower; the town shrunk to 100, then less and dwindled to almost nothing. The Fountain Saloon typified the spirit and enterprise of Rawhide, with "business as usual despite Hell or High Water," but the watery ride of the bartender and patrons really marked the highwater point of a gallant and courageous mining camp. The old town still stands, an easy drive from Fallon or Schurz over a fine gravel road. But it takes a good imagination to people the weather-beaten buildings with the thousands of adventurous men and women who once gave Rawhide its place in Nevada history. The wooden buildings have baked under the desert sun to a blackened tan, with the grain etched deeply by sand storms. Gaunt headframes dot the nearby hillsides like a mechanical forest. Tin roofs, tin can dumps, are rusted to a deep maroon. And little whirlwinds spiral dust columns in the empty street.

Medicine Man's Penalty

Paul Neyland

FORTUNATE INDEED are the present day members of the medical profession in Nevada that they are not practicing under the system common in this State 100 years ago, and in fact, as recently as 1910. The ancient Paiutes and Shoshones of Nevada had a way of discouraging Medicine Men who "lost too many cases."

How long this custom continued is unknown, the last case of record being what appeared to be a routine Indian killing in April, 1910, on the old Moapa Road, eight miles north of Las Vegas. Indian Harry York, a medicine man, was killed by two Indians while four passively looked on. The Indians talked openly about it and the local sheriff investigated.

The trial revealed that five sisters of Bismark, (the Indian who used a shotgun on York), had died under the medicine man's care. Bismark, recalling the ancient Paiute limit which allowed a medicine man three failures only, called up a committee of five friends. They waylaid York on the road, and Bismark shot the medicine man. He fell but still lived, and Long Black Charley shot him with a rifle. Still the hardy medicine man lived, so Bismark polished him off at short range with the shotgun. Looking

on, and nodding approval were four other Indians, Vegas Wash Joe, Jack, Worky, and Mike, who obviously felt that any medicine man who was 60 per cent over quota had slight need for any sympathy.

The committee had reconsidered a day later, deeming the dead medicine man worthy of burial, and they had dragged the body some 300 yards from the road, and buried it, face down, in a shallow grave. There was no attempt at concealment, however, and all Indians talked freely at the trial. They appeared puzzled that white men should make so much fuss. After all, if York had not been checked in his career, there would be no telling how many Indians might die. And when the trial brought a verdict of not guilty "because the accused were acting under tribal law", the Indians accepted it as simple justice.

There were many other records kept in earlier times, of tribal medicine men who paid the supreme penalty for failure in their profession, the execution often being carried out by stoning at the hands of special delegations of tribesmen. The medicine man enjoyed great power and prestige among his fellows as long as he was successful, but the alternative was death.

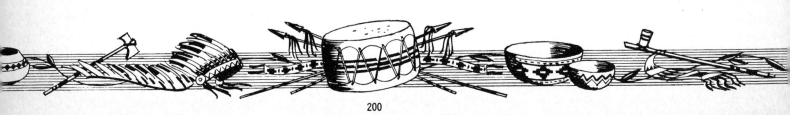

Last Indian Battle

LHE LAST INDIAN BATTLE in America took place February 26, 1911, near Kelly Creek, Humboldt County, and came as a climax to a dramatic chase across the frozen wastelands of northern Nevada. The story widely published at the time, and easily verified today by surviving members of the posse, tells of the fanatical massacre, on January 19, 1911, of four prominent Washoe County sheepmen in Little Highrock Canyon some 40 miles north of Gerlach.

Inspecting their sheep, Harry Cambron, Indianano, Laxague, and Erramospe, were shot down in ambush by a band of renegade Shoshone. Their faces were mutilated for gold teeth, their bodies stripped of warm clothing, and thrown in a snowbank on Little Highrock Creek.

Taking horses, guns, clothing and equipment, the little band of Indians fled eastward, across the bitter cold Black Rock Desert, the windswept Quinn River country, and over into the deep drifts of the rolling Kelly Creek area, just north of the modern day Getchell Mine. The band had at various times killed at least four men.

The news of the massacre struck all Nevada like a thunderbolt and posses were hastily formed by the sheriffs of Humboldt, Elko, and Washoe counties also over the line in California. One group of 18 hardy men, including Captain Donnelly, superintendent of the Nevada State Police, an Indian tracker, and a number of young cow punchers took up the trail at Little Highrock. They followed the Shoshone through driving hail, ice, sleet, snow and sub-zero weather in one of the most terrible winters in Nevada history. For 16 days they lived in the saddle, at times catching a little sleep or hot food at scattered ranches. And something like a panic gripped northern Nevada isolated sheep camps, ranches, and prospectors' cabins.

On Sunday, February 26th, at noon, the posse was plodding through a light snow storm near Rabbit Creek. Suddenly, without warning, they came upon the Indian encampment in a shallow sagebrush draw. As the posse hastily dismounted, pulling rifles from scabbards and gloves from stiffened, numbed fingers, the Indians opened fire and began to retreat down the draw. The squaws, with their babies on their backs, uttered wild cries and made a dash for the ponies hobbled out on the hillside, but one flank of the spreading posse cut them off.

It was said the men, women, and even the children took an active part in the fighting. Squaws and children used bows and arrows, and improvised spears with parts of sheepshears lashed on broom handles. Posse members related that the squaws painted their faces and performed a sort of death chant, as the heavy fire of the posse cut down the Indians one by one. One member of the posse, Ed. Hogle, accompanied by two cowboys, walked down one side of the gully and almost on top of an Indian concealed behind the sagebrush. The Indian fired first, shooting Hogle in the center of the heart a split second before Hogle's companions blasted in return. The Indian band had been exterminated with one exception of a young girl named Snake, the child, and the two papooses still strapped to the bodies of their mothers. It was the last Indian battle.

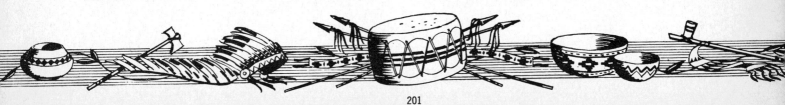

COPPER TOWN

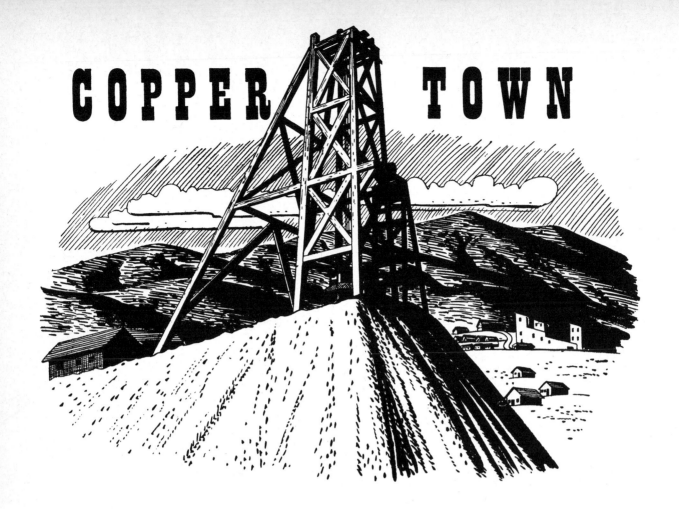

NEARLY A MILLION DOLLARS in gold and silver came from the mines of the Cope district in northern Elko County during the years between '69 and the early '80's, and Mountain City, twelve miles from the Idaho line, grew to a sizeable town of a thousand residents as prospectors combed the hills for elusive wealth. As the riches dwindled, miners moved on, leaving only a hundred or so hardy souls who maintained that hidden riches were still locked in the hills. Their belief in the future of this northern Nevada mining camp was rewarded by the persistency of S. Frank Hunt, miner, geologist, and, above all, practical prospector whose background of experience included ventures in Colorado, Alaska, and other Nevada camps. Twelve years of toil, near heartbreak and personal rebuff, overcome by this one man's dogged determination, resulted in discovery of Rio Tinto's multi-million dollar copper lode.

In his middle years, lamed and often ill, Hunt, the prospector was strong on determination. Visiting northern Elko County in 1919 he was disappointed in his quest for gold or silver and was ready to shake the dust of Mountain City when he came upon a leached, drab gossan outcrop some three miles south of the little mining town. His keen sense of geological values visualized a rich copper deposit buried beneath this bare rock. Up went the familiar stone monument enclosing a tobacco can carrying the location notice claiming Rio Tinto. For nearly ten years every cent he could earn or save plus a grubstake went into development of an incline shaft which went down 50 feet. Hunt felt sure he would have to sink at least two hundred and it was a pessimistic world at the depth of depression that turned a deaf ear to his Nevada Katanga. Copper was five and six cents on the market and prospects were black until his unfailing determination interested Ogden C. Chase of Salt Lake City. Rio Tinto was organized for two million shares and stock offered free to those willing to pay a five cent assessment. The money raised sent Hunt and his co-workers back to the shaft and during a snowbound winter they struck the sulphide ore body at approximately 250 feet, revealing forty per cent copper ore. Stock boomed on the market. International Smelting bought control and within 4½ years after discovery, production was 450 tons daily with earnings at the rate of $4,000,000 annually. Anaconda built a model apartment city near the workings and through the Rio Tinto mine, Mountain City took a new lease on life.

Believing that the commonwealth which so bountifully rewarded his zeal should share his good fortune, the founder created the S. Frank Hunt Foundation for the Mackay School of Mines at the University of Nevada, endowing it with stock and cash gifts upwards of $200,000. Today the fund is used to finance field trips and the study of geology, mineralogy, and mining, as well as to fulfill the late Mr. Hunt's hobby of making more "good" prospectors.

Last of the Basket Makers

WHEN THE HISTORY of Western art is recorded for future generations, the rhythmic name of a Washoe Indian squaw will attain a prominent place, for in her perfect work she symbolized the hopes and fears, the fables and timid superstitions of her race. Not unlike the bards of old, her talents achieved a harmony of true art, but it was not in music or songs; rather it was the eloquent expression of a weaver. In thin white willow her nimble fingers passed on the legends of her people. With no formal training she was instinctively an historian, an astronomer, a religeuse and a draughtsman with a keen eye for beauty and a fine sense of symmetry. . . . The last of the great Washoe basket makers. She was Dat-So-La-Lee..

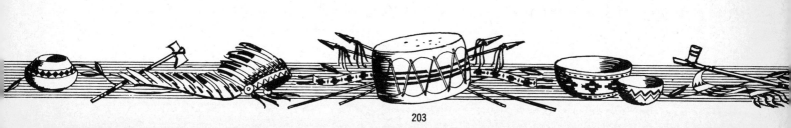

With charactertistic tribal stoicism she was given the name Da-bu-da at birth. In strict translation it means "broad hips," but like many another artist, her original name goes unknown today, for she had married, adopted another name and advanced well beyond middle age before she overcame the fears which kept her talents hidden for half a century.

There is no true record of Dat-So-La-Lee's birth, but she was a girl in her early 'teens when John C. Fremont's little band of explorers reached the eastern rim of the Sierras in 1844. Until her death in 1925 when she was well over 90 years of age, she treasured some tiny medallions and buttons that Fremont's men left with her tribe.

Abe Cohen, a Carson City merchant, first brought to light her true talents when he discovered that an ancient tribal defeat kept her from weaving the ceremonial baskets. In some distant age the Paiutes had defeated the Washoes and driven them to the hills. They had destroyed all of the artistic Washoe baskets, so perfect that they were used as a medium of exchange, and had issued an ultimatum that the Washoes would never again weave such baskets.

Cohen convinced Dat-So-La-Lee that no harm would come to her if she wove these baskets, and then she gave full expression to her heritage. Under Mr. Cohen's guidance she produced 120 basket masterpieces, many of which were over a year in the making.

Some of them now grace historical museums throughout the United States; others bring fabulous sums as collectors' items. Most famous of Dat-So-La-Lee's creations is the basket which develops the legend "Myriads of Stars shine on the graves of our ancestors." With her died the age-old secrets of Washoe weaving . . . Dat-So-La-Lee was the last of the Basket Makers.

Modern Day GOLD RUSH

FROM Miami and New York, from the midwest and deep south, fortune hunters pricked up their ears in March 1927, for another Nevada bonanza was in the making. Model T's and Chevies, Diannas and Willys, Jewetts and Oaklands took to the nation's roadways and headed for Weepah where a fabulous new strike showed assays of $78,000 a ton in gold and silver.

It was a helter-skelter rush to no-man's-land in the desert with household goods and provisions tied precariously to jouncing vehicles. This was not the slow plodding of pioneers to a new Klondyke, but a race of the budding mechanical age, where the speediest vehicle might gain for its owner untold riches in the new strike. In Florida the automobile club was deluged with requests for maps and routing to Weepah. Detailed mimeographed information was the club's immediate response.

In five weeks time the forlorn sagebrush desert of the Lone Mountain country near Tonopah was a seething boom camp of fifteen hundred persons. Tents flowered along the desert floor overnight, sixty new frame buildings arose as if by magic, seventy men were drawing regular mining pay checks and at least fifteen syndicates were preparing to work claims adjacent to the new find. Mining men described the town as a "monstrosity." Hardiest veterans of the trail said they had never witnessed such an aggregation, "combining the ballyhoo of a cheap circus with the selvedge of a monster county fair, where an almost interminable row of hot dog stands lined the main street." Prospectors and working miners did not take kindly to this invasion of their domain, and several threats of lynching warned off would-be claim jumpers.

Weepah mushroomed from the mystery of a midnight visit to Tonopah by three mining men, Frank Horton, Jr., Leonard Traynor and W. E. Schmidt. They possessed samples of white quartz plastered with gold and slabs of talcy stuff carrying free gold. Refusing to reveal location of the find they suddenly disappeared, carrying only meager supplies. Gold excitement reached fever pitch. News stories on the press wires of the nation aroused even more interest in the east than in Nevada. Returning to Tonopah in a couple of days, Horton and Traynor brought one hundred pounds of samples that ran thirty-nine dollars a pound in gold and carried 168 ounces of silver. The strike, they said, was on the property of the old Electric Mines, 27 miles from Tonopah—the rush was on.

After the first rush, Weepah produced fitfully. Interested capital built a mill and bunkhouses in the thirties to carry on open pit mining, but in 1940 buildings and equipment were dismantled and moved. Today sagebrush covers the townsite, and only glory holes pock marking the hills reveal the location of a modern day gold rush.

INDEX

APPENDIX

Acknowledgement for valuable assistance in compiling this material is gratefully made to the various newspapers of Nevada who opened their old files; to the officials of the State Museum, State Department of Highways, officials of the State of New Mexico, and the Republic of Mexico in charge of archives; the Bancroft Library, Berkeley, California; the California State Historical Society, San Francisco, California; the California State Library, Sacramento, California; the Chalfant Press, Bishop and Lone Pine, California; the County Recorder's Office, Washoe County, Nevada; the Historical Society of the L.D.S. Church, Salt Lake City, Utah; the Library of Congress, Washington, D. C.; Dr. S. L. Lee, Carson City; the National Park Service, Boulder City, Nevada; the Nevada State Historical Society, Reno, Nevada; the Nevada State Library, Carson City, Nevada; the Reno Evening Gazette and Nevada State Journal Offices, Reno, Nevada; the University of Nevada Library, Reno, Nevada; the Washoe County Library, Reno, Nevada; the Wells Fargo Museum and Library, San Francisco, California; Alice B. Addenbrooke, Reno, Nevada; Hal Bulmer (Mining Engineer) Reno, Nevada; Mrs. Laura Bulmer, Reno, Nevada; Marco Chatovich, Silver Peak, Nevada; Mr. and Mrs. Richard Cowles, Reno, Nevada; Anne Crump, Verdi, Nevada; Albert Daniels (dec.), Reno, Nevada. Mrs. Laura Darrough, Smoky Valley, Nevada; Mr. and Mrs. George L. Dugan, Reno, Nevada; F. N. Fletcher (at that time in Carson City, Nevada); Mrs. Lida Gilbert, Reno, Nevada; M. R. Grater, Boulder City, Nevada; Eugene Grutt, Reno, Nevada; Ed Hand, Reno, Nevada; M. R. Harrington, Southwest Museum, Los Angeles, California; Frank Humphrey, (dec.), Reno, Nevada; Mrs. Marguerite Humphrey, Reno, Nevada; Mrs. Bertha Innman, Terrebonne, Oregon; Joseph Leonesio, Reno, Nevada; Parker Liddell, Reno, Nevada; Judge A. J. Maestretti, Reno, Nevada; Laura Mills, Fallon, Nevada; Ernest Molini, Reno, Nevada; Patrick Mooney, Sr., Reno, Nevada; Mrs. Charlotte Nay, Tonopah, Nevada; Roy Noble, Reno, Nevada; Walter G. Reid, Virginia City, Nevada; Mrs. Alice Robinson (dec.), Big Pine, California; Douglas Robinson, Bishop, California; Mrs. Mildred Ryan, Tonopah, Nevada; Mrs. Mary Sharp, Tonopah, Nevada; Mrs. John Shirley, Ernest and Louis Shirley, Silver Peak, Nevada; Howard Smith, Fallon, Nevada; Mrs. Lydia Summerfield (dec.), Hawthorne, Nevada; Maude Sawin Taylor, Reno, Nevada; Jeanne Elizabeth Wier (dec.), Reno, Nevada.

There are several score more persons whom space does not permit us to mention here, yet who gave very valuable assistance. We hope to acknowledge their help later, and perhaps at the same time, those whose cooperation in recent months came too close to press time to be included in this volume.

Research for the series has been directed by Mrs. Myrtle Myles of Reno; artwork is by Paul Nyeland of the San Francisco firm of Shawl, Nyeland & Seavey, artists; copy for three years by Jack Myles; original idea, supervision, and copy for three years by Thomas C. Wilson. Cover and book design for this volume are by Mel Mathewson.